Potatoes & Vegetables

p

This is a Parragon Book
This edition published in 2003

Parragon
Queen Street House
4 Queen Street
Bath BA1 1HE, UK

A copy of the CIP data for this book is available from the British
Library, upon request

Printed in China

Note

Cup measurements used in this book are for American cups.
Tablespoons are assumed to be 15 ml. Unless otherwise stated,
milk is assumed to be full fat, eggs are medium and pepper is
freshly ground black pepper.

Contents

Introduction

Everybody, whether meat-eating, vegetarian or vegan, should eat a good balance of nutritious and flavoursome foods in their diet. This book features 246 recipes, all of which show just how versatile and healthy cooking with vegetables can be.

Potatoes are one of the world's most popular vegetables and they have enormous nutritional value. They lend themselves to most culinary styles and are perhaps the most versatile staple food available in the world today. It is one of the most important crops cultivated for human consumption, with Russia, Poland and Germany being the highest consumers, closely followed by Holland, Cyprus and Ireland.

On average we eat 109 kg/242 lb per head per annum, which is good news when you consider the nutritional properties of this best-loved tuber. The average 225 g/8 oz potato, containing 180 calories, has protein, starch for energy and fibre, as well as being a good source of vitamin C. Most of the vitamins are found just beneath the skin, so it is often suggested they are cooked in their skins and then peeled. If not cooked with fat, the potato even has a great role to play in the slimming diet.

However, the potato has not always been held in such high regard. It originated in South America and is thought to date back to as far as 3000 BC. First known as the papa and eaten by the Incas, the potato was unknown to the rest of the world until the sixteenth century, when Spanish conquistador Francisco Pizarro captured Peru, which was famed for its richness in minerals. The mineral trade brought many people to Peru, who, in turn, carried the potato to the rest of the world. The potato was known by many names, which reflected the different cooking methods used by the Indians. Even this far back in its history, the potato was eaten fresh in season and dried by the Incas for use in the winter. Nowadays the storage life of potatoes and the different methods of preservation have increased its popularity in the food market.

The potato first arrived in Europe via Spain, and its name gradually changed from papa to battata. It became famous for both its nutritional and healing properties – the Italians believed it could heal a wound if the cooked flesh was rubbed into the infected area. One person who believed this was Pope Pious IV, who grew his own crop in Italy. It spread to Belgium, Germany, Switzerland and France, but did not reach the British Isles until Frances Drake stopped in the New World and shared his cargo of potatoes with English colonists.

Later repatriated by Sir Walter Raleigh, the colonists brought the potato to Britain, where Raleigh grew the crop on his land. He was also responsible for taking the potato to Ireland, discovering that Irish soil was perfect for growing it. The Irish soon adopted the potato and it became a mainstay of their diet.

Today there are many varieties of potato, each being suitable for different cooking methods, be it roasting, boiling, steaming, baking, mashing or frying. What makes it particularly versatile is the fact that it absorbs other flavours very readily and it has a consistency which lends itself to many uses.

CHOOSING AND USING POTATOES

Look for a firm, regular-shaped potato, either red or yellow in colour, with a smooth, tight skin. Avoid potatoes which are turning green or sprouting, as the flavour will be bitter and they will have higher levels of natural toxicants called glycoalkaloids. Store potatoes in a cool, dark, dry place, as too much light turns them green.

The recipes that follow in this book open up a world of delightful dishes, from light salads and snacks to hearty main meals and beautiful bakes, many potato-based. In addition, there are many tempting recipes, from nourishing soups to healthy snacks, which make skilfull use of myriad other vegetables – all of these vegetable-based dishes are suitable for vegetarian cooking.

TYPES OF POTATO

There are about 3,000 known varieties of potato, but only about 100 of these are regularly grown. Of these, about 20 are found with ease on our greengrocers' and supermarket shelves. The following is a brief description of the most popular varieties and their uses, as a guide for the recipes in this book.

Charlotte New Potatoes

Craig Royal Red: *a main crop potato, ready in July, it is non-floury (mealy) and has a pink or red skin. A waxy potato, it is best for frying and boiling or using in salads.*

Cyprus New Potato: *found in late winter and spring, it is best simply scrubbed and boiled. Not a good mashing potato.*

Desiree: *a high quality, pink-skinned floury (mealy) potato, good for baking, frying, boiling and mashing.*

Home Guard: *generally the first of the new potatoes. It blackens easily and collapses on cooking, so it is best boiled lightly in its skin.*

Jersey Royal: *a delicious new potato. It appears from May to October, but is at its peak in August. It has a flaky skin and firm yellow flesh.*

King Edward: *a large potato which is creamy white, or sometimes yellow in colour. Ideal for all cooking methods, it is a very popular variety.*

Maris Piper: *a medium-firm potato with creamy white flesh. It is good for boiling and frying.*

New Potatoes: *these generally have a white flesh and grow quickly. They are dug up in early summer and are best scraped and boiled to use in salads or eaten with melted butter.*

Pentland Crown: *a thin-skinned, creamy white potato which is at its best in late winter. It has a floury (mealy) texture, making it ideal for mashing and baking.*

Francine

Pentland Hawk: *a firm, pale potato with pale yellow flesh, it is a general, all-purpose potato.*

Pentland Squire: *a firm, white-fleshed potato, which is suitable for all methods of cooking.*

Pink Fir Apple: *this long, knobbly potato has pink flesh and a firm, waxy texture. Good in salads.*

Anya

White Sweet Potato: *smaller than the yam, although interchangeable, it is yellow-fleshed with a drier texture. Best fried, boiled or casseroled, it is ideal with spices.*

Yam: *a red sweet potato which is orange-fleshed. It is best mashed in cakes and soufflés or roasted.*

Pentland Squire

Many of the recipes in this book are designed to appeal to vegetarians and vegans and they dispel the myth that all vegetarian food is brown, stodgy and bland. When browsing through the recipes you will discover just how versatile, and flavoursome, cooking with vegetables can be.

Fresh produce is now brought from all over the world to give us a whole array of fresh fruit and vegetables with which to work. In addition, the use of spices, fresh herbs and garlic makes for a very exciting and healthy diet.

Eating a balanced, nutritional diet is very important, and can be easily achieved by combining the recipes in this book when planning your meal to include protein, carbohydrate, vitamins, minerals and some fats.

It is very important in any diet, and especially a vegetarian diet, that a good balance is achieved and sufficient protein is eaten.

The recipes in this book come from all over the world, but there are also traditional recipes such as Vegetable-Toad-in-the-Hole, a family dish in which it is guaranteed you won't miss the meat. As a number of the potato-based dishes include meat, there is something for everyone here. It is the perfect way to introduce your friends to a healthy and delicious diet.

When cooking the following recipes, feel free to substitute some ingredients to suit your specific diets, for example, using soya milk in place of cow's milk. Cooking with vegetables has progressed from nut cutlets to a colourful and imaginative way of eating. Go ahead and enjoy!

THE STORE-CUPBOARD

Flour

You will need to keep a selection of flour: selfraising and wholemeal (wholewheat) are the most useful. You may also like to keep some rice flour and cornflour (cornstarch) for thickening sauces and to add to cakes, biscuits and puddings. Buckwheat, chickpea (garbanzo bean) and soya flours can also be bought. These are useful for combining with other flours to add different flavours and textures.

Grains

A good variety of grains is essential. For rice, choose from long-grain, basmati, Italian arborio, short-grain and wild rice. Look out for fragrant Thai rice, jasmine rice and combinations of different varieties to add colour and texture to your dishes. When choosing your rice, remember that brown rice is a better source of vitamin B1 and fibre.

Other grains add variety to the diet. Try to include some barley millet, bulgur wheat, polenta, oats, semolina, sago and tapioca.

Pasta

Pasta is so popular nowadays, and there are many types and shapes to choose from. Keep a good selection, such as basic lasagne sheets, tagliatelle or fettuccine (flat ribbons) and spaghetti. For a change, sample some of the many fresh pastas now available. Better still, make your own – handrolling pasta can be very satisfying, and you can buy a special machine for rolling the dough and cutting certain shapes.

Pulses (legumes)

Pulses (legumes) are a valuable source of protein, vitamins and minerals. Stock up on soya beans, haricot (navy) beans, red kidney beans, cannellini beans, chickpeas (garbanzo beans), lentils, split peas and butter beans. Buy dried pulses (legumes) for soaking and cooking yourself, or canned varieties for speed and convenience.

Spices and herbs

A good selection of spices and herbs is important for adding variety to your cooking. There are some good spice mixtures available – try Cajun, Chinese five-spice, Indonesian piri-piri and the different curry blends. Although spices will keep well, don't leave them in the cupboard for too long, as they may lose some of their strength. Buy small amounts as you need them. Fresh herbs are preferable to dried, but it is essential to have dried ones in stock as a useful back-up.

Chillies

These come both fresh and dried and in many colours. The 'hotness' varies so use with caution. The seeds are hottest and are usually discarded. Chilli powder should also be used sparingly. Check whether the powder is pure chilli or a chilli seasoning or blend, which should be milder.

Nuts and seeds

As well as adding protein, vitamins and useful fats to the diet, nuts and seeds add important flavour and texture to vegetarian meals. Make sure that you keep a good supply of nuts, such as hazelnuts, pine kernels (nuts) and walnuts. Coconut is useful too.

For your seed collection, have sesame, sunflower, pumpkin and poppy. Pumpkin seeds in particular are a good source of zinc.

Dried fruits

Currants, raisins, sultanas (golden raisins), dates, apples, apricots, figs, pears, peaches, prunes, paw-paws (papayas), mangoes, figs, bananas and pineapples can all be purchased dried and can be used in lots of different recipes. When buying dried fruits, look for untreated varieties: for example, buy figs that have not been rolled in sugar, and choose unsulphured apricots, if they are available.

Oils and fats

Oils are useful for adding subtle flavourings to foods, so it is a good idea to have a selection in your store-cupboard. Use a light olive oil for cooking and extra-virgin olive oil for salad dressings. Use sunflower oil as a good general-purpose oil. Sesame oil is wonderful in stir-fries; hazelnut and walnut oils are superb in salad dressings. Oils and fats add flavour to foods, and contain the important fat-soluble vitamins A, D, E and K. Remember all fats and oils are high in calories, and that oils are higher in calories than butter or margarine.

Vinegars

Choose three or four vinegars – red or white wine, cider, light malt, tarragon, sherry or balsamic vinegar, to name just a few. Each will add its own character to your recipes.

Mustards

Mustards are made from black, brown or white mustard seeds which are ground and mixed with spices. Meaux mustard is made from mixed mustard seeds and has a grainy texture with a warm, taste. Dijon mustard, made from husked and ground mustard seeds, has a sharp flavour. Its versatility in salads and with barbecues makes it ideal for the vegetarian. German mustard is mild and is best used in Scandinavian and German dishes.

Bottled sauces

Soy sauce is widely used in Eastern cookery and is made from fermented yellow soya beans mixed with wheat, salt, yeast and sugar. Light soy sauce tends to be rather salty, whereas dark soy sauce tends to be sweeter. Teriyaki sauce gives an authentic Japanese flavouring to stir-fries. Black bean and yellow bean sauces add an instant authentic Chinese flavour to stir-fries.

Soups & Salads

Potatoes form the basis of many delicious and easy-to-prepare home-made soups, as they are the perfect thickening ingredient while adding a subtle flavour. With the addition of just a few ingredients such as vegetables, you have a whole selection of inexpensive soups at your fingertips. Add herbs, onion, garlic, meat or fish, top with herbs or croûtons and vegetables, or serve with crusty bread.

Also featured in this chapter are salads based on potatoes and vegetables. In addition to the creamy potato salads with herbs that are so popular, there are many other recipes to tempt your palate. Starters should be colourful and flavoursome but should complement the remainder of the meal. Avoid repeating ingredients in following courses. In this chapter are well-known classics as well as innovative alternatives. There are salads suitable for light lunches as well as hearty main-course salads. Many are also ideal for barbecues (grills) and picnics.

Sweet Potato & Onion Soup

Serves 4

INGREDIENTS

2 tbsp vegetable oil	300 ml/½ pint/1¼ cups	TO GARNISH:
900 g/2 lb sweet potatoes, diced	unsweetened orange juice	coriander (cilantro) sprigs
1 carrot, diced	225 ml/8 fl oz/1 cup natural yogurt	orange rind
2 onions, sliced	2 tbsp chopped fresh coriander	
2 garlic cloves, crushed	(cilantro)	
600 ml/1 pint/2½ cups vegetable stock	salt and pepper	

1 Heat the vegetable oil in a large saucepan and add the diced sweet potatoes and carrot, sliced onions and garlic. Sauté gently for 5 minutes, stirring constantly.

2 Pour in the vegetable stock and orange juice and bring them to the boil.

3 Reduce the heat to a simmer, cover the saucepan and cook the vegetables for 20 minutes or until the sweet potato and carrot cubes are tender.

4 Transfer the mixture to a food processor or blender in batches and process for 1 minute until puréed. Return the purée to the rinsed-out saucepan.

5 Stir in the natural yogurt and chopped coriander (cilantro) and season to taste. Serve the soup garnished with coriander (cilantro) sprigs and orange rind.

COOK'S TIP

This soup can be chilled before serving, if preferred. If chilling it, stir the yogurt into the dish just before serving. Serve in chilled bowls.

Potato, Apple & Rocket (Arugula) Soup

Serves 4

INGREDIENTS

4 tbsp butter
900 g/2 lb waxy potatoes, diced
1 red onion, quartered
1 tbsp lemon juice
1 litre/1³/₄pints/4¹/₂ cups chicken
   stock

450 g/1 lb dessert apples, peeled
   and diced
pinch of ground allspice
50 g/1³/₄ oz rocket (arugula)
   leaves
salt and pepper

TO GARNISH:
slices of red apple
chopped spring onions (scallions)

1 Melt the butter in a large saucepan and add the diced potatoes and sliced red onion. Sauté gently for 5 minutes, stirring constantly.

2 Add the lemon juice, chicken stock, diced apples and the ground allspice.

3 Bring to the boil, then reduce the heat to a simmer, cover the pan and cook for 15 minutes.

4 Add the rocket (arugula) to the soup and cook for a further 10 minutes until the potatoes are cooked through.

5 Transfer half of the soup to a food processor or blender and process for 1 minute. Return to the pan and stir the purée into the remaining soup.

6 Season to taste with salt and pepper. Ladle into

hot soup bowls and garnish with the apple slices and chopped spring onions (scallions). Serve at once with warm crusty bread.

COOK'S TIP

If rocket (arugula) is unavailable, use baby spinach instead for a similar flavour.

Indian Potato & Pea Soup

Serves 4

INGREDIENTS

2 tbsp vegetable oil	1 tsp ground coriander (cilantro)	100 g/3½ oz frozen peas
225 g/8 oz floury (mealy) potatoes, diced	1 tsp ground cumin	4 tbsp natural yogurt
1 large onion, chopped	900 ml/1½ pints/3¾cups vegetable stock	salt and pepper
2 garlic cloves, crushed	1 red chilli, chopped	chopped fresh coriander (cilantro), to garnish
1 tsp garam masala		

1 Heat the vegetable oil in a large saucepan and add the diced potatoes, onion and garlic. Sauté gently for about 5 minutes, stirring constantly.

2 Add the ground spices and cook for 1 minute, stirring all the time.

3 Stir in the vegetable stock and chopped red chilli and bring the mixture to the boil. Reduce the heat, cover the pan and simmer for 20 minutes until the potatoes begin to break down.

4 Add the peas and cook for a further 5 minutes. Stir in the yogurt and season to taste.

5 Pour into warmed soup bowls, garnish with chopped fresh coriander (cilantro) and serve hot with warm bread.

COOK'S TIP

Potatoes blend perfectly with spices, this soup being no exception. For an authentic Indian dish, serve this soup with warm naan bread.

VARIATION

For slightly less heat, deseed the chilli before adding it to the soup. Always wash your hands after handling chillies as they contain volatile oils that can irritate the skin and make your eyes burn if you touch your face.

Broccoli & Potato Soup

Serves 4

INGREDIENTS

2 tbsp olive oil	125 g/4^1/$_2$ oz blue cheese,	150 ml/^{1}/$_4$ pint/^{2}/$_3$ cup double
2 potatoes, diced	crumbled	(heavy) cream
1 onion, diced	1 litre/1^3/$_4$ pints/4^1/$_2$ cups	pinch of paprika
225 g/8 oz broccoli florets	vegetable stock	salt and pepper

1 Heat the oil in a large saucepan and add the diced potatoes and onion. Sauté gently for 5 minutes, stirring constantly.

2 Reserve a few broccoli florets for the garnish and add the remaining broccoli to the pan. Add the cheese and stock.

3 Bring to the boil, then reduce the heat, cover the pan and simmer for 25 minutes until the potatoes are tender.

4 Transfer the soup to a food processor or blender in 2 batches and process until the mixture is a smooth purée.

5 Return the purée to a clean saucepan and stir in the cream and a pinch of paprika. Season to taste with salt and pepper.

6 Blanch the reserved broccoli florets in a little boiling water for about 2 minutes, then drain with a perforated spoon.

7 Pour the soup into warmed bowls and garnish with the broccoli florets and a sprinkling of paprika. Serve immediately.

COOK'S TIP

This soup freezes very successfully. Follow the method described here up to step 4, and freeze the soup after it has been puréed. Add the cream and paprika just before serving.

Potato & Dried Mushroom Soup

Serves 4

INGREDIENTS

2 tbsp vegetable oil

2 large floury (mealy) potatoes,
   sliced

1 onion, sliced

2 garlic cloves, crushed

1 litre/1³/4 pints/4¹/2 cups beef stock

25 g/1 oz dried mushrooms

2 celery sticks, sliced

2 tbsp brandy

salt and pepper

TOPPING:

3 tbsp butter

2 thick slices white bread, crusts

removed

3 tbsp grated Parmesan cheese

TO GARNISH:

rehydrated dried mushrooms

parsley sprigs

1 Heat the vegetable oil in a large frying pan (skillet) and add the potato and onion slices and the garlic. Sauté gently for 5 minutes, stirring constantly.

2 Add the beef stock, dried mushrooms and the sliced celery. Bring to the boil, then reduce the heat to a simmer, cover the saucepan and cook the soup for 20 minutes until the potatoes are tender.

3 Meanwhile, melt the butter for the topping in the frying pan (skillet). Sprinkle the bread slices with the grated cheese and fry the slices in the butter for 1 minute on each side until crisp. Cut each slice into triangles.

4 Stir the brandy into the soup, season with salt and pepper. Pour into warmed bowls and top with the triangles. Serve garnished with mushrooms and parsley.

COOK'S TIP

Probably the most popular dried mushroom is the cep, but any variety will add a lovely flavour to this soup. If you do not wish to use dried mushrooms, add 125 g/4 oz sliced fresh mushrooms of your choice to the soup.

Potato, Split Pea & Cheese Soup

Serves 4

INGREDIENTS

2 tbsp vegetable oil
2 floury (mealy) potatoes, diced
  with skins left on
2 onions, diced
75 g/2³/₄ oz split green peas

1 litre/1³/₄ pints/4¹/₂ cups
  vegetable stock
5 tbsp grated Gruyère cheese
salt and pepper

CROUTONS:
3 tbsp butter
1 garlic clove, crushed
1 tbsp chopped fresh parsley
1 thick slice white bread, cubed

1 Heat the vegetable oil in a large saucepan and add the diced potatoes and onions. Sauté gently for about 5 minutes, stirring constantly.

2 Add the split green peas to the pan and stir to mix together well.

3 Pour the vegetable stock into the pan and bring to the boil. Reduce the heat to a simmer and cook for 35 minutes until the potatoes are tender and the split peas cooked.

4 Meanwhile, make the croutons. Melt the butter in a frying pan (skillet). Add the garlic, chopped parsley and bread cubes and cook for about 2 minutes, turning frequently until the bread cubes are golden brown on all sides.

5 Stir the grated cheese into the soup and season to taste with salt and pepper.

6 Pour the soup into warmed bowls and sprinkle the croutons on top. Serve at once.

VARIATION

Red lentils could be used instead of split green peas if preferred, for a richly coloured soup. Add a large pinch of brown sugar to the recipe for sweetness if red lentils are used.

Leek, Potato & Bacon Soup

Serves 4

INGREDIENTS

25 g/1 oz/2 tbsp butter
175 g/6 oz potatoes, diced
4 leeks, shredded
2 garlic cloves, crushed
100 g/3½ oz smoked bacon, diced

900 ml/1½ pints/3¾ cups vegetable stock
225 ml/8 fl oz/1 cup double (heavy) cream
2 tbsp chopped fresh parsley
salt and pepper

TO GARNISH:
vegetable oil
1 leek, shredded

1 Melt the butter in a large saucepan and add the diced potatoes, shredded leeks, garlic and diced bacon. Sauté gently for 5 minutes, stirring constantly.

2 Add the vegetable stock and bring to the boil. Reduce the heat, cover the saucepan and simmer for 20 minutes until the potatoes are cooked. Stir in the double (heavy) cream.

3 Meanwhile, make the garnish. Half-fill a pan with oil and heat to 180°C–190°C/350°F–375°F or until a cube of bread browns in 30 seconds. Add the shredded leek and deep-fry for 1 minute until browned and crisp, taking care as the leek contains water. Drain the leek thoroughly on paper towels and reserve.

4 Reserve a few pieces of potato, leek and bacon and set aside. Put the rest of the soup in a food processor or blender in batches and process each batch for 30 seconds. Return the puréed soup to a clean saucepan and heat through.

5 Stir in the reserved vegetables, bacon and parsley and season to taste. Pour into warmed bowls and garnish with the fried leeks.

VARIATION

For a lighter soup, omit the cream and stir yogurt or crème fraîche into the soup at the end of the cooking time.

Potato, Cabbage & Chorizo Soup

Serves 4

INGREDIENTS

2 tbsp olive oil	1 litre/1³/₄ pints/4¹/₂ cups pork or	50 g/1³/₄ oz chorizo sausage,
3 large potatoes, cubed	vegetable stock	sliced
2 red onions, quartered	150 g/5¹/₂ oz Savoy cabbage,	salt and pepper
1 garlic clove, crushed	shredded	paprika, to garnish

1 Heat the olive oil in a large saucepan and add the cubed potatoes, quartered red onions and garlic. Sauté gently for 5 minutes, stirring constantly.

2 Add the pork or vegetable stock and bring to the boil. Reduce the heat and cover the saucepan. Simmer the vegetables for about 20 minutes until the potatoes are tender.

3 Process the soup in a food processor or blender in 2 batches for 1 minute each. Return the puréed soup to a clean pan.

4 Add the shredded Savoy cabbage and sliced chorizo sausage to the pan and cook for a further 7 minutes. Season to taste.

5 Ladle the soup into warmed soup bowls, garnish with a sprinkling of paprika and serve.

COOK'S TIP

Chorizo sausage requires no pre-cooking. In this recipe, it is added towards the end of the cooking time so that it does not overpower the other flavours in the soup.

VARIATION

If chorizo sausage is not available, you could use any other spicy sausage or even salami in its place.

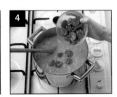

Chinese Potato & Pork Broth

Serves 4

INGREDIENTS

1 litre/1¾ pints/4½ cups chicken
    stock
2 large potatoes, diced
2 tbsp rice wine vinegar
125 g/4½ oz pork fillet, sliced

2 tbsp cornflour (cornstarch)
4 tbsp water
1 tbsp light soy sauce
1 tsp sesame oil
1 carrot, cut into very thin
    strips

1 tsp ginger root, chopped
3 spring onions (scallions), sliced
    thinly
1 red (bell) pepper, sliced
225 g/8 oz can bamboo shoots,
    drained

1 Add the chicken stock, diced potatoes and 1 tbsp of the rice wine vinegar to a saucepan and bring to the boil. Reduce the heat until the stock is just simmering.

2 In a small bowl, mix the cornflour (cornstarch) with the water. Stir the mixture into the hot stock.

3 Bring the stock back to the boil, stirring until thickened, then reduce the heat until it is just simmering again.

4 Place the pork slices in a shallow dish and season with the remaining rice wine vinegar, soy sauce and sesame oil.

5 Add the pork slices, carrot strips and chopped ginger to the stock and cook for 10 minutes. Stir in the sliced spring onions (scallions), red (bell) pepper and bamboo shoots. Cook for a further 5 minutes.

6 Pour the soup into warmed bowls and serve immediately.

COOK'S TIP

Sesame oil is very strongly flavoured and is, therefore, only used in small quantities.

VARIATION

For extra heat, add 1 chopped red chilli or 1 tsp of chilli powder to the soup in step 5.

Chunky Potato & Beef Soup

Serves 4

INGREDIENTS

2 tbsp vegetable oil

225 g/8 oz braising or frying
     steak, cut into strips

225 g/8 oz new potatoes, halved

1 carrot, diced

2 celery sticks, sliced

2 leeks, sliced

900 ml/1½ pints/3¾ cups beef
     stock

8 baby sweetcorn cobs, sliced

1 bouquet garni

2 tbsp dry sherry

salt and pepper

chopped fresh parsley, to garnish

1 Heat the vegetable oil in a large saucepan. Add the strips of meat and cook for 3 minutes, turning constantly.

2 Add the halved potatoes, diced carrot and sliced celery and leeks. Cook for a further 5 minutes, stirring.

3 Pour the beef stock into the saucepan and bring to the boil. Reduce the heat until the liquid is simmering, then add the sliced baby sweetcorn cobs and the bouquet garni.

4 Cook the soup for a further 20 minutes or until the meat and all of the vegetables are cooked through.

5 Remove the bouquet garni from the saucepan and discard. Stir the dry sherry into the soup and then season to taste with salt and pepper.

6 Pour the soup into warmed bowls and garnish with the chopped fresh parsley. Serve at once, accompanied by chunks of fresh crusty bread.

COOK'S TIP

Make double the quantity of soup and freeze the remainder in a rigid container for later use. When ready to use, leave in the refrigerator to defrost thoroughly, then heat until piping hot.

Potato & Mixed Fish Soup

Serves 4

INGREDIENTS

2 tbsp vegetable oil	225 ml/8 fl oz/1 cup dry white	2 tomatoes, peeled, seeded and
450 g/1 lb small new potatoes,	wine	chopped
halved	600 ml/1 pint/2¹/₂ cups fish stock	100 g/3¹/₂ oz peeled cooked
1 bunch spring onions (scallions),	225 g/8 oz white fish fillet,	prawns (shrimp)
sliced	skinned and cubed	150 ml/¹/₄ pint/²/₃ cup double
1 yellow (bell) pepper, sliced	225 g/8 oz smoked cod fillet,	(heavy) cream
2 garlic cloves, crushed	skinned and cubed	2 tbsp shredded fresh basil

1 Heat the vegetable oil in a large saucepan and add the halved potatoes, sliced spring onions (scallions) and (bell) pepper and the garlic. Sauté gently for 3 minutes, stirring constantly.

2 Add the white wine and fish stock and bring to the boil. Reduce the heat and simmer for 10–15 minutes.

3 Add the cubed fish fillets and the tomatoes to the soup and continue to cook for 10 minutes or until the fish is cooked through.

4 Stir in the prawns (shrimp), cream and shredded basil and cook for 2–3 minutes. Pour the soup into warmed bowls and serve.

COOK'S TIP

The basil is added at the end of the cooking time as the flavour is destroyed by heat.

VARIATION

For a soup which is slightly less rich, omit the wine and stir natural yogurt into the soup instead of the double (heavy) cream.

Mixed Bean Soup

Serves 4

INGREDIENTS

1 tbsp vegetable oil
1 red onion, halved and sliced
100 g/3½ oz/⅔ cup potato,
   diced
1 carrot, diced
1 leek, sliced

1 green chilli, sliced
3 garlic cloves, crushed
1 tsp ground coriander (cilantro)
1 tsp chilli powder
1 litre/1¾ pints/4 cups
   vegetable stock

450 g/1 lb mixed canned beans,
   such as red kidney, borlotti,
   black eye or flageolet, drained
salt and pepper
2 tbsp chopped coriander
   (cilantro), to garnish

1 Heat the vegetable oil in a large saucepan and add the prepared onion, potato, carrot and leek. Sauté for about 2 minutes, stirring, until the vegetables are slightly softened.

2 Add the sliced chilli and crushed garlic and cook for a further 1 minute.

3 Stir in the ground coriander (cilantro), chilli powder and the vegetable stock.

4 Bring the soup to the boil, reduce the heat and cook for 20 minutes or until the vegetables are tender.

5 Stir in the beans, season well with salt and pepper and cook for a further 10 minutes, stirring occasionally.

6 Transfer the soup to a warm tureen or individual bowls, garnish with chopped coriander (cilantro) and serve.

COOK'S TIP

Serve this soup with slices of warm corn bread or a cheese loaf.

Vegetable & Corn Chowder

Serves 4

INGREDIENTS

1 tbsp vegetable oil
1 red onion, diced
1 red (bell) pepper, diced
3 garlic cloves, crushed
1 large potato, diced
2 tbsp plain (all-purpose) flour

600 ml/1 pint/2½ cups milk
300 ml/½ pint/1¼ cups
    vegetable stock
50 g/1¾ oz broccoli florets
300 g/10½ oz/3 cups canned
    sweetcorn in brine, drained

75 g/2¾ oz/¾ cup vegetarian
    Cheddar cheese, grated
salt and pepper
1 tbsp chopped fresh coriander
    (cilantro), to garnish

1 Heat the oil in a large saucepan and sauté the onion, (bell) pepper, garlic and potato for 2–3 minutes, stirring.

2 Stir in the flour and cook for 30 seconds. Stir in the milk and stock.

3 Add the broccoli and sweetcorn. Bring the mixture to the boil, stirring, then reduce the heat and simmer for about 20 minutes or until the vegetables are tender.

4 Stir in 50 g/1¾ oz/ ½ cup of the cheese until it melts.

5 Season and spoon the chowder into a warm soup tureen. Garnish with the remaining cheese and the coriander (cilantro) and serve.

COOK'S TIP

Vegetarian cheeses are made with rennets of non-animal origin, using microbial or fungal enzymes.

COOK'S TIP

Add a little double (heavy) cream to the soup after adding the milk for a really creamy flavour.

Cauliflower & Broccoli Soup with Gruyère

Serves 4

INGREDIENTS

3 tbsp vegetable oil
1 red onion, chopped
2 garlic cloves, crushed
300 g/10½ oz cauliflower florets
300 g/10½ oz broccoli florets

1 tbsp plain (all-purpose) flour
600 ml/1 pint/2½ cups milk
300 ml/½ pint/1¼ cups
　vegetable stock
75 g/2¾ oz/¾ cup vegetarian
　Gruyère cheese, grated

pinch of paprika
150 ml/¼ pint/⅔ cup single
　(light) cream
paprika and vegetarian Gruyère
　cheese shavings, to garnish

1 Heat the oil in a large saucepan and sauté the onion, garlic, cauliflower and broccoli for 3–4 minutes, stirring constantly. Add the flour and cook for a further 1 minute, stirring.

2 Stir in the milk and stock and bring to the boil. Reduce the heat and simmer for 20 minutes.

3 Remove about a quarter of the vegetables and set aside.

4 Put the remaining soup in a food processor and blend for 30 seconds until smooth. Transfer the soup to a clean saucepan.

5 Return the reserved vegetable pieces to the soup.

6 Stir in the grated cheese, paprika and single (light) cream and heat gently for 2–3 minutes without boiling, or until the cheese starts to melt.

7 Transfer to warm serving bowls, garnish with shavings of Gruyère and dust with paprika.

COOK'S TIP

The soup must not start to boil after the cream has been added otherwise it will curdle. Use natural (unsweetened) yogurt instead of the cream if preferred, but again do not allow to boil.

Celery, Stilton & Walnut Soup

Serves 4

INGREDIENTS

50 g/1¾ oz/4 tbsp butter
2 shallots, chopped
3 celery sticks, chopped
1 garlic clove, crushed
2 tbsp plain (all-purpose) flour

600 ml/1 pint/2½ cups
  vegetable stock
300 ml/½ pint/1¼ cups milk
150 g/5½ oz/1½ cups blue Stilton
  cheese, crumbled, plus extra to
  garnish

2 tbsp walnut halves, roughly
  chopped
150 ml/¼ pint/⅔ cup natural
  (unsweetened) yogurt
salt and pepper
chopped celery leaves, to garnish

1 Melt the butter in a large saucepan and sauté the shallots, celery and garlic for 2–3 minutes, stirring, until softened.

2 Add the flour and cook for 30 seconds.

3 Gradually stir in the vegetable stock and milk and bring to the boil.

4 Reduce the heat to a gentle simmer and add the crumbled blue Stilton cheese and walnut halves. Cover and leave to simmer for 20 minutes.

5 Stir in the natural (unsweetened) yogurt and heat for a further 2 minutes without boiling.

6 Season the soup, then transfer to a warm soup tureen or individual serving bowls, garnish with chopped celery leaves and extra crumbled blue Stilton cheese and serve at once.

COOK'S TIP

As well as adding protein, vitamins and useful fats to the diet, nuts add important flavour and texture to vegetarian meals.

VARIATION

Use an alternative blue cheese, such as Dolcelatte or Gorgonzola, if preferred or a strong vegetarian Cheddar cheese, grated.

Curried Parsnip Soup

Serves 4

INGREDIENTS

1 tbsp vegetable oil	2 tsp garam masala	grated rind and juice of 1 lemon
1 tbsp butter	1/2 tsp chilli powder	salt and pepper
1 red onion, chopped	1 tbsp plain (all-purpose) flour	lemon zest, to garnish
3 parsnips, chopped	850 ml/1 1/2 pints/3 3/4 cups	
2 garlic cloves, crushed	vegetable stock	

1 Heat the oil and butter in a large saucepan until the butter has melted.

2 Add the onion, parsnips and garlic and sauté for 5–7 minutes, stirring, until the vegetables have softened.

3 Add the garam masala and chilli powder and cook for 30 seconds, stirring well.

4 Sprinkle in the flour, mixing well and cook for a further 30 seconds.

5 Stir in the stock, lemon rind and juice and bring to the boil. Reduce the heat and simmer for 20 minutes.

6 Remove some of the vegetable pieces with a slotted spoon and reserve until required. Blend the remaining soup and vegetables in a food processor for 1 minute or until smooth.

7 Return the soup to a clean saucepan and stir in the reserved vegetables. Heat the soup through for 2 minutes.

8 Season then transfer to soup bowls, garnish with grated lemon zest and serve.

VARIATION

Use 1 medium orange instead of the lemon if preferred and garnish with grated orange zest.

Jerusalem Artichoke Soup

Serves 4

INGREDIENTS

675 g/1½ lb Jerusalem
    artichokes
5 tbsp orange juice
25 g/1 oz/2 tbsp butter
1 leek, chopped

1 garlic clove, crushed
300 ml/½ pint/1¼ cups
    vegetable stock
150 ml/¼ pint/⅔ cup milk

2 tbsp chopped coriander
    (cilantro)
150 ml/¼ pint/⅔ cup natural
    (unsweetened) yogurt
grated orange rind, to garnish

1 Rinse the Jerusalem artichokes and place in a large saucepan with 2 tablespoons of the orange juice and enough water to cover. Bring to the boil, reduce the heat and cook for 20 minutes or until the artichokes are tender.

2 Drain the artichokes, reserving 425 ml/¾ pint/2 cups of the cooking liquid. Leave the artichokes to cool.

3 Once cooled, peel the artichokes and place in a large bowl. Mash the flesh with a potato masher.

4 Melt the butter in a large saucepan and sauté the leek and garlic for 2–3 minutes, stirring until the leek softens.

5 Stir in the artichoke flesh, the reserved cooking water, the stock, milk and remaining orange juice. Bring the soup to the boil, reduce the heat and simmer for 2–3 minutes.

6 Remove a few pieces of leek with a slotted spoon and reserve. Transfer the remainder of the soup to a food processor and blend for 1 minute until smooth.

7 Return the soup to a clean saucepan and stir in the reserved leeks, coriander (cilantro) and yogurt.

8 Transfer to individual soup bowls, garnish with orange rind and serve.

VARIATION

If Jerusalem artichokes are unavailable, you could use sweet potatoes instead.

Red (Bell) Pepper & Chilli Soup

Serves 4

INGREDIENTS

225 g/8 oz red (bell) peppers,
    seeded and sliced
1 onion, sliced
2 garlic cloves, crushed
1 green chilli, chopped

300 ml/$\frac{1}{2}$ pint/1$\frac{1}{2}$ cups passata
    (sieved tomatoes)
600 ml/1 pint/2$\frac{1}{2}$ cups
    vegetable stock
2 tbsp chopped basil

fresh basil sprigs, to garnish

1 Put the (bell) peppers in a large saucepan with the onion, garlic and chilli. Add the passata (sieved tomatoes) and vegetable stock and bring to the boil, stirring well.

2 Reduce the heat to a simmer and cook for 20 minutes or until the (bell) peppers have softened. Drain, reserving the liquid and vegetables separately.

3 Sieve the vegetables by pressing through a sieve (strainer) with the back of a spoon.

Alternatively, blend in a food processor until smooth.

4 Return the vegetable purée to a clean saucepan with the reserved cooking liquid. Add the basil and heat through until hot. Garnish the soup with fresh basil sprigs and serve.

COOK'S TIP

Basil is a useful herb to grow at home. It can be grown easily in a window box.

VARIATION

This soup is also delicious served cold with 150 ml/$\frac{1}{4}$ pint/$\frac{2}{3}$ cup of natural (unsweetened) yogurt swirled into it.

Dahl Soup

Serves 4

INGREDIENTS

25 g/1 oz/2 tbsp butter	1 tsp ground cumin	vegetable stock
2 garlic cloves, crushed	1 kg/2 lb 4 oz canned, chopped	300 ml/¹/₂ pint/1¹/₄ cups coconut milk
1 onion, chopped	tomatoes, drained	salt and pepper
¹/₂ tsp turmeric	175 g/6 oz/1 cup red lentils	chopped coriander (cilantro) and
1 tsp garam masala	2 tsp lemon juice	lemon slices, to garnish
¹/₄ tsp chilli powder	600 ml/1 pint/2¹/₂ cups	naan bread, to serve

1 Melt the butter in a large saucepan and sauté the garlic and onion for 2–3 minutes, stirring. Add the spices and cook for a further 30 seconds.

2 Stir in the tomatoes, red lentils, lemon juice, vegetable stock and coconut milk and bring to the boil.

3 Reduce the heat and simmer for 25–30 minutes until the lentils are tender and cooked.

4 Season to taste and spoon the soup into a warm tureen. Garnish and serve with warm naan bread.

COOK'S TIP

You can buy cans of coconut milk from supermarkets and delicatessens. It can also be made by grating creamed coconut, which comes in the form of a solid bar, and mixing it with water.

COOK'S TIP

Add small quantities of hot water to the pan whilst the lentils are cooking if they begin to absorb too much of the liquid.

Avocado & Vegetable Soup

Serves 4

INGREDIENTS

1 large, ripe avocado	2 tomatoes, peeled and seeded	vegetable stock
2 tbsp lemon juice	1 garlic clove, crushed	150 ml/ $^1/_4$ pint/ $^2/_3$ cup milk
1 tbsp vegetable oil	1 leek, chopped	shredded leeks, to garnish
50 g/1 $^3/_4$ oz/ $^1/_2$ cup canned	1 red chilli, chopped	
sweetcorn, drained	425 ml/ $^3/_4$ pint/2 cups	

1 Peel and mash the avocado with a fork, stir in the lemon juice and reserve until required.

2 Heat the oil in a pan and sauté the sweetcorn, tomatoes, garlic, leek and chilli for 2–3 minutes or until the vegetables are softened.

3 Put half of the vegetable mixture in a food processor or blender with the avocado and blend until smooth. Transfer to a clean saucepan.

4 Add the stock, milk and reserved vegetables and cook gently for 3–4 minutes until hot. Garnish and serve.

COOK'S TIP

To remove the stone from an avocado, first cut the avocado in half, then holding one half in your hand, rap the stone with a knife until it is embedded in the stone, then twist the knife until the stone is dislodged.

COOK'S TIP

If serving chilled, transfer from the food processor to a bowl, stir in the stock and milk, cover and chill in the refrigerator for at least 4 hours.

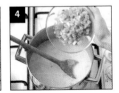

Spanish Tomato Soup with Garlic Bread Croûtons

Serves 4

INGREDIENTS

4 tbsp olive oil	225 g/8 oz French or	GARLIC BREAD:
1 onion, chopped	Italian bread, cubed	4 slices ciabatta or French bread
3 garlic cloves, crushed	1 litre/1¾ pints/4 cups	4 tbsp olive oil
1 green (bell) pepper, chopped	vegetable stock	2 garlic cloves, crushed
½ tsp chilli powder		25 g/1 oz/¼ cup grated
450 g/1 lb tomatoes, chopped		vegetarian Cheddar
		chilli powder, to garnish

1 Heat the olive oil in a large frying pan (skillet) and add the prepared onion, garlic and (bell) pepper. Sauté the vegetables for 2–3 minutes or until the onion has softened.

2 Add the chilli powder and tomatoes and cook over a medium heat until the mixture has thickened.

3 Stir in the bread cubes and stock and cook for 10–15 minutes until the soup is thick and fairly smooth.

4 To make the garlic bread, toast the bread slices under a medium grill (broiler). Drizzle the oil over the top of the bread, rub with the garlic, sprinkle with the cheese and return to the grill (broiler) for 2–3 minutes until the cheese has melted. Sprinkle with chilli powder and serve with the soup.

VARIATION

Replace the green (bell) pepper with red (bell) pepper, if you prefer.

Broad (Fava) Bean & Mint Soup

Serves 4

INGREDIENTS

2 tbsp olive oil
1 red onion, chopped
2 garlic cloves, crushed
2 potatoes, diced
450 g/1 lb/3 cups broad (fava)

beans, thawed if frozen
850 ml/1½ pints/3¾ cups
    vegetable stock
2 tbsp freshly chopped mint

fresh mint sprigs and yogurt,
    to garnish

1 Heat the olive oil in a large saucepan and sauté the onion and garlic for 2–3 minutes until softened and transluscent

2 Add the potatoes and cook for 5 minutes, stirring well.

3 Stir in the beans and the stock, cover and simmer for 30 minutes or until the beans and potatoes are tender.

4 Remove a few vegetables with a slotted spoon and set aside

until required. Place the remainder of the soup in a food processor or blender and purée until smooth.

5 Return the soup to a clean saucepan and add the reserved vegetables and mint. Stir well and heat through gently.

6 Transfer the soup to a warm tureen or individual serving bowls. Garnish with swirls of yogurt and sprigs of fresh mint and serve immediately.

VARIATION

Use fresh coriander (cilantro) and ½ tsp ground cumin as flavourings in the soup, if you prefer.

Tuscan Bean & Vegetable Soup

Serves 4

INGREDIENTS

1 medium onion, chopped
1 garlic clove, finely chopped
2 celery sticks, sliced
1 large carrot, diced
400 g/14 oz can chopped
   tomatoes
150 ml/5 fl oz/²⁄₃ cup Italian dry
   red wine

1.2 litres/2 pints/5 cups fresh
   vegetable stock
1 tsp dried oregano
425 g/15 oz can mixed beans
   and pulses
2 medium courgettes
   (zucchini), diced

1 tbsp tomato purée (paste)
salt and pepper

TO SERVE:
low-fat pesto sauce
  crusty bread

1 Place the onion, garlic, celery and carrot in a large saucepan. Stir in the tomatoes, red wine, vegetable stock and oregano.

2 Bring the vegetable mixture to the boil, cover and leave to simmer for 15 minutes. Stir the beans and courgettes (zucchini) into the mixture, and continue to cook, uncovered, for a further 5 minutes.

3 Add the tomato purée (paste) to the mixture and season well with salt and pepper to taste. Then heat through, stirring occasionally, for 2–3 minutes, but do not allow the mixture to boil again.

4 Ladle the soup into warm bowls and top with a spoonful of low-fat pesto on each portion. Serve the soup accompanied with plenty of fresh crusty bread.

VARIATION

For a more substantial soup, add 350 g/12 oz diced lean cooked chicken or turkey with the tomato purée (paste) in step 3.

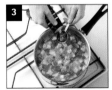

Lentil, Pasta & Vegetable Soup

Serves 4

INGREDIENTS

1 tbsp olive oil

1 medium onion, chopped

4 garlic cloves, finely chopped

350 g/12 oz carrot, sliced

1 stick celery, sliced

225 g/8 oz/1¼ cups red lentils

600 ml/1 pint/2½ cups fresh
   vegetable stock

700 ml/1¼ pint/scant 3 cups
   boiling water

150 g/5½ oz/scant 1 cup pasta

150 ml/5 fl oz/⅔ cup natural
   low-fat fromage frais
   (unsweetened yogurt)

salt and pepper

2 tbsp fresh parsley, chopped,
   to garnish

1 Heat the oil in a large saucepan and gently fry the prepared onion, garlic, carrot and celery, stirring gently, for 5 minutes until the vegetables begin to soften.

2 Add the lentils, stock and boiling water. Season with salt and pepper to taste, stir and bring back to the boil. Simmer, uncovered, for 15 minutes until the lentils are completely tender. Allow to cool for 10 minutes.

3 Meanwhile, bring another saucepan of water to the boil and cook the pasta according to the instructions on the packet. Drain well and set aside.

4 Place the soup in a blender and process until smooth. Return to a saucepan and add the pasta. Bring back to a simmer and heat for 2–3 minutes until piping hot. Remove from the heat and stir in the fromage frais (yogurt). Season if necessary.

5 Serve sprinkled with chopped parsley.

COOK'S TIP

Avoid boiling the soup once the fromage frais (yogurt) has been added. Otherwise it will separate and become watery, spoiling the appearance of the soup.

Tomato & Red (Bell) Pepper Soup

Serves 4

INGREDIENTS

2 large red (bell) peppers
1 large onion, chopped
2 sticks celery, trimmed and
    chopped
1 garlic clove, crushed

600 ml/1 pint/2½ cups fresh
    vegetable stock
2 bay leaves
2 x 400 g/14 oz cans plum
    tomatoes

salt and pepper
2 spring onions (scallions), finely
    shredded, to garnish
crusty bread, to serve

1 Preheat the grill (broiler) to hot. Halve and deseed the (bell) peppers, arrange them on the grill (broiler) rack and cook, turning occasionally, for 8–10 minutes until softened and charred.

2 Leave to cool slightly, then carefully peel off the charred skin. Reserving a small piece for garnish, chop the (bell) pepper flesh and place in a large saucepan.

3 Mix in the onion, celery and garlic. Add the stock and the bay leaves. Bring to the boil, cover and simmer for 15 minutes. Remove from the heat.

4 Stir in the tomatoes and transfer to a blender. Process for a few seconds until smooth. Return to the saucepan.

5 Season to taste and heat for 3–4 minutes until piping hot. Ladle into warm bowls and garnish with the reserved (bell) pepper cut into strips and the spring onion (scallion). Serve with crusty bread.

COOK'S TIP

If you prefer a coarser, more robust soup, lightly mash the tomatoes with a wooden spoon and omit the blending process in step 4.

Carrot, Apple & Celery Soup

Serves 4

INGREDIENTS

900 g/2 lb carrots, finely diced
1 medium onion, chopped
3 sticks celery, diced
1 litre/1¾ pints/1 quart fresh
   vegetable stock

3 medium-sized eating
   (dessert) apples
2 tbsp tomato purée (paste)
1 bay leaf
2 tsp caster (superfine) sugar

½ large lemon
salt and pepper
celery leaves, washed and
   shredded, to garnish

1 Place the carrots, onion and celery in a large saucepan and add the stock. Bring to the boil, cover and simmer for 10 minutes.

2 Meanwhile, peel, core and dice 2 of the eating (dessert) apples. Add the pieces of apple, tomato purée (paste), bay leaf and caster (superfine) sugar to the saucepan and bring to the boil. Reduce the heat, half cover and allow to simmer for 20 minutes. Remove and discard the bay leaf.

3 Meanwhile, wash, core and cut the remaining apple into thin slices, leaving on the skin. Place the apple slices in a small saucepan and squeeze over the lemon juice. Heat gently and simmer for 1–2 minutes until tender. Drain and set aside.

4 Place the carrot and apple mixture in a blender or food processor and blend until smooth. Alternatively, press the carrot and apple mixture through a sieve with the back of a wooden spoon.

5 Gently re-heat the soup if necessary and season with salt and pepper to taste. Ladle the soup into warm bowls and serve topped with the reserved apple slices and shredded celery leaves.

COOK'S TIP

Soaking light coloured fruit in lemon juice helps to prevent it from turning brown.

Potato, Mixed Bean & Apple Salad

Serves 4

INGREDIENTS

225 g/8 oz new potatoes,
  scrubbed and quartered
225 g/8 oz mixed canned beans,
  such as red kidney beans,
  flageolet and borlotti beans,
  drained and rinsed

1 red dessert apple, diced and
  tossed in 1 tbsp lemon juice
1 small yellow (bell) pepper, diced
1 shallot, sliced
½ head fennel, sliced
oak leaf lettuce leaves

DRESSING:
1 tbsp red wine vinegar
2 tbsp olive oil
½ tbsp American mustard
1 garlic clove, crushed
2 tsp chopped fresh thyme

1 Cook the quartered
potatoes in a saucepan of
boiling water for 15 minutes
until tender. Drain and
transfer to a mixing bowl.

2 Add the mixed beans
to the potatoes with
the diced apple and yellow
(bell) pepper, and the sliced
shallots and fennel. Mix
well, taking care not to
break up the cooked
potatoes.

3 In a bowl, whisk all
the dressing ingredients
together, then pour it over
the potato salad.

4 Line a plate or salad
bowl with the oak leaf
and spoon the potato
mixture into the centre.
Serve immediately.

VARIATION

*Use Dijon or wholegrain
mustard in place of English
mustard for a different
flavour.*

COOK'S TIP

*Canned beans are used
here for convenience, but
dried beans may be used
instead. Soak for 8 hours
or overnight, drain and
place in a saucepan.
Cover with water, bring
to the boil and boil for
10 minutes, then simmer
until tender.*

Potato, Beetroot & Cucumber Salad with Dill Dressing

Serves 4

INGREDIENTS

450 g/1 lb waxy potatoes, diced
4 small cooked beetroot, sliced
½ small cucumber, sliced thinly
2 large dill pickles, sliced

1 red onion, halved and sliced
dill sprigs, to garnish

DRESSING:
1 garlic clove, crushed
2 tbsp olive oil
2 tbsp red wine vinegar
2 tbsp chopped fresh dill
salt and pepper

1 Cook the diced potatoes in a saucepan of boiling water for 15 minutes or until tender. Drain and leave to cool.

2 When cool, mix the potato and beetroot together in a bowl and set aside.

3 Line a salad platter with the slices of cucumber, dill pickles and red onion. Spoon the potato and beetroot mixture into the centre of the platter.

4 In a small bowl, whisk all the dressing ingredients together, then pour it over the salad.

5 Serve the salad immediately, garnished with dill sprigs.

COOK'S TIP

If making the salad in advance, do not mix the beetroot and potatoes until just before serving, as the beetroot will bleed its colour.

VARIATION

Line the salad platter with 2 heads of chicory (endive), separated into leaves, and arrange the cucumber, dill pickle and red onion slices on top of the leaves.

Potato, Radish & Cucumber Salad

Serves 4

INGREDIENTS

450 g/1 lb new potatoes,
   scrubbed and halved
½ cucumber, sliced thinly

2 tsp salt
1 bunch radishes, sliced thinly

DRESSING:
1 tbsp Dijon mustard
2 tbsp olive oil
1 tbsp white wine vinegar
2 tbsp mixed chopped herbs

1 Cook the potatoes in a saucepan of boiling water for 10-15 minutes or until tender. Drain and leave to cool.

2 Meanwhile spread out the cucumber slices on a plate and sprinkle with the salt. Leave to stand for 30 minutes, then rinse under cold running water and pat dry with paper towels.

3 Arrange the cucumber and radish slices on a serving plate in a decorative pattern and pile the cooked potatoes in the centre of the slices.

4 In a small bowl, mix the dressing ingredients together. Pour the dressing over the salad, tossing well to coat all of the salad ingredients. Leave to chill in the refrigerator before serving.

VARIATION

Dijon mustard has a mild clean taste which is perfect for this salad as it does not overpower the other flavours. If unavailable, use another mild mustard – English mustard is too strong for this salad.

COOK'S TIP

The cucumber adds not only colour but a real freshness to the salad. It is salted and left to stand to remove the excess water which would make the salad soggy. Wash the cucumber well to remove all of the salt, before adding to the salad.

Sweet Potato & Banana Salad

Serves 4

INGREDIENTS

450 g/1 lb sweet potatoes, diced
50 g/1³/₄ oz/10 tsp butter
1 tbsp lemon juice
1 garlic clove, crushed
1 red (bell) pepper, diced

1 green (bell) pepper, diced
2 bananas, sliced thickly
2 thick slices white bread, crusts
    removed, diced
salt and pepper

DRESSING:

2 tbsp clear honey
2 tbsp chopped fresh chives
2 tbsp lemon juice
2 tbsp olive oil

1 Cook the sweet potatoes in a saucepan of boiling water for 10–15 minutes until tender. Drain thoroughly and reserve.

2 Meanwhile, melt the butter in a frying pan (skillet). Add the lemon juice, garlic and (bell) peppers and cook for 3 minutes, turning constantly.

3 Add the banana slices to the pan and cook for 1 minute. Remove the bananas from the pan with a slotted spoon and stir into the potatoes.

4 Add the bread cubes to the frying pan (skillet) and cook for 2 minutes, turning frequently until they are golden brown on all sides.

5 Mix the dressing ingredients together in a small saucepan and heat until the honey is runny.

6 Spoon the potato mixture into a serving dish and season to taste with salt and pepper. Pour the dressing over the potatoes and sprinkle the croûtons over the top. Serve

COOK'S TIP

Use firm, slightly underripe bananas in this recipe as they won't turn soft and mushy when fried.

Sweet Potato & Nut Salad

Serves 4

INGREDIENTS

450 g/1 lb sweet potatoes, diced
2 celery sticks, sliced
125 g/4$^{1}/_{2}$ oz celeriac, grated
2 spring onions (scallions), sliced
50 g/1$^{3}/_{4}$ oz pecan nuts, chopped

2 heads chicory (endive),
    separated
1 tsp lemon juice
thyme sprigs, to garnish

DRESSING:
4 tbsp vegetable oil
1 tbsp garlic wine vinegar
1 tsp soft light brown sugar
2 tsp chopped fresh thyme

1 Cook the sweet potatoes in a saucepan of boiling water for 5 minutes until tender. Drain thoroughly and leave to cool.

2 When cooled, stir in the celery, celeriac, spring onions (scallions) and pecan nuts.

3 Line a salad plate with the chicory (endive) leaves and sprinkle with lemon juice.

4 Spoon the potato mixture into the centre of the leaves.

5 In a small bowl, whisk the dressing ingredients together.

6 Pour the dressing over the salad and serve at once, garnished with thyme sprigs.

COOK'S TIP

Sweet potatoes do not store as well as ordinary potatoes. It is best to store them in a cool, dark place (not the refrigerator) and use within 1 week of purchase.

VARIATION

For variety, replace the garlic wine vinegar in the dressing with a different flavoured oil, such as chilli or herb.

Indian Potato Salad

Serves 4

INGREDIENTS

4 medium floury (mealy)
potatoes, diced
75 g/2³/₄ oz small broccoli florets
1 small mango, diced
4 spring onions (scallions), sliced
salt and pepper

small cooked spiced poppadoms,
to serve

DRESSING:
¹/₂ tsp ground cumin
¹/₂ tsp ground coriander

1 tbsp mango chutney
150 ml/¹/₄ pint/²/₃ cup natural
yogurt
1 tsp ginger root, chopped
2 tbsp chopped fresh coriander
(cilantro)

1 Cook the potatoes in
a saucepan of boiling
water for 10 minutes or until
tender. Drain and place in a
mixing bowl.

2 Meanwhile, blanch the
broccoli florets in a
separate saucepan of boiling
water for 2 minutes. Drain
well and add to the potatoes
in the bowl.

3 When the potatoes
and broccoli have
cooled, add the diced mango
and sliced spring onions
(scallions). Season to taste

with salt and pepper and
mix well to combine.

4 In a small bowl, stir
all of the dressing
ingredients together.

5 Spoon the dressing
over the potato mixture
and mix together carefully,
taking care not to break up
the potatoes and broccoli.

6 Serve the salad at once,
accompanied by small
cooked spiced poppadoms.

COOK'S TIP

*Mix the dressing ingredients
together in advance and
leave to chill in the
refrigerator for a few hours
in order for a stronger
flavour to develop.*

Mexican Potato Salad

Serves 4

INGREDIENTS

4 large waxy potatoes, sliced
1 ripe avocado
1 tsp olive oil
1 tsp lemon juice
1 garlic clove, crushed

1 onion, chopped
2 large tomatoes, sliced
1 green chilli, chopped
1 yellow (bell) pepper, sliced

2 tbsp chopped fresh coriander (cilantro)
salt and pepper
lemon wedges, to garnish

1 Cook the potato slices in a saucepan of boiling water for 10–15 minutes or until tender. Drain and leave to cool.

2 Meanwhile, cut the avocado in half and remove the stone. Using a spoon, scoop the avocado flesh from the 2 halves and place in a mixing bowl.

3 Mash the avocado flesh with a fork and stir in the olive oil, lemon juice, garlic and chopped onion. Cover the bowl with cling film (plastic wrap) and set aside.

4 Mix the tomatoes, chilli and yellow (bell) pepper together and transfer to a salad bowl with the potato slices.

5 Spoon the avocado mixture on top and sprinkle with the coriander (cilantro). Season to taste and serve garnished with lemon wedges.

COOK'S TIP

Mixing the avocado flesh with lemon juice prevents it from turning brown once exposed to the air.

VARIATION

Omit the green chilli from this salad if you do not like hot dishes.

Potato Nests of Chinese Salad

Serves 4

INGREDIENTS

POTATO NESTS:
450 g/1 lb floury (mealy)
    potatoes, grated
125 g/4½ oz/1 cup cornflour
    (cornstarch)
vegetable oil, for frying
fresh chives, to garnish

SALAD:
125 g/4½ oz pineapple, cubed
1 green (bell) pepper, cut into strips
1 carrot, cut into thin strips
50 g/1¾ oz mangetout
    (snowpeas), sliced thickly
4 baby sweetcorn cobs, halved
    lengthways

25 g/1 oz beansprouts
2 spring onions (scallions), sliced

DRESSING:
1 tbsp clear honey
1 tsp light soy sauce
1 garlic clove, crushed
1 tsp lemon juice

1 To make the nests, rinse the potatoes several times in cold water. Drain well on paper towels and place them in a mixing bowl. Add the cornflour (cornstarch), mixing well to coat the potatoes.

2 Half fill a wok with vegetable oil and heat until smoking. Line a 15 cm/6 inch diameter wire sieve with a quarter of the potato mixture and press another sieve of the same size on top.

3 Lower the sieves into the oil and cook for 2 minutes until the potato nest is golden brown and crisp. Remove from the wok, allowing the excess oil to drain off.

4 Repeat 3 more times to use up all of the mixture and make a total of 4 nests. Leave to cool.

5 Mix the salad ingredients together in a bowl, then spoon into the potato baskets.

6 Mix the dressing ingredients together in a bowl. Pour the dressing over the salad, garnish with chives and serve immediately.

COOK'S TIP

For this recipe, the potatoes must be washed well before use to remove excess starch. Make sure the potatoes are completely dry before cooking in the fat to prevent spitting.

Potato, Rocket (Arugula) & Apple Salad

Serves 4

INGREDIENTS

2 large potatoes, unpeeled and
    sliced
2 green dessert apples, diced
1 tsp lemon juice
25 g/1 oz walnut pieces
125 g/4$^{1}/_{2}$ oz goat's cheese,

cubed
150 g/5$^{1}/_{2}$ oz rocket (arugula)
    leaves
salt and pepper

DRESSING:
2 tbsp olive oil
1 tbsp red wine vinegar
1 tsp clear honey
1 tsp fennel seeds

1 Cook the potatoes in a pan of boiling water for 15 minutes until tender. Drain and leave to cool. Transfer the cooled potatoes to a serving bowl.

2 Toss the diced apples in the lemon juice, drain and stir into the cold potatoes.

3 Add the walnut pieces, cheese cubes and rocket (arugula) leaves, then toss the salad to mix.

4 In a small bowl, whisk the dressing ingredients together and pour the dressing over the salad. Serve immediately.

VARIATION

Use smoked or blue cheese instead of goat's cheese, if you prefer. In addition, if rocket (arugula) is unavailable use baby spinach instead.

COOK'S TIP

Serve this salad immediately to prevent the apple from discolouring. Alternatively, prepare all of the other ingredients in advance and add the apple at the last minute.

Potato & Mixed Vegetable Salad with Lemon Mayonnaise

Serves 4

INGREDIENTS

450 g/1 lb waxy new potatoes, scrubbed
1 carrot, cut into matchsticks
225 g/8 oz cauliflower florets
225 g/8 oz baby sweetcorn cobs, halved lenghtways
175 g/6 oz French (green) beans
175 g/6 oz ham, diced

50 g/1³/₄ oz mushrooms, sliced
salt and pepper

DRESSING:
2 tbsp chopped fresh parsley
150 ml/¹/₄ pint/²/₃ cup mayonnaise

150 ml/¹/₄ pint/²/₃ cup natural yogurt
4 tsp lemon juice
rind of 1 lemon
2 tsp fennel seeds

1 Cook the potatoes in a pan of boiling water for 15 minutes or until tender. Drain and leave to cool. When the potatoes are cold, slice them thinly.

2 Meanwhile, cook the carrot matchsticks, cauliflower florets, baby sweetcorn cobs and French (green) beans in a pan of boiling water for 5 minutes. Drain well and leave to cool.

3 Reserve 1 tsp of the chopped parsley for the garnish. In a bowl, mix the remaining dressing ingredients together.

4 Arrange the vegetables on a salad platter and top with the ham strips and sliced mushrooms.

5 Spoon the dressing over the the salad and garnish with the reserved parsley. Serve at once.

COOK'S TIP

For a really quick salad, use a frozen packet of mixed vegetables, thawed, instead of fresh vegetables.

Indonesian Potato & Chicken Salad

Serves 4

INGREDIENTS

4 large waxy potatoes, diced

300 g/10½ oz fresh pineapple, diced

2 carrots, grated

175 g/6 oz beansprouts

1 bunch spring onions (scallions), sliced

1 large courgette (zucchini), cut into matchsticks

3 celery sticks, cut into matchsticks

175 g/6 oz unsalted peanuts

2 cooked chicken breast fillets, about 125 g/4½ oz each, sliced

DRESSING:

6 tbsp crunchy peanut butter

6 tbsp olive oil

2 tbsp light soy sauce

1 red chilli, chopped

2 tsp sesame oil

4 tsp lime juice

1 Cook the diced potatoes in a saucepan of boiling water for 10 minutes or until tender. Drain and leave to cool.

2 Transfer the cooled potatoes to a salad bowl.

3 Add the pineapple, carrots, beansprouts, spring onions (scallions), courgette (zucchini), celery, peanuts and sliced chicken to the potatoes. Toss well to mix all the salad ingredients together.

4 To make the dressing, put the peanut butter in a small bowl and gradually whisk in the olive oil and light soy sauce.

5 Stir in the chopped red chilli, sesame oil and lime juice. Mix until well combined.

6 Pour the spicy dressing over the salad and toss lightly to coat all of the ingredients. Serve the salad immediately, garnished with the lime wedges.

COOK'S TIP

Unsweetened canned pineapple may be used in place of the fresh pineapple for convenience. If only sweetened canned pineapple is available, drain it and rinse under cold running water before using.

Potato & Spicy Chicken Salad

Serves 4

INGREDIENTS

2 skinned chicken breast fillets,
  about 125 g/4^{1}/2 oz each
25 g/1 oz/2 tbsp butter
1 red chilli, chopped
1 tbsp clear honey
^{1}/2 tsp ground cumin
2 tbsp chopped fresh coriander

(cilantro)
2 large potatoes, diced
50 g/1^{3}/4 oz thin green beans,
  halved
1 red (bell) pepper, cut into thin
  strips
2 tomatoes, seeded and diced

DRESSING:
2 tbsp olive oil
pinch of chilli powder
1 tbsp garlic wine vinegar
pinch of caster sugar
1 tbsp chopped fresh coriander
  (cilantro)

1 Cut the chicken into thin strips. Melt the butter in a pan over a medium heat and add the chicken, chilli, honey and cumin. Cook for 10 minutes, turning until cooked through.

2 Transfer the mixture to a bowl, leave to cool, then stir in the coriander (cilantro).

3 Meanwhile, cook the diced potatoes in a saucepan of boiling water for 10 minutes until tender. Drain and leave to cool.

4 Blanch the green beans in boiling water for 3 minutes, drain and leave to cool. Mix the green beans and potatoes together in a salad bowl.

5 Add the (bell) pepper strips and diced tomatoes to the potatoes and beans. Stir in the spicy chicken mixture.

6 In a small bowl, whisk the dressing ingredients together and pour the dressing over the salad, tossing well. Serve at once.

VARIATION

If you prefer, use lean turkey meat instead of the chicken for a slightly stronger flavour. Use the white meat for the best appearance and flavour.

Grilled (Broiled) New Potato Salad

Serves 4

INGREDIENTS

650 g/1½ lb new potatoes, scrubbed	4 rashers smoked bacon	DRESSING:
	salt and pepper	4 tbsp mayonnaise
3 tbsp olive oil	parsley sprig, to garnish	1 tbsp garlic wine vinegar
2 tbsp chopped fresh thyme		2 garlic cloves, crushed
1 tsp paprika		1 tbsp chopped fresh parsley

1 Cook the new potatoes in a saucepan of boiling water for 10 minutes. Drain thoroughly.

2 Mix the olive oil, chopped thyme and paprika together and pour the mixture over the warm potatoes.

3 Place the bacon rashers under a preheated medium grill (broiler) and cook for 5 minutes, turning once until crisp. When cooked, roughly chop the bacon and keep warm.

4 Transfer the potatoes to the grill (broiler) pan and cook for 10 minutes, turning once.

5 Mix the dressing ingredients in a small serving bowl. Transfer the potatoes and bacon to a large serving bowl. Season with salt and pepper and mix together.

6 Spoon over the dressing, garnish with a parsley sprig and serve immediately for a warm salad. Alternatively, leave to cool and serve chilled.

VARIATION

Add spicy sausage to the salad in place of bacon – you do not need to cook it under the grill (broiler) before adding to the salad.

Potato & Italian Sausage Salad

Serves 4

INGREDIENTS

450 g/1 lb waxy potatoes
1 raddichio or lollo rosso lettuce
1 green (bell) pepper, sliced
175 g/6 oz Italian sausage, sliced
1 red onion, halved and sliced

125 g/4¹/₂ oz sun-dried
    tomatoes, sliced
2 tbsp shredded fresh basil

DRESSING:
1 tbsp balsamic vinegar
1 tsp tomato purée (paste)
2 tbsp olive oil
salt and pepper

1 Cook the potatoes in a saucepan of boiling water for 20 minutes or until cooked through. Drain and leave to cool.

2 Line a large serving platter with the radicchio or lollo rosso lettuce leaves.

3 Slice the cooled potatoes and arrange them in layers on the lettuce-lined serving platter together with the sliced green (bell) pepper, sliced Italian sausage, red onion, sun-dried tomatoes and shredded fresh basil.

4 In a small bowl, whisk the balsamic vinegar, tomato purée (paste) and olive oil together and season to taste with salt and pepper. Pour the dressing over the potato salad and serve immediately.

COOK'S TIP

You can use either packets of sun-dried tomatoes or jars of sun-dried tomatoes in oil. If using tomatoes packed in oil, simply rinse the oil from the tomatoes and pat them dry on paper towels before using.

VARIATION

Any sliced Italian sausage or salami can be used in this salad. Italy is home of the salami and there are numerous varieties to choose from – those from the south tend to be more highly spiced than those from the north of the country.

Potato & Lobster Salad
with Lime Dressing

Serves 4

INGREDIENTS

450 g/1 lb waxy potatoes, scrubbed and sliced	2 tbsp lime juice	2 hard-boiled (hard-cooked) eggs, quartered
225 g/8 oz cooked lobster meat	finely grated rind of 1 lime	1 tbsp quartered stoned (pitted) green olives
150 ml/¼ pint/⅔ cup mayonnaise	1 tbsp chopped fresh parsley	salt and pepper
	2 tbsp olive oil	
	2 tomatoes, seeded and diced	

1 Cook the potatoes in a saucepan of boiling water for 10-15 minutes or until cooked through. Drain and reserve.

2 Remove the lobster meat from the shell and separate it into large pieces.

3 In a bowl, mix together the mayonnaise, 1 tbsp of the lime juice, half the grated lime rind and half the chopped parsley, then set aside.

4 In a separate bowl, whisk the remaining lime juice with the olive oil and pour the dressing over the potatoes. Arrange the potatoes on a serving plate.

5 Top with the lobster meat, tomatoes, eggs and olives. Season with salt and pepper and sprinkle with the reserved parsley.

6 Spoon the mayonnaise on to the centre of the salad, top with the reserved rind and serve.

COOK'S TIP

As shellfish is used in this salad, serve it immediately, or keep covered and chilled for up to 1 hour before serving.

VARIATION

Crabmeat or prawns (shrimp) may be used instead of the lobster, if you prefer.

Potato & Tuna Salad

Serves 4

INGREDIENTS

450 g/1 lb new potatoes,
    scrubbed and quartered
1 green (bell) pepper, sliced
50 g/1³/₄ oz canned sweetcorn,
    drained
1 red onion, sliced

300 g/10¹/₂ oz canned tuna in
    brine, drained and flaked
2 tbsp chopped stoned (pitted)
    black olives
salt and pepper
lime wedges, to garnish

DRESSING:
2 tbsp mayonnaise
2 tbsp soured cream
1 tbsp lime juice
2 garlic cloves, crushed
finely grated rind of 1 lime

1 Cook the potatoes in a saucepan of boiling water for 15 minutes until tender. Drain and leave to cool in a mixing bowl.

2 Gently stir in the sliced green (bell) pepper, sweetcorn and sliced red onion.

3 Spoon the potato mixture into a large serving bowl and arrange the flaked tuna and chopped black olives over the top. Season the salad generously with salt and pepper.

4 To make the dressing, mix together the mayonnaise, soured cream, lime juice, garlic and lime rind in a bowl.

5 Spoon the dressing over the tuna and olives, garnish with lime wedges and serve.

COOK'S TIP

Served with a crisp white wine, this salad makes the perfect light lunch for summer or winter.

VARIATION

Green beans and hard-boiled (hard-cooked) egg slices can be added to the salad for a more traditional Salade Niçoise.

Aubergine (Eggplant) Salad

Serves 4

INGREDIENTS

1 large aubergine (eggplant)	pinch of paprika	GARNISH:
3 tbsp tahini paste	1 tbsp chopped coriander	strips of pimiento
(sesame seed paste)	(cilantro)	lemon wedges
juice and rind of 1 lemon	salt and pepper	toasted sesame seeds
1 garlic clove, crushed	little Gem lettuce leaves	

1 Cut the aubergine (eggplant) in half, place in a colander and sprinkle with salt. Leave to stand for 30 minutes, rinse under cold running water and drain well. Pat dry with paper towels.

2 Place the aubergine (eggplant) halves, skin-side uppermost, on an oiled baking tray (cookie sheet). Cook in a preheated oven, 230°C/450°F/ Gas Mark 8, for 10–15 minutes. Remove from the oven and allow to cool.

3 Cut the aubergine (eggplant) into cubes and set aside until required. Mix the tahini paste (sesame seed paste), lemon juice and rind, garlic, paprika and coriander (cilantro) together. Season to taste and stir in the aubergine (eggplant).

4 Line a serving dish with lettuce leaves and spoon the aubergine (eggplant) into the centre. Garnish the salad with pimiento slices, lemon wedges and toasted sesame seeds and serve.

COOK'S TIP

Tahini paste (sesame seed paste) is a nutty-flavoured sauce available from most health food shops. It is good served with many Middle Eastern dishes.

Salad with Garlic & Yogurt Dressing

Serves 4

INGREDIENTS

75 g/2¾ oz cucumber,
   cut into sticks

6 spring onions (scallions),
   halved

2 tomatoes, seeded
   and cut into eight

1 yellow (bell) pepper, cut into
   strips

2 celery sticks, cut into strips

4 radishes, quartered

75 g/2¾ oz rocket (arugula)

1 tbsp chopped mint, to serve

DRESSING:

2 tbsp lemon juice

1 garlic clove, crushed

150 ml/ ¼ pint/⅔ cup natural
   (unsweetened) yogurt

2 tbsp olive oil

salt and pepper

1 Mix the cucumber, spring onions (scallions), tomatoes, (bell) pepper, celery, radishes and rocket (arugula) together in a large serving bowl.

2 To make the dressing, stir the lemon juice, garlic, natural (unsweetened) yogurt and olive oil together. Season well with salt and pepper.

3 Spoon the dressing over the salad and toss to mix.

4 Sprinkle the salad with chopped mint and serve.

COOK'S TIP

Do not toss the dressing into the salad until just before serving, otherwise it will turn soggy.

COOK'S TIP

Rocket (arugula) has a distinct warm, peppery flavour which is ideal in green salads. Once you have grown it in your garden or greenhouse you will always have plenty as it re-seeds all over the place! If rocket (arugula) is unavailable, lamb's lettuce (corn salad) makes a good substitute.

Courgette (Zucchini), Yogurt & Mint Salad

Serves 4

INGREDIENTS

2 courgettes (zucchini), cut
into sticks
100 g/3¹/₂ oz French (green)
beans, cut into three
1 green (bell) pepper, cut
into strips

2 celery sticks, sliced
1 bunch watercress

DRESSING:
200 ml/7 fl oz/³/₄ cup natural
(unsweetened) yogurt

1 garlic clove, crushed
2 tbsp chopped mint
pepper

1 Cook the courgettes
(zucchini) and
French (green) beans in a
saucepan of salted boiling
water for 7–8 minutes.
Drain and leave to cool
completely.

2 Mix the courgettes
(zucchini) and
French (green) beans
with the (bell) pepper,
celery and watercress in a
large bowl.

3 To make the dressing,
mix together the
natural (unsweetened)

yogurt, garlic and chopped
mint in a bowl. Season with
pepper to taste.

4 Spoon the dressing on
to the salad and
serve immediately.

COOK'S TIP

*The salad must be served
as soon as the yogurt
dressing has been added –
the dressing will start to
separate if kept for any
length of time.*

COOK'S TIP

*Watercress is available all
year round. Its fresh peppery
flavour makes it a delicious
addition to many salads.*

Bean, Avocado & Tomato Salad

Serves 4

INGREDIENTS

lollo rosso lettuce	175 g/6 oz/2 cups mixed canned	2 tbsp garlic wine vinegar
2 ripe avocados	beans, drained	pinch of caster (superfine) sugar
2 tsp lemon juice	DRESSING:	pinch of chilli powder
4 medium tomatoes	4 tbsp olive oil	1 tbsp chopped parsley
1 onion	drop of chilli oil	

1 Line a serving bowl with the lettuce.

2 Using a sharp knife, thinly slice the avocados and sprinkle with the lemon juice.

3 Thinly slice the tomato and onion. Arrange the avocado, tomatoes and onion around the salad bowl, leaving a space in the centre.

4 Spoon the beans into the centre of the salad and whisk the dressing ingredients together. Pour the dressing over the salad and serve.

COOK'S TIP

Instead of whisking the dressing, place all the ingredients in a screw-top jar and shake vigorously. Any leftover dressing can then be kept and stored in the same jar.

COOK'S TIP

The lemon juice is sprinkled on to the avocados to prevent discoloration when in contact with the air. For this reason the salad should be prepared, assembled and served quite quickly.

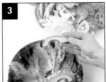

Gado Gado

Serves 4

INGREDIENTS

100 g/3¹/₂ oz/1 cup white
cabbage, shredded
100 g/3¹/₂ oz French (green)
beans, cut into 3
100 g/3¹/₂ oz carrots, cut into
matchsticks
100 g/3¹/₂ oz cauliflower florets
100 g/3¹/₂ oz bean sprouts

DRESSING:
100 ml/3¹/₂ fl oz/¹/₂ cup
vegetable oil
100 g/3¹/₂ oz/1 cup unsalted
peanuts
2 garlic cloves, crushed
1 small onion, finely chopped
¹/₂ tsp chilli powder
¹/₃ tsp light brown sugar

425 ml/³/₄ pint/2 cups water
juice of ¹/₂ lemon
salt
sliced spring onions (scallions),
to garnish

1 Cook the vegetables separately in a saucepan of salted boiling water for 4–5 minutes, drain well and chill.

2 To make the dressing, heat the oil in a frying pan (skillet) and fry the peanuts for 3–4 minutes, turning.

3 Remove from the pan with a slotted spoon and leave to drain on absorbent paper towels. Grind the peanuts in a blender or crush with a rolling pin until a fine mixture is formed.

4 Pour all but 1 tbsp oil from the pan and fry the garlic and onion for 1 minute. Add the chilli powder, sugar, a pinch of salt and the water and bring to the boil.

5 Stir in the peanuts. Reduce the heat and simmer for 4–5 minutes until the sauce thickens. Add the lemon juice and leave to cool.

6 Arrange the vegetables in a serving dish and spoon the peanut dressing into the centre. Garnish and serve.

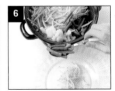

Grilled (Broiled) Vegetable Salad with Mustard Dressing

Serves 4

INGREDIENTS

1 courgette (zucchini), sliced
1 yellow (bell) pepper, sliced
1 aubergine (eggplant), sliced
1 fennel bulb, cut into eight
1 red onion, cut into eight
16 cherry tomatoes
3 tbsp olive oil

1 garlic clove, crushed
fresh rosemary sprigs, to garnish

DRESSING:
4 tbsp olive oil
2 tbsp balsamic vinegar
2 tsp chopped rosemary
1 tsp Dijon mustard
1 tsp clear honey
2 tsp lemon juice

1 Put all of the vegetables except for the cherry tomatoes on to a baking tray (cookie sheet).

2 Mix the oil and garlic and brush over the vegetables. Cook under a medium-hot grill (broiler) for 10 minutes until tender and beginning to char. Leave to cool. Spoon the vegetables into a serving bowl.

3 Mix the dressing ingredients and pour over the vegetables. Cover and chill for 1 hour. Garnish and serve.

COOK'S TIP

This dish could also be served warm – heat the dressing in a pan and then toss into the vegetables.

COOK'S TIP

Balsamic vinegar is made in and around Modena in Italy. It is dark and mellow with a sweet-sour flavour. Although it is rather expensive, you only need a small amount to give a wonderful taste to the dressing. If it is unavailable, use sherry vinegar or white wine vinegar instead.

Red Cabbage & Pear Salad

Serves 4

INGREDIENTS

350 g/12 oz/4 cups red cabbage,
    finely shredded
2 Conference pears,
    thinly sliced
4 spring onions (scallions), sliced
1 carrot, grated

fresh chives, to garnish
lollo biondo leaves, to serve

DRESSING:
4 tbsp pear juice
1 tsp wholegrain mustard
3 tbsp olive oil
1 tbsp garlic wine vinegar
1 tbsp chopped chives

1 Toss the cabbage, pears and spring onions (scallions) together in a bowl.

2 Line a serving dish with lettuce leaves and spoon the cabbage and pear mixture into the centre.

3 Sprinkle the carrot into the centre of the cabbage to form a domed pile.

4 To make the dressing, mix together the pear juice, wholegrain mustard, olive oil, garlic wine vinegar and chives.

5 Pour the dressing over the salad, garnish and serve immediately.

COOK'S TIP

Mix the salad just before serving to prevent the colour from the red cabbage bleeding into the other ingredients.

VARIATION

Experiment with different types of salad leaves. The slightly bitter flavour of chicory (endive) or radicchio would work well with the sweetness of the pears.

Alfalfa, Beetroot & Spinach Salad

Serves 4

INGREDIENTS

100 g/3½ oz baby spinach
75 g/2¾ oz alfalfa sprouts
2 celery sticks, sliced
4 cooked beetroot, cut into eight

DRESSING:
4 tbsp olive oil
1½ tbsp garlic wine vinegar
1 garlic clove, crushed

2 tsp clear honey
1 tbsp chopped chives

1 Place the spinach and alfalfa sprouts in a large bowl and mix together.

2 Add the celery and mix well.

3 Toss in the beetroot and mix well.

4 To make the dressing, mix the oil, wine vinegar, garlic, honey and chopped chives.

5 Pour the dressing over the salad, toss well and serve immediately.

COOK'S TIP

If the spinach leaves are too large, tear them up rather than cutting them because cutting bruises the leaves.

COOK'S TIP

Alfalfa sprouts should be available from most supermarkets, if not, use bean sprouts instead.

VARIATION

Add the segments of 1 large orange to the salad to make it even more colourful and refreshing. Replace the garlic wine vinegar with a different flavoured oil such as chilli or herb, if you prefer.

Snacks & Light Meals

Sometimes we may not feel like eating a full-scale meal but still want something appetizing and satisfying. Potatoes and vegetables are so versatile that they can be used as a base to create a whole array of tempting light meals and satisfying snacks. They are also extremely nutritious, as the carbohydrate that they contain will give a welcome energy boost.

This chapter contains a range of tempting snacks which are quick and easy to make and will satisfy those mid-morning or mid-afternoon hunger pangs! They also come in handy if an unexpected visitor drops by. The chapter also contains a range of delicious yet light meals which are ideal if you feel slightly peckish rather than ravenously hungry. They cater to all tastes, including vegetarian, and all times of day. Many can be prepared ahead of time and will not detain you in the kitchen too long.

Potato & Bean Pâté

Serves 4

INGREDIENTS

100 g/3$\frac{1}{2}$ oz floury (mealy)
   potatoes, diced
225 g/8 oz mixed canned beans,
   such as borlotti, flageolet and
   kidney beans, drained

1 garlic clove, crushed
2 tsp lime juice
1 tbsp chopped fresh coriander
   (cilantro)
2 tbsp natural yogurt

salt and pepper
chopped fresh coriander
   (cilantro), to garnish

1 Cook the potatoes in a saucepan of boiling water for 10 minutes until tender. Drain well and mash.

2 Transfer the potato to a food processor or blender and add the beans, garlic, lime juice and the fresh coriander (cilantro). Season the mixture and process for 1 minute to make a smooth purée. Alternatively, mix the beans with the potato, garlic, lime juice and coriander (cilantro) and mash.

3 Turn the purée into a bowl and add the yogurt. Mix well.

4 Spoon the pâté into a serving dish and garnish with the chopped coriander (cilantro). Serve at once or leave to chill.

VARIATION

If you do not have a food processor or you would prefer to make a chunkier pâté, simply mash the ingredients with a fork.

COOK'S TIP

To make Melba toast, toast ready-sliced white or brown bread lightly on both sides under a preheated high grill (broiler) and remove the crusts. Holding the bread flat, slide a sharp knife between the toasted bread to split it horizontally. Cut into triangles and toast the untoasted side until the edges curl.

Smoked Fish & Potato Pâté

Serves 4

INGREDIENTS

650 g/1¹⁄₂ lb floury (mealy)
potatoes, diced
300 g/10¹⁄₂ oz smoked mackerel,
skinned and flaked
75 g/2³⁄₄ oz cooked gooseberries

2 tsp lemon juice
2 tbsp crème fraîche
1 tbsp capers
1 gherkin, chopped
1 tbsp chopped dill pickle

1 tbsp chopped fresh dill
salt and pepper
lemon wedges, to garnish

1 Cook the diced potatoes in a saucepan of boiling water for 10 minutes until tender, then drain well.

2 Place the cooked potatoes in a food processor or blender.

3 Add the skinned and flaked smoked mackerel and process for 30 seconds until fairly smooth. Alternatively, mash with a fork.

4 Add the cooked gooseberries with the lemon juice and crème fraîche. Blend for a further 10 seconds or mash well.

5 Stir in the capers, gherkin, dill pickle and chopped fresh dill. Season well with salt and pepper.

6 Turn the fish pâté into a serving dish, garnish with lemon wedges and serve with slices of toast or warm crusty bread in chunks or slices.

COOK'S TIP

Use stewed, canned or bottled cooked gooseberries for convenience and to save time, or when fresh gooseberries are out of season.

VARIATION

Use other tart fruits, such as stewed apples, instead of the gooseberries if they are unavailable.

Potato Kibbeh

Serves 4

INGREDIENTS

175 g/6 oz bulgar wheat
350 g/12 oz floury (mealy)
    potatoes, diced
2 small eggs
25 g/1 oz/2 tbsp butter, melted
pinch of ground cumin
pinch of ground coriander (cilantro)

pinch of grated nutmeg
salt and pepper
oil for deep-frying

STUFFING:
175 g/6 oz minced lamb
1 small onion, chopped

1 tbsp pine kernels (nuts)
25 g/1 oz dried apricots, chopped
pinch of grated nutmeg
pinch of ground cinnamon
1 tbsp chopped fresh coriander
    (cilantro)
2 tbsp lamb stock

1 Put the bulgar wheat in a bowl and cover with boiling water. Soak for 30 minutes until the water has been absorbed and the bulgar wheat has swollen.

2 Meanwhile, cook the diced potatoes in a saucepan of boiling water for 10 minutes or until cooked through. Drain and mash until smooth.

3 Add the bulgar wheat to the mashed potato with the eggs, the melted butter, the ground cumin and coriander (cilantro), and the grated nutmeg. Season well with salt and pepper.

4 To make the stuffing, dry fry the lamb for 5 minutes, add the onion and cook for a further 2–3 minutes. Add the remaining stuffing ingredients and cook for 5 minutes until the lamb stock has been absorbed. Leave the mixture to cool slightly, then divide into 8 portions. Roll each one into a ball.

5 Divide the potato mixture into 8 portions and flatten each into a round. Place a portion of stuffing in the centre of each round. Shape the coating around the stuffing to encase it completely.

6 In a large saucepan or deep fat fryer, heat the oil to 180°C–190°C/ 350°F–375°F or until a cube of bread browns in 30 seconds, and cook the kibbeh for 5–7 minutes until golden brown. Drain well and serve at once.

Potato & Meatballs in Spicy Sauce

Serves 4

INGREDIENTS

225 g/8 oz floury (mealy)
potatoes, diced
225 g/8 oz minced beef or lamb
1 onion, finely chopped
1 tbsp chopped fresh coriander
(cilantro)
1 celery stick, finely chopped
2 garlic cloves, crushed

25 g/1 oz/2 tbsp butter
1 tbsp vegetable oil
salt and pepper
chopped fresh coriander (cilantro),
to garnish

SAUCE:
1 tbsp vegetable oil

1 onion, finely chopped
2 tsp soft brown sugar
400 g/14 oz can chopped tomatoes
1 green chilli, chopped
1 tsp paprika
150 ml/¼ pint/⅔ cup vegetable
stock
2 tsp cornflour (cornstarch)

1 Cook the diced potatoes in a saucepan of boiling water for 25 minutes until cooked through. Drain well and transfer to a large mixing bowl. Mash until smooth.

2 Add the minced beef or lamb, onion, coriander (cilantro), celery and garlic and mix well.

3 Bring the mixture together with your hands and roll it into 20 small balls.

4 To make the sauce, heat the oil in a pan and sauté the onion for 5 minutes. Add the remaining sauce ingredients and bring to the boil, stirring. Lower the heat and simmer for 20 minutes.

5 Meanwhile, heat the butter and oil for the potato and meat balls in a frying pan (skillet). Add the balls in batches and cook for 10–15 minutes until browned, turning frequently. Keep warm whilst cooking the

remainder. Serve the potato and meatballs in a warm shallow ovenproof dish with the sauce poured around them and garnished with coriander (cilantro).

COOK'S TIP

Make the potato and meatballs in advance and chill or freeze them for later use. Make sure you defrost them thoroughly before cooking.

Potato & Fish Balls with Tomato Sauce

Serves 4

INGREDIENTS

450 g/1 lb floury (mealy)
    potatoes, diced
2 smoked fish fillets, such as cod,
    about 225 g/8 oz total
    weight, skinned
40 g/1 1/2 oz/3 tbsp butter

2 eggs, beaten
1 tbsp chopped fresh dill
1/2 tsp cayenne pepper
oil for deep-frying
salt and pepper
dill sprigs, to garnish

SAUCE:
300 ml/1/2 pint/1 1/4 cups passata
1 tbsp tomato purée (paste)
2 tbsp chopped fresh dill
150 ml/1/4 pint/2/3 cup fish stock

1 Cook the diced potatoes in a saucepan of boiling water for 10 minutes or until cooked. Drain well, then add the butter to the potato and mash until smooth. Season well with salt and pepper.

2 Meanwhile, poach the fish in boiling water for 10 minutes, turning once. Drain and mash the fish. Stir it into the potato mixture and leave to cool.

3 While the potato and fish mixture is cooling,

make the sauce. Put the passata, tomato purée (paste), dill and stock in a pan and bring to the boil. Reduce the heat, cover the pan and simmer for 20 minutes until thickened.

4 Add the eggs, dill and cayenne pepper to the potato and fish mixture and beat until well mixed.

5 In a large saucepan or deep fat fryer, heat the oil to 180°C–190°C/ 350°F–375°F, or until a cube of bread browns in 30

seconds. Drop dessert spoons of the potato mixture into the oil and cook for 3–4 minutes until golden brown. Drain on paper towels.

6 Garnish the potato and fish balls with dill sprigs and serve with the tomato sauce.

VARIATION

Smoked fish is used for extra flavour, but white fish fillets or minced prawns (shrimp) may be used, if preferred.

Thai Potato Crab Cakes

Serves 4

INGREDIENTS

450 g/1 lb floury (mealy)
potatoes, diced
175 g/6 oz white crab meat,
drained if canned
4 spring onions (scallions),
chopped
1 tsp light soy sauce
½ tsp sesame oil

1 tsp chopped lemon grass
1 tsp lime juice
3 tbsp plain (all-purpose) flour
2 tbsp vegetable oil
salt and pepper

SAUCE:
4 tbsp finely chopped cucumber

2 tbsp clear honey
1 tbsp garlic wine vinegar
½ tsp light soy sauce
1 red chilli, chopped

TO GARNISH:
1 red chilli, sliced
cucumber slices

1 Cook the diced potatoes in a saucepan of boiling water for 10 minutes until cooked through. Drain well and mash.

2 Mix the crab meat into the potato with the spring onions (scallions), soy sauce, sesame oil, lemon grass, lime juice and flour. Season with salt and pepper.

3 Divide the potato mixture into 8 portions of equal size and shape them into small rounds, using floured hands.

4 Heat the oil in a wok or frying pan (skillet) and cook the cakes, 4 at a time, for 5–7 minutes, turning once. Keep warm and repeat with the remaining cakes.

5 Meanwhile, make the sauce. In a small serving bowl, mix the cucumber, honey, vinegar, soy sauce and chopped red chilli.

6 Garnish the cakes with the sliced red chilli and cucumber slices and serve with the sauce.

COOK'S TIP

Do not make the cucumber sauce too far in advance as the water from the cucumber will make the sauce runny and dilute the flavour.

Potato & Mixed Mushroom Cakes

Serves 4

INGREDIENTS

450 g/1lb floury (mealy)
   potatoes, diced
25 g/1 oz/2 tbsp butter
175 g/6 oz mixed mushrooms,
   chopped

2 garlic cloves, crushed
1 small egg, beaten
1 tbsp chopped fresh chives, plus
   extra to garnish
flour, for dusting

oil, for frying
salt and pepper

1 Cook the potatoes in a pan of boiling water for 10 minutes or until cooked through. Drain well, mash and set aside.

2 Meanwhile, melt the butter in a frying pan (skillet) and cook the mushrooms and garlic for 5 minutes, stirring. Drain well.

3 Stir the mushrooms and garlic into the potato together with the beaten egg and chives.

4 Divide the mixture equally into 4 portions and shape them into round cakes. Toss them in the flour until the outside of the cakes is completely coated.

5 Heat the oil in a frying pan (skillet) and cook the potato cakes over a medium heat for 10 minutes until they are golden brown, turning them over halfway through. Serve the cakes at once, with a simple crisp salad.

COOK'S TIP

Prepare the cakes in advance, cover and leave to chill in the refrigerator for up to 24 hours, if you wish.

VARIATION

If chives are unavailable, use other fresh herbs of your choice. Sage, tarragon and coriander (cilantro) all combine well with mixed mushrooms.

Potato, Cheese & Onion Rosti

Serves 4

INGREDIENTS

900 g/2 lb Maris Piper potatoes
1 onion, grated
50 g/2 oz Gruyère cheese, grated
2 tbsp chopped fresh parsley

1 tbsp olive oil
25 g/1 oz/2 tbsp butter
salt and pepper

TO GARNISH:
shredded spring onion (scallion)
1 small tomato, quartered

1 Parboil the potatoes in a pan of boiling water for 10 minutes and leave to cool. Peel the potatoes and grate with a coarse grater. Place the grated potatoes in a large mixing bowl.

2 Stir in the onion, cheese and parsley. Season well with salt and pepper. Divide the potato mixture into 4 portions of equal size and form them into cakes.

3 Heat half of the olive oil and butter in a frying pan (skillet) and cook 2 of the potato cakes over a high heat for 1 minute, then reduce the heat and cook for 5 minutes until they are golden underneath. Turn them over and cook for a further 5 minutes.

4 Repeat with the other half of the oil and butter to cook the remaining 2 cakes. Transfer to serving plates, garnish and serve.

COOK'S TIP

The potato cakes should be flattened as much as possible during cooking, otherwise the outside will be cooked before the centre.

VARIATION

To make these rosti into a more substantial meal, add chopped cooked bacon or ham to the potato mixture.

Potato & Cauliflower Fritters

Serves 4

INGREDIENTS

225 g/8 oz floury (mealy)
potatoes, diced
225 g/8 oz cauliflower florets
2 tbsp grated Parmesan cheese

1 egg
1 egg white for coating
oil, for frying

paprika, for dusting (optional)
salt and pepper
crispy bacon slices, chopped,
to serve

1 Cook the potatoes in a saucepan of boiling water for 10 minutes until cooked through. Drain well and mash.

2 Cook the cauliflower florets in a separate pan of boiling water for 10 minutes.

3 Drain the cauliflower florets and mix into the mashed potato. Stir in the grated Parmesan cheese and season well with salt and pepper.

4 Separate the whole egg and beat the yolk into the potato and cauliflower, mixing well.

5 Lightly whisk both the egg whites in a clean bowl, then carefully fold into the potato and cauliflower mixture.

6 Divide the potato mixture into 8 equal portions and shape them into rounds.

7 Heat the oil in a frying pan (skillet) and cook

the fritters for 3–5 minutes, turning once halfway through cooking.

8 Dust the cooked fritters with a little paprika, if preferred, and serve at once accompanied by the crispy chopped bacon.

VARIATION

Any other vegetable, such as broccoli, can be used in this recipe instead of the cauliflower florets, if you prefer.

Potato Fritters with Garlic Sauce

Serves 4

INGREDIENTS

450 g/1 lb waxy potatoes, cut
  into large cubes
125 g/4¹/₂ oz Parmesan cheese,
  grated
oil, for deep-frying

SAUCE:
25 g/1 oz/2 tbsp butter
1 onion, halved and sliced
2 garlic cloves, crushed
25 g/1 oz/¹/₄ cup plain
  (all-purpose) flour
300 ml/¹/₂ pint/1¹/₄ cups milk

1 tbsp chopped fresh parsley

BATTER:
50 g/1³/₄ oz/¹/₂ cup plain
  (all-purpose) flour
1 small egg
150 ml/¹/₄ pint/²/₃ cup milk

1 To make the sauce, melt the butter in a saucepan and cook the sliced onion and garlic for 2–3 minutes. Add the flour and cook for 1 minute.

2 Remove from the heat and stir in the milk and parsley. Return to the heat and bring to the boil. Keep warm.

3 Meanwhile, cook the cubed potatoes in a saucepan of boiling water for 5–10 minutes until just firm. Do not overcook or they will fall apart.

4 Drain the potatoes and toss them in the Parmesan cheese.

5 To make the batter, place the flour in a mixing bowl and gradually beat in the egg and milk until smooth. Dip the potato cubes into the batter to coat them.

6 In a large saucepan or deep fat fryer, heat the oil to 180°–C190°C/ 350°F–375°F, or until a cube of bread browns in 30 seconds, and cook the fritters for 3–4 minutes or until golden. Drain the fritters with a perforated spoon and transfer them to a serving bowl. Serve with the sauce.

COOK'S TIP

Coat the potatoes in the Parmesan whilst still slightly wet to ensure that the cheese sticks and coats well.

Potato Croquettes with Ham & Cheese

Serves 4

INGREDIENTS

450 g/1 lb floury (mealy)
potatoes, diced
300 ml/¹/₂ pint/1¹/₂ cups milk
25 g/1 oz/2 tbsp butter
4 spring onions (scallions), chopped
75 g/2³/₄ oz Cheddar cheese
50 g/1³/₄ oz smoked ham, chopped
1 celery stick, diced
1 egg, beaten

50 g/1³/₄ oz/¹/₂ cup plain
(all-purpose) flour
oil, for deep frying
salt and pepper

COATING:
2 eggs, beaten
125 g/4¹/₂ oz fresh wholemeal
(whole wheat) breadcrumbs

SAUCE:
25 g/1 oz/2 tbsp butter
25 g/1 oz/ ¹/₄ cup plain
(all-purpose) flour
150 ml/¹/₄ pint/²/₃ cup milk
150 ml/¹/₄ pint/²/₃ cup vegetable
stock
75 g/2²/₃oz Cheddar cheese, grated
1 tsp Dijon mustard
1 tbsp chopped coriander (cilantro)

1 Place the potatoes in a pan with the milk and bring to the boil. Reduce to a simmer until the liquid has been absorbed and the potatoes are cooked.

2 Add the butter and mash the potatoes. Stir in the spring onions (scallions), cheese, ham, celery, egg and flour. Season and leave to cool.

3 To make the coating, whisk the eggs in a bowl. Put the breadcrumbs in a separate bowl.

4 Shape the potato mixture into 8 balls. First dip them in the egg, then in the breadcrumbs.

5 To make the sauce, melt the butter in a small pan. Add the flour and cook for 1 minute.

Remove from the heat and stir in the milk, stock, cheese, mustard and herbs. Bring to the boil, stirring until thickened. Reduce the heat and keep warm.

6 In a deep fat fryer, heat the oil to 180°C–190°C/ 350°F–375°F and fry the croquettes for 5 minutes until golden. Drain well and serve with the sauce.

Hash Browns with Tomato Sauce

Serves 4

INGREDIENTS

450 g/1 lb waxy potatoes
1 carrot, diced
1 celery stick, diced
50 g/2 oz button mushrooms, diced
1 onion, diced
2 garlic cloves, crushed
25 g/1 oz frozen peas, thawed
50 g/2 oz Parmesan cheese, grated

4 tbsp vegetable oil
25 g/1 oz/2 tbsp butter
salt and pepper

SAUCE:
300 ml/¹/₂ pint/1¹/₄ cups passata
2 tbsp chopped fresh coriander
(cilantro)

1 tbsp Worcestershire sauce
¹/₂ tsp chilli powder
2 tsp brown sugar
2 tsp American mustard
85 ml/3 fl oz/¹/₃ cup vegetable stock

1 Cook the potatoes in a saucepan of boiling water for 10 minutes. Drain and leave to cool. Meanwhile, cook the carrot in boiling water for 5 minutes.

2 When cool, grate the potato with a coarse grater.

3 Drain the carrot and add it to the grated potato with the celery, mushrooms, onion, peas and cheese. Season well.

4 Place all of the sauce ingredients in a pan and bring to the boil. Reduce the heat and simmer for 15 minutes.

5 Divide the potato mixture into 8 portions of equal size and shape into flattened rectangles with your hands.

6 Heat the oil and butter in a frying pan (skillet) and cook the hash browns over a low heat for 4–5 minutes on each side until crisp and golden brown.

7 Serve the hash browns with the tomato sauce.

COOK'S TIP

Use any mixture of vegetables for this recipe. For a non-vegetarian dish, add bacon pieces or diced ham for added flavour.

Potato Pancakes with Soured Cream & Salmon

Serves 4

INGREDIENTS

450 g/1 lb floury (mealy)
   potatoes, grated
2 spring onions (scallions),
   chopped
2 tbsp self-raising flour
2 eggs, beaten

2 tbsp vegetable oil
salt and pepper
fresh chives, to garnish

TOPPING:
150 ml/¼ pint/⅔ cup soured
   cream
125 g/4½ oz smoked salmon

1 Rinse the grated potatoes under cold running water, drain and pat dry on paper towels. Transfer to a mixing bowl.

2 Mix the chopped spring onions (scallions), flour and eggs into the potatoes and season well with salt and pepper.

3 Heat 1 tbsp of the oil in a frying pan (skillet). Drop about 4 tablespoonfuls of the mixture into the pan

and spread each one with the back of a spoon to form a round (the mixture should make 16 pancakes). Cook for 5–7 minutes, turning once, until golden. Drain well.

4 Heat the remaining oil and cook the remaining mixture in batches.

5 Top the pancakes with the soured cream and smoked salmon, garnish with fresh chives and serve hot.

COOK'S TIP

Smaller versions of this dish may be made and served as appetizers.

VARIATION

These pancakes are equally delicious topped with prosciutto or any other dry-cured ham instead of the smoked salmon.

Potato Omelette with Feta Cheese & Spinach

Serves 4

INGREDIENTS

75 g/3 oz/¹⁄₃ cup butter
6 waxy potatoes, diced
3 garlic cloves, crushed
1 tsp paprika

2 tomatoes, skinned, seeded
   and diced
12 eggs
pepper

FILLING:
225 g/8 oz baby spinach
1 tsp fennel seeds
125 g/4¹⁄₂ oz feta cheese, diced
4 tbsp natural yogurt

1 Heat 2 tbsp of the butter in a frying pan (skillet) and cook the potatoes over a low heat for 7–10 minutes until golden, stirring constantly. Transfer to a bowl.

2 Add the garlic, paprika and tomatoes and cook for a further 2 minutes.

3 Whisk the eggs together in a jug and season with pepper. Pour the eggs into the potatoes and mix well.

4 Place the spinach in boiling water for 1 minute until just wilted. Drain and refresh the spinach under cold running water and pat dry with paper towels. Stir in the fennel seeds, feta cheese and yogurt.

5 Heat 1 tbsp of the butter in a 15 cm/6 inch omelette or frying pan (skillet). Ladle a quarter of the egg and potato mixture into the pan. Cook for 2 minutes, turning once, until set.

6 Transfer the omelette to a serving plate. Spoon a quarter of the spinach mixture on to one half of the omelette, then fold the omelette in half over the filling. Repeat to make 4 omelettes.

VARIATION

Use any other cheese, such as blue cheese, instead of the feta and blanched broccoli in place of the baby spinach, if you prefer.

Spanish Tortilla

Serves 4

INGREDIENTS

1 kg/ 2.2 lb waxy potatoes, thinly sliced
4 tbsp vegetable oil
1 onion, sliced
2 garlic cloves, crushed

1 green (bell) pepper, diced
2 tomatoes, deseeded and chopped
25 g/1 oz canned sweetcorn, drained

6 large eggs, beaten
2 tbsp chopped fresh parsley
salt and pepper

1 Parboil the potatoes in a saucepan of boiling water for 5 minutes. Drain well.

2 Heat the oil in a large frying pan (skillet), add the potato and onions and sauté gently for 5 minutes, stirring constantly, until the potatoes have browned.

3 Add the garlic, diced (bell) pepper, chopped tomatoes and sweetcorn, mixing well.

4 Pour in the eggs and add the chopped parsley. Season well with salt and pepper. Cook for 10–12 minutes until the underside is cooked through.

5 Remove the frying pan (skillet) from the heat and continue to cook the tortilla under a preheated medium grill (broiler) for 5–7 minutes or until the tortilla is set and the top is golden brown.

6 Cut the tortilla into wedges or cubes, depending on your preference, and serve with salad. In Spain tortillas are served hot, cold or warm.

COOK'S TIP

Ensure that the handle of your pan is heatproof before placing it under the grill (broiler) and be sure to use an oven glove when removing it as it will be very hot.

Paprika Crisps

Serves 4

INGREDIENTS

2 large potatoes
3 tbsp olive oil

1/2 tsp paprika pepper
salt

1 Using a sharp knife, slice the potatoes very thinly so that they are almost transparent. Drain the potato slices thoroughly and pat dry with paper towels.

2 Heat the oil in a large frying pan (skillet) and add the paprika, stirring constantly, to ensure that the paprika doesn't catch and burn.

3 Add the potato slices to the frying pan (skillet) and cook them in a single layer for about 5 minutes or until the potato

slices just begin to curl slightly at the edges.

4 Remove the potato slices from the pan using a perforated spoon and transfer them to paper towels to drain thoroughly.

5 Thread the potato slices on to several wooden kebab (kabob) skewers.

6 Sprinkle the potato slices with a little salt and cook over a medium hot barbecue (grill) or under a medium grill (broiler) for 10 minutes, turning frequently, until

the potato slices begin to crispen. Sprinkle with a little more salt, if preferred, and serve.

VARIATION

You could use curry powder or any other spice to flavour the crisps instead of the paprika, if you prefer.

Creamy Mushrooms & Potatoes

Serves 4

INGREDIENTS

25 g/1 oz dried ceps
225 g/8 oz floury (mealy) potatoes, diced
25 g/1 oz/2 tbsp butter, melted
4 tbsp double (heavy) cream

2 tbsp chopped fresh chives
25 g/1 oz Emmental cheese, grated
8 large open capped mushrooms

150 ml/¼ pint/⅔ cup vegetable stock
salt and pepper
fresh chives, to garnish

1 Place the dried ceps in a bowl, cover with boiling water and leave to soak for 20 minutes.

2 Meanwhile, cook the potatoes in a saucepan of boiling water for 10 minutes until cooked. Drain well and mash.

3 Drain the soaked ceps and chop them finely. Mix them into the mashed potato.

4 Mix the butter, cream and chives together and pour into the cep and potato mixture. Season with salt and pepper.

5 Remove the stalks from the open-capped mushrooms. Chop the stalks and stir them into the potato mixture. Spoon the mixture into the open-capped mushrooms and sprinkle the cheese over the top.

6 Place the filled mushrooms in a shallow ovenproof dish and pour in the vegetable stock.

7 Cover the dish and cook in a preheated oven, 220°C/425°F/Gas Mark 7, for 20 minutes. Remove the lid and cook for 5 minutes until golden on top.

8 Garnish the mushrooms with fresh chives and serve at once.

VARIATION

Use fresh mushrooms instead of the dried ceps, if preferred, and stir a mixture of chopped nuts into the mushroom stuffing mixture for extra crunch.

Potato Noodles with Cheese, Mushrooms & Bacon

Serves 4

INGREDIENTS

450 g/1 lb floury (mealy)
   potatoes, diced
225 g/8 oz/2 cups plain
   (all-purpose) flour
1 egg, beaten
1 tbsp milk
salt and pepper

parsley sprig, to garnish
SAUCE:
1 tbsp vegetable oil
1 onion, chopped
1 garlic clove, crushed
125 g/4^1/2 oz open-capped
   mushrooms, sliced

3 smoked bacon slices, chopped

50 g/2 oz Parmesan cheese,
   grated
300 ml/^{1}/2 pint/1^1/4 cups double
   (heavy) cream
2 tbsp chopped fresh parsley

1 Cook the diced potatoes in a saucepan of boiling water for 10 minutes until cooked through. Drain well. Mash the potatoes until smooth, then beat in the flour, egg and milk. Season with salt and pepper and bring together to form a stiff paste.

2 On a lightly floured surface, roll out the paste to form a thin sausage shape. Cut the sausage into 2.5 cm/1 inch lengths. Bring a large pan of salted water to the boil, drop in the dough pieces and cook for 3–4 minutes. They will rise to the top when cooked.

3 To make the sauce, heat the oil in a pan and sauté the onion and garlic for 2 minutes. Add the mushrooms and bacon and cook for 5 minutes. Stir in the cheese, cream and parsley and season.

4 Drain the noodles and transfer to a warm pasta bowl. Spoon the sauce over the top and toss to mix. Garnish with a parsley sprig and serve.

COOK'S TIP

Make the dough in advance, then wrap and store the noodles in the refrigerator for up to 24 hours.

Potato & Mushroom Bake

Serves 4

INGREDIENTS

25 g/1 oz butter
450 g/1 lb waxy potatoes, thinly
  sliced
150 g/5 oz mixed mushrooms,
  sliced

1 tbsp chopped fresh rosemary
4 tbsp chopped fresh chives
2 garlic cloves, crushed
150 ml/^{1}/4 pint/^{2}/3 cup double
  (heavy) cream

salt and pepper
fresh chives, to garnish

1 Grease a shallow round ovenproof dish with butter.

2 Parboil the sliced potatoes in a saucepan of boiling water for 10 minutes. Drain well. Layer a quarter of the potatoes in the base of the dish.

3 Arrange a quarter of the mushrooms on top of the potatoes and sprinkle with a quarter of the rosemary, chives and garlic.

4 Continue layering in the same order, finishing with a layer of potatoes on top.

5 Pour the cream over the top of the potatoes. Season well.

6 Cook in a preheated oven, 190°C/375°F/ Gas Mark 5, for 45 minutes or until the bake is golden brown.

7 Garnish with fresh chives and serve at once.

COOK'S TIP

For a special occasion, the bake may be made in a lined cake tin (pan) and turned out to serve.

VARIATION

Use 50 g/2 oz re-hydrated dried mushrooms instead of the fresh mixed mushrooms, for a really intense flavour.

Spicy Potato-Filled Naan Breads

Serves 4

INGREDIENTS

225 g/8 oz waxy potatoes, scrubbed and diced	½ tsp chilli powder	RAITHA:
	1 tbsp tomato purée (paste)	150 ml/¼ pint/⅔ cup natural
1 tbsp vegetable oil	3 tbsp vegetable stock	yogurt
1 onion, chopped	75 g/2¾ oz baby spinach,	4 tbsp diced cucumber
2 garlic cloves, crushed	shredded	1 tbsp chopped mint
1 tsp ground cumin	4 small or 2 large naan breads	
1 tsp ground coriander (cilantro)	lime pickle, to serve	

1 Cook the diced potatoes in a saucepan of boiling water for 10 minutes. Drain thoroughly.

2 Heat the vegetable oil in a separate saucepan and cook the onion and garlic for 3 minutes, stirring. Add the spices and cook for a further 2 minutes.

3 Stir in the potatoes, tomato purée (paste), vegetable stock and spinach. Cook for 5 minutes until the potatoes are tender.

4 Warm the naan breads in a preheated oven, 150°C/300°F/Gas Mark 2, for about 2 minutes.

5 To make the raitha, mix the yogurt, cucumber and mint together in a small bowl.

6 Remove the naan breads from the oven. Using a sharp knife, cut a pocket in the side of each naan bread. Spoon the spicy potato mixture into each pocket.

7 Serve the filled naan breads at once, accompanied by the raitha and lime pickle.

COOK'S TIP

To give the raitha a much stronger flavour, make it in advance and leave to chill in the refrigerator until ready to serve.

Potato & Spinach Filo Triangles

Serves 4

INGREDIENTS

225 g/8 oz waxy potatoes, diced
    finely
450 g/1 lb baby spinach
1 tomato, seeded and chopped
$^1/_4$ tsp chilli powder

$^1/_2$ tsp lemon juice
225 g/8 oz packet filo pastry,
    thawed if frozen
25 g/1 oz butter, melted
salt and pepper

MAYONNAISE:
150 ml/$^1/_4$ pint/$^2/_3$ cup
    mayonnaise
2 tsp lemon juice
rind of 1 lemon

1 Lightly grease a baking (cookie) sheet with a little butter.

2 Cook the potatoes in a saucepan of boiling water for 10 minutes or until cooked through. Drain thoroughly and place in a mixing bowl.

3 Meanwhile, put the spinach in a saucepan with 2 tbsp of water, cover and cook over a low heat for 2 minutes until wilted. Drain the spinach thoroughly and add to the potato.

4 Stir in the chopped tomato, chilli powder and lemon juice. Season to taste with salt and pepper.

5 Lightly butter 8 sheets of filo pastry. Spread out 4 of the sheets and lay the other 4 on top of each. Cut them into 20 x 10 cm/ 8 x 4 inch rectangles.

6 Spoon the potato and spinach mixture on to one end of each rectangle. Fold a corner of the pastry over the filling, fold the pointed end back over the pastry strip, then fold over

the remaining pastry to form a triangle.

7 Place the triangles on the baking (cookie) sheet and bake in a preheated oven, 190°C/375°F/Gas Mark 5, for 20 minutes or until golden brown.

8 To make the mayonnaise, mix the mayonnaise, lemon juice and lemon rind together in a small bowl. Serve the potato and spinach filo triangles warm or cold with the lemon mayonnaise and a crisp green salad.

Garlic Mushrooms on Toast

Serves 4

INGREDIENTS

75 g/2¾ oz/6 tbsp vegetarian
   margarine
2 garlic cloves, crushed
350 g/12 oz/4 cups mixed
   mushrooms, such as open-
   cap, button, oyster and

shiitake, sliced
8 slices French bread
1 tbsp chopped parsley
salt and pepper

1 Melt the margarine in a frying pan (skillet). Add the crushed garlic and cook for 30 seconds, stirring.

2 Add the mushrooms and cook for 5 minutes, turning occasionally.

3 Toast the French bread slices under a preheated medium grill (broiler) for 2–3 minutes, turning once.

4 Transfer the toasts to a serving plate.

5 Toss the parsley into the mushrooms, mixing well, and season well with salt and pepper to taste.

6 Spoon the mushroom mixture over the bread and serve immediately.

COOK'S TIP

Store mushrooms for 24–36 hours in the refrigerator, in paper bags, as they sweat in plastic. Wild mushrooms should be washed but other varieties can simply be wiped with paper towels.

COOK'S TIP

Add seasonings, such as curry powder or chilli powder, to the mushrooms for extra flavour, if liked.

Potato, (Bell) Pepper & Mushroom Hash

Serves 4

INGREDIENTS

675 g/1¹/₂ lb potatoes, cubed

1 tbsp olive oil

2 garlic cloves, crushed

1 green (bell) pepper, cubed

1 yellow (bell) pepper, cubed

3 tomatoes, diced

75 g/2³/₄ oz/1 cup button
   mushrooms, halved

1 tbsp vegetarian Worcester
   sauce

2 tbsp chopped basil

salt and pepper

fresh basil sprigs, to garnish

warm, crusty bread, to serve

1 Cook the potatoes in a saucepan of boiling salted water for 7–8 minutes. Drain well and reserve.

2 Heat the oil in a large, heavy-based frying pan (skillet) and cook the potatoes for 8–10 minutes, stirring until browned.

3 Add the garlic and (bell) peppers and cook for 2–3 minutes.

4 Stir in the tomatoes and mushrooms and cook, stirring, for 5–6 minutes.

5 Stir in the vegetarian Worcester sauce and basil and season well. Garnish and serve with crusty bread.

VARIATION

This dish can also be eaten cold as a salad.

COOK'S TIP

Most brands of Worcester sauce contain anchovies so make sure you choose a vegetarian variety.

Vegetable Samosas

Makes 12

INGREDIENTS

FILLING:

2 tbsp vegetable oil

1 onion, chopped

1/2 tsp ground coriander
(cilantro)

1/2 tsp ground cumin

pinch of turmeric

1/2 tsp ground ginger

1/2 tsp garam masala

1 garlic clove, crushed

225 g/8 oz/1 1/2 cups potatoes,
diced

100 g/3 1/2 oz/1 cup frozen peas,
thawed

150 g/5 1/2 oz/2 cups spinach,
chopped

PASTRY:

12 sheets filo pastry

oil, for deep-frying

1 To make the filling, heat the oil in a frying pan (skillet) and sauté the onion for 1–2 minutes, stirring until softened. Stir in all of the spices and garlic and cook for 1 minute.

2 Add the potatoes and cook over a gentle heat for 5 minutes, stirring until they begin to soften.

3 Stir in the peas and spinach and cook for a further 3–4 minutes.

4 Lay the filo pastry sheets out on a clean work surface (counter) and fold each sheet in half lengthwise.

5 Place 2 tbsp of the vegetable filling at one end of each folded pastry sheet. Fold over one corner to make a triangle. Continue folding in this way to make a triangular package and seal the edges with water.

6 Repeat with the remaining pastry and filling.

7 Heat the oil for deep-frying to 180°C/350°F or until a cube of bread browns in 30 seconds. Fry the samosas, in batches, for 1–2 minutes until golden. Drain on absorbent paper towels and keep warm whilst cooking the remainder. Serve.

Scrambled Tofu (Bean Curd) on Toast

Serves 4

INGREDIENTS

75 g/2³/₄ oz/6 tbsp
  vegetarian margarine
450 g/1 lb marinated,
  firm tofu (bean curd)

1 red onion, chopped
1 red (bell) pepper, chopped
4 ciabatta rolls
2 tbsp chopped mixed herbs

salt and pepper
fresh herbs, to garnish

1 Melt the margarine in a frying pan (skillet) and crumble the tofu (bean curd) into the pan.

2 Add the onion and (bell) pepper and cook for 3–4 minutes, stirring occasionally.

3 Meanwhile, slice the ciabatta rolls in half and toast under a hot grill (broiler) for about 2–3 minutes, turning once. Remove the toasts and transfer to a serving plate.

4 Add the herbs to t he tofu (bean curd) mixture, combine and season.

5 Spoon the tofu (bean curd) mixture on to the toast and garnish with fresh herbs. Serve at once.

COOK'S TIP

Marinated tofu (bean curd) adds extra flavour to this dish. Smoked tofu (bean curd) could be used instead.

COOK'S TIP

Rub the cut surface of a garlic clove over the toasted ciabatta rolls for extra flavour.

Mixed Bean Pan-Fry

Serves 4

INGREDIENTS

350 g/12 oz/4 cups mixed green
    beans, such as French (green)
    and broad (fava) beans
2 tbsp vegetable oil
2 garlic cloves, crushed

1 red onion, halved and sliced
225 g/8 oz firm marinated
    tofu (bean curd), diced
1 tbsp lemon juice
1/2 tsp turmeric

1 tsp ground mixed spice
150 ml/ 1/4 pint/2/3 cup
    vegetable stock
2 tsp sesame seeds

1 Trim and chop the French (green) beans and set aside until required.

2 Heat the oil in a frying pan (skillet) and sauté the garlic and onion for 2 minutes, stirring well.

3 Add the tofu (bean curd) and cook for 2–3 minutes until just beginning to brown.

4 Add the French (green) beans and broad (fava) beans. Stir in the lemon juice, turmeric, mixed spice and vegetable stock and bring to the boil.

5 Reduce the heat and simmer for 5–7 minutes or until the beans are tender. Sprinkle with sesame seeds and serve immediately.

VARIATION

Add lime juice instead of lemon, for an alternative citrus flavour.

VARIATION

Use smoked tofu (bean curd) instead of marinated tofu (bean curd) for an alternative flavour.

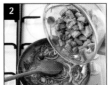

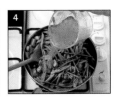

Calzone with Sun-Dried Tomatoes & Vegetables

Makes 4

INGREDIENTS

DOUGH:
450 g/1 lb/3½ cups strong
    white flour
2 tsp easy-blend dried yeast
1 tsp caster (superfine) sugar
150 ml/¼ pint/⅔ cup
    vegetable stock
150 ml/¼ pint/⅔ cup passata
    (sieved tomatoes)
beaten egg

FILLING:
1 tbsp vegetable oil
1 onion, chopped
1 garlic clove, crushed
2 tbsp chopped sun-dried
    tomatoes
100 g/3½ oz spinach, chopped
3 tbsp canned and drained
    sweetcorn
25 g/1 oz/¼ cup French (green)

beans, cut into three
1 tbsp tomato purée (paste)
1 tbsp chopped oregano
50 g/1¾ oz Mozzarella
    cheese, sliced
salt and pepper

1 Sieve the flour into a bowl. Add the yeast and sugar and beat in the stock and passata (sieved tomatoes) to make a smooth dough.

2 Knead the dough on a lightly floured surface for 10 minutes, then place in a clean, lightly oiled bowl and leave to rise in a warm place for 1 hour.

3 Heat the oil in a frying pan (skillet) and sauté the onion for 2–3 minutes. Stir in the garlic, tomatoes, spinach, corn and beans and cook for 3–4 minutes. Add the tomato purée (paste) and oregano and season well.

4 Divide the risen dough into 4 equal portions and roll each on to a floured surface to form an 18 cm/7 inch circle. Spoon a quarter of the filling on to one half of each circle and top with cheese. Fold the dough over to encase the filling, sealing the edge with a fork. Glaze with beaten egg. Put the calzone on a lightly greased baking tray (cookie sheet) and cook in a preheated oven, 220°C/425°F/Gas Mark 7, for 25–30 minutes until risen and golden. Serve warm.

Vegetable Enchiladas

Serves 4

INGREDIENTS

4 flour tortillas
75 g/2¾ oz/ ¾ cup vegetarian
   Cheddar, grated

FILLING:
75 g/2¾ oz spinach
2 tbsp olive oil
8 baby sweetcorn cobs, sliced
25 g/1 oz/1 tbsp frozen
   peas, thawed

1 red (bell) pepper, diced
1 carrot, diced
1 leek, sliced
2 garlic cloves, crushed
1 red chilli, chopped
salt and pepper

SAUCE:
300 ml/½ pint/1¼ cups passata
   (sieved tomatoes)
2 shallots, chopped
1 garlic clove, crushed
300 ml/½ pint/1¼ cups
   vegetable stock
1 tsp caster (superfine) sugar
1 tsp chilli powder

1 To make the filling, blanch the spinach in a pan of boiling water for 2 minutes, drain well and chop.

2 Heat the oil in a frying pan (skillet) and sauté the corn, peas, (bell) pepper, carrot, leek, garlic and chilli for 3–4 minutes, stirring briskly. Stir in the spinach and season well with salt and pepper to taste.

3 Put all of the sauce ingredients in a saucepan and bring to the boil, stirring. Cook over a high heat for 20 minutes, stirring, until thickened and reduced by a third.

4 Spoon a quarter of the filling along the centre of each tortilla. Roll the tortillas around the filling and place in an ovenproof dish, seam-side down.

5 Pour the sauce over the tortillas and sprinkle the cheese on top. Cook in a preheated oven, 180°C/350°F/Gas Mark 4, for 20 minutes or until the cheese has melted and browned.
Serve immediately.

Spinach Gnocchi with Tomato & Basil Sauce

Serves 4

INGREDIENTS

450 g/1 lb baking potatoes
75 g/2¾ oz spinach
1 tsp water
25 g/1 oz/3 tbsp butter or
    vegetarian margarine
1 small egg, beaten

150 g/5½ oz/¾ cup plain
    (all-purpose) flour
fresh basil sprigs, to garnish

TOMATO SAUCE:
1 tbsp olive oil
1 shallot, chopped

1 tbsp tomato purée (paste)
225 g/8 oz can chopped
    tomatoes
2 tbsp chopped basil
85 ml/3 fl oz/6 tbsp red wine
1 tsp caster (superfine) sugar
salt and pepper

1 Cook the potatoes in their skins in a pan of boiling salted water for 20 minutes. Drain well and press through a sieve into a bowl. Cook the spinach in 1 tsp water for 5 minutes until wilted. Drain and pat dry with paper towels. Chop and stir into the potatoes.

2 Add the butter or margarine, egg and half of the flour to the spinach mixture, mixing well. Turn out on to a floured surface, gradually kneading in the remaining flour to form a soft dough. With floured hands, roll the dough into thin ropes and cut off 2 cm/ ¾ inch pieces. Press the centre of each dumpling with your finger, drawing it towards you to curl the sides of the gnocchi. Cover and leave to chill.

3 Heat the oil for the sauce in a pan and sauté the chopped shallots for 5 minutes.

Add the tomato purée (paste), tomatoes, basil, red wine and sugar and season well. Bring to the boil and then simmer for 20 minutes.

4 Bring a pan of salted water to the boil and cook the gnocchi for 2–3 minutes or until they rise to the top of the pan. Drain well and transfer to serving dishes. Spoon the tomato sauce over the top. Garnish and serve.

Vegetable Jambalaya

Serves 4

INGREDIENTS

75 g/2³/₄ oz/¹/₂ cup brown rice	50 g/1³/₄ oz/¹/₂ cup frozen peas	1 tsp creole seasoning
2 tbsp olive oil	100 g/3¹/₂ oz small broccoli	¹/₂ tsp chilli flakes
2 garlic cloves, crushed	florets	salt and pepper
1 red onion, cut into eight	150 ml/5 floz/²/₃ cup	
1 aubergine (eggplant), diced	vegetable stock	
1 green (bell) pepper, diced	225 ml/8 fl oz can chopped	
50 g/1³/₄ oz/¹/₂ cup baby corn	tomatoes	
cobs, halved lengthwise	1 tbsp tomato purée (paste)	

1 Cook the rice in a saucepan of boiling water for 20 minutes or until cooked through. Drain and set aside.

2 Heat the oil in a heavy-based frying pan (skillet) and cook the garlic and onion for 2–3 minutes, stirring.

3 Add the aubergine (eggplant), (bell) pepper, corn, peas and broccoli to the pan and cook, stirring occasionally, for 2–3 minutes.

4 Stir in the vegetable stock and canned tomatoes, tomato purée (paste), creole seasoning and chilli flakes.

5 Season to taste and cook over a low heat for 15–20 minutes or until the vegetables are tender.

6 Stir the brown rice in to the vegetable mixture and cook, mixing well, for 3–4 minutes or until hot. Transfer the vegetable jambalaya to warm serving dishes and serve immediately.

COOK'S TIP

Use a mixture of rice, such as wild or red rice, for colour and texture. Cook the rice in advance for a speedier recipe.

Stuffed Mushrooms

Serves 4

INGREDIENTS

8 open-cap mushrooms
1 tbsp olive oil
1 small leek, chopped
1 celery stick, chopped
100 g/3½ oz firm tofu (bean curd), diced
1 courgette (zucchini), chopped

1 carrot, chopped
100 g/3½ oz/1 cup wholemeal (whole wheat) breadcrumbs
2 tbsp chopped basil
1 tbsp tomato purée (paste)
2 tbsp pine kernels (nuts)
75 g/2¾ oz/¾ cup vegetarian

Cheddar cheese, grated
150 ml/¼ pint/⅔ cup vegetable stock
salt and pepper
green salad, to serve

1 Remove the stalks from the mushrooms and chop finely.

2 Heat the oil in a frying pan (skillet). Add the chopped mushroom stalks, leek, celery, tofu (bean curd), courgette (zucchini) and carrot and cook for 3–4 minutes, stirring.

3 Stir in the breadcrumbs, basil, tomato purée (paste) and pine kernels (nuts). Season with salt and pepper to taste.

4 Spoon the mixture into the mushrooms and top with the cheese.

5 Place the mushrooms in a shallow ovenproof dish and pour the vegetable stock around them.

6 Cook in a preheated oven at 220°C/425°F/Gas Mark 7 for 20 minutes or until cooked through and the cheese has melted. Remove the mushrooms from the dish and serve immediately with a green salad.

COOK'S TIP

Vary the vegetables used for flavour and colour or according to those you have available.

Vegetable Crêpes

Serves 4

INGREDIENTS

PANCAKES:

100 g/3¹/₂ oz plain
  (all-purpose) flour
pinch of salt
1 egg, beaten
300 ml/¹/₂ pint/1¹/₄ cups milk
vegetable oil, for frying

FILLING:

2 tbsp vegetable oil
1 leek, shredded
¹/₂ tsp chilli powder
¹/₂ tsp ground cumin
50 g/1³/₄ oz mangetout
  (snow peas)
100 g/3¹/₂ oz button mushrooms,
1 red (bell) pepper, sliced
25 g/1 oz/¹/₄ cup cashew nuts,
  chopped

SAUCE:

25 g/1 oz/2 tbsp vegetarian
  margarine
25 g/1 oz/3 tbsp plain
  (all-purpose) flour
150 ml/¹/₄ pint/²/₃ cup
  vegetable stock
150 ml/¹/₄ pint/²/₃ cup milk
1 tsp Dijon mustard
75 g/2³/₄ oz vegetarian Cheddar
  cheese, grated
2 tbsp chopped coriander (cilantro)

1 For the pancakes, sieve the flour and salt into a bowl. Beat in the egg and milk to make a batter. For the filling, heat the oil in a pan (skillet) and sauté the leek for 2–3 minutes. Add the rest of the ingredients and cook for 5 minutes, stirring. To make the sauce, melt the margarine in a pan and add the flour. Cook for 1 minute and remove from the heat.

Stir in the stock and milk and return to the heat. Bring to the boil, stirring until thick. Add the mustard, half of the cheese and the coriander (cilantro); cook for 1 minute.

2 Heat 1 tbsp of oil in a non-stick 15 cm/6 inch frying pan (skillet). Pour the oil from the pan and add an eighth of the batter, to cover the base of the pan. Cook

for 2 minutes, turn the pancake and cook the other side for 1 minute. Repeat with the remaining batter. Spoon a little of the filling along the centre of each pancake and roll up. Place in a heatproof dish and pour the sauce on top. Top with cheese and heat under a hot grill (broiler) for 3–5 minutes or until the cheese melts and turns golden.

Vegetable Pasta Nests

Serves 4

INGREDIENTS

175 g/6 oz spaghetti
1 aubergine (eggplant), halved
    and sliced
1 courgette (zucchini), diced
1 red (bell) pepper, seeded and

chopped diagonally
6 tbsp olive oil
2 garlic cloves, crushed
50 g/1¾ oz/4 tbsp butter or
    vegetarian margarine, melted

15 g/½ oz/1 tbsp dry white
    breadcrumbs
salt and pepper
fresh parsley sprigs, to garnish

1 Bring a large saucepan of water to the boil and cook the spaghetti until 'al dente' or according to the instructions on the packet. Drain well and set aside until required.

2 Place the aubergine (eggplant), courgette (zucchini) and (bell) pepper on a baking tray (cookie sheet).

3 Mix the oil and garlic together and pour over the vegetables, tossing to coat.

4 Cook under a preheated hot grill (broiler) for about 10 minutes, turning, until tender and lightly charred. Set aside and keep warm.

5 Divide the spaghetti among 4 lightly greased Yorkshire pudding tins (pans). Using a fork, curl the spaghetti to form nests.

6 Brush the pasta nests with melted butter or margarine and sprinkle with the breadcrumbs. Bake in a preheated oven, at 200°C/400°F/ Gas Mark 6, for 15 minutes or until lightly golden. Remove the pasta nests from the tins (pans) and transfer to serving plates. Divide the grilled (broiled) vegetables between the pasta nests, season and garnish.

COOK'S TIP

'Al dente' means 'to the bite' and describes cooked pasta that is not too soft, but still has a bite to it.

Vegetable Burgers & Chips (Fries)

Serves 4

INGREDIENTS

VEGETABLE BURGERS:
100 g/3¹/₂ oz spinach
1 tbsp olive oil
1 leek, chopped
2 garlic cloves, crushed
100 g/3¹/₂ oz /1¹/₂ cups
   mushrooms, chopped
300 g/10¹/₂ oz firm tofu (bean
   curd), chopped

1 tsp chilli powder
1 tsp curry powder
1 tbsp chopped coriander
   (cilantro)
75 g/2³/₄ oz /1¹/₂ cups fresh
   wholemeal (whole wheat)
   breadcrumbs
1 tbsp olive oil

CHIPS (FRIES):
2 large potatoes
2 tbsp flour
1 tsp chilli powder
2 tbsp olive oil
burger bap or roll
   and salad, to serve

1 To make the burgers, cook the spinach in a little water for 2 minutes. Drain thoroughly and pat dry with paper towels.

2 Heat the oil in a frying pan (skillet) and sauté the leek and garlic for 2–3 minutes. Add the remaining ingredients except for the breadcrumbs and cook for 5–7 minutes until the vegetables have softened. Toss in the spinach and cook for 1 minute.

3 Transfer the mixture to a food processor and blend for 30 seconds until almost smooth. Stir in the breadcrumbs, mixing well, and leave until cool enough to handle. Using floured hands, form the mixture into four equal-sized burgers. Leave to chill for 30 minutes.

4 To make the chips (fries), cut the potatoes into thin wedges and cook in a pan of boiling water for 10 minutes. Drain and toss in the flour and chilli. Lay the chips on a baking tray (cookie sheet) and sprinkle with the oil. Cook in a preheated oven, 200°C/400°F/ Gas Mark 6, for 30 minutes or until golden.

5 Meanwhile, heat 1 tbsp oil in a frying pan (skillet) and cook the burgers for 8–10 minutes, turning once. Serve with salad in a bap.

Vegetable Dim Sum

Serves 4

INGREDIENTS

2 spring onions (scallions), chopped

25 g/1 oz green beans, chopped

½ small carrot, finely chopped

1 red chilli, chopped

25 g/1 oz/⅓ cup bean sprouts, chopped

25 g/1 oz/⅓ cup button mushrooms, chopped

25 g/1 oz/¼ cup unsalted cashew nuts, chopped

1 small egg, beaten

2 tbsp cornflour (cornstarch)

1 tsp light soy sauce

1 tsp hoi-sin sauce

1 tsp sesame oil

32 wonton wrappers

oil, for deep-frying

1 tbsp sesame seeds

1 Mix all of the vegetables together in a bowl.

2 Add the nuts, egg, cornflour (cornstarch), soy sauce, hoi-sin sauce and sesame oil to the bowl, stirring to mix well.

3 Lay the wonton wrappers out on a chopping board and spoon small quantities of the mixture into the centre of each. Gather the wrapper around the filling at the top, to make little parcels, leaving the top open.

4 Heat the oil for deep-frying in a wok to 180°C/350°F or until a cube of bread browns in 30 seconds.

5 Fry the wontons, in batches, for 1–2 minutes or until golden brown. Drain on absorbent paper towels and keep warm whilst frying the remaining wontons.

6 Sprinkle the sesame seeds over the wontons. Serve the vegetable dim sum with a soy or plum dipping sauce.

COOK'S TIP

If preferred, arrange the wontons on a heatproof plate and then steam in a steamer for 5-7 minutes for a healthier cooking method.

Cheese & Garlic Mushroom Pizzas

Serves 4

INGREDIENTS

DOUGH:
450 g/1 lb/3 ½ cups strong
  white flour
2 tsp easy-blend yeast
2 garlic cloves, crushed
2 tbsp chopped thyme
2 tbsp olive oil
300 ml/½ pint/1¼ cups
  tepid water

TOPPING:
25 g/1 oz/2 tbsp butter or
  vegetarian margarine
350 g/12 oz/5 cups mixed
  mushrooms, sliced
2 garlic cloves, crushed
2 tbsp chopped parsley
2 tbsp tomato purée (paste)
6 tbsp passata (sieved tomatoes)

75 g/2¾ oz Mozzarella cheese,
  grated
salt and pepper
chopped parsley, to garnish

1 Put the flour, yeast, garlic and thyme in a bowl. Make a well in the centre and gradually stir in the oil and water. Bring together to form a soft dough.

2 Turn the dough on to a floured surface and knead for 5 minutes or until smooth. Roll into a 35 cm/14 inch round and place on a greased baking tray (cookie sheet). Leave in a warm place for 20 minutes or until the dough puffs up.

3 Meanwhile, make the topping. Melt the margarine or butter in a frying pan (skillet) and sauté the mushrooms, garlic and parsley for 5 minutes.

4 Mix the tomato purée (paste) and passata (sieved tomatoes) and spoon on to the pizza base, leaving a 1 cm/½ inch edge of dough. Spoon the mushroom mixture on top. Season well and sprinkle the cheese on top. Cook the pizza in a preheated oven, 190°C/375°F/Gas Mark 5, for 20–25 minutes or until the base is crisp and the cheese has melted. Garnish with chopped parsley and serve.

Watercress & Cheese Tartlets

Makes 4

INGREDIENTS

100 g/3½ oz/¾ cup plain (all-purpose) flour	2–3 tbsp cold water	cheese, grated
pinch of salt	2 bunches watercress	4 tbsp natural (unsweetened) yogurt
75 g/2¾ oz /½ cup butter or vegetarian margarine	2 garlic cloves, crushed	½ tsp paprika
	1 shallot, chopped	
	150 g/5½ oz vegetarian Cheddar	

1 Sieve the flour into a mixing bowl and add the salt. Rub 50 g/1¾ oz/⅓ cup of the butter or margarine into the flour until the mixture resembles breadcrumbs.

2 Stir in the cold water to make a firm dough.

3 Roll the dough out on a floured surface and use to line four 10 cm/4 inch tartlet tins (pans). Prick the bases with a fork and leave to chill.

4 Heat the remaining butter or margarine in a frying pan (skillet). Discard the stems from the watercress and add to the pan with the garlic and shallot, cooking for 1–2 minutes until the watercress is wilted.

5 Remove the pan from the heat and stir in the cheese, yogurt and paprika.

6 Spoon the mixture into the pastry cases and cook in a preheated oven, 180°C/350°F/Gas Mark 4, for 20 minutes or until the filling is firm. Turn out the tartlets and serve.

VARIATION

Use spinach instead of the watercress, making sure it is well drained before mixing with the remaining filling ingredients.

Vegetable-Filled Ravioli

Serves 4

INGREDIENTS

FILLING:

25 g/1 oz/3 tbsp butter or
vegetarian margarine
2 garlic cloves, crushed
1 small leek, chopped
2 celery sticks, chopped

200 g/7 oz/2¹⁄₃ cups open-cap
mushrooms, chopped
1 egg, beaten
2 tbsp grated vegetarian Parmesan
cheese
salt and pepper

RAVIOLI:

4 sheets filo pastry
25 g/1 oz/3 tbsp vegetarian
margarine
oil, for deep-frying

1 To make the filling, melt the butter or margarine in a frying pan (skillet) and sauté the garlic and leek for 2–3 minutes until softened.

2 Add the celery and mushrooms and cook for a further 4–5 minutes until all of the vegetables are tender.

3 Turn off the heat and stir in the egg and grated Parmesan cheese. Season with salt and pepper to taste.

4 Lay the pastry sheets on a chopping board and cut each into nine squares.

5 Spoon a little of the filling into the centre half of the squares and brush the edges of the pastry with butter or margarine. Lay another square on top and seal the edges to make a parcel.

6 Heat the oil for deep-frying to 180°C/350°F or until a cube of bread browns in 30 seconds. Fry the ravioli, in batches, for 2–3 minutes or until golden brown. Remove from the oil with a slotted spoon and pat dry on absorbent paper towels. Transfer to a warm serving plate and serve.

COOK'S TIP

Parmesan cheese is generally non-vegetarian, however, there is an Italian Parmesan called Grano Padano, which is usually vegetarian. Alternatively you could use Pecorino.

Bulgur-Filled Aubergines (Eggplants)

Serves 4

INGREDIENTS

4 medium aubergines (eggplants)
salt
175 g/6 oz/³/4 cup bulgur wheat
300 ml/¹/2 pint/1¹/4 cups
    boiling water
3 tbsp olive oil
2 garlic cloves, crushed

2 tbsp pine kernels (nuts)
¹/2 tsp turmeric
1 tsp chilli powder
2 celery sticks, chopped
4 spring onions (scallions),
    chopped
1 carrot, grated

50 g/1³/4 oz/³/4 cup button
    mushrooms, chopped
2 tbsp raisins
2 tbsp chopped fresh coriander
    (cilantro)
green salad, to serve

1 Cut the aubergines (eggplants) in half lengthwise and scoop out the flesh with a teaspoon. Chop the flesh and set aside. Rub the insides of the aubergines (eggplants) with a little salt and leave to stand for 20 minutes.

2 Meanwhile, put the bulgur wheat in a mixing bowl and pour the boiling water over the top. Leave to stand for 20 minutes or until the water has been absorbed.

3 Heat the oil in a frying pan (skillet). Add the garlic, pine kernels (nuts), turmeric, chilli powder, celery, spring onions (scallions), carrot, mushrooms and raisins and cook for 2–3 minutes.

4 Stir in the reserved aubergine (eggplant) flesh and cook for a further 2–3 minutes. Add the coriander (cilantro), mixing well.

5 Remove the pan from the heat and stir in the

bulgur wheat. Rinse the aubergine (eggplant) shells under cold water and pat dry with paper towels.

6 Spoon the bulgur filling into the aubergines (eggplants) and place in a roasting tin (pan). Pour in a little boiling water and cook in a preheated oven, 180°C/350°F/Gas Mark 4, for 15–20 minutes.

7 Serve hot with a green salad.

Lentil Croquettes

Serves 4

INGREDIENTS

225 g/8 oz/1 ¼ cups split red lentils	½ tsp chilli powder	1 tsp turmeric
1 green (bell) pepper, finely chopped	1 tsp ground cumin	1 tsp chilli powder
1 red onion, finely chopped	2 tsp lemon juice	4 tbsp vegetable oil
2 garlic cloves, crushed	2 tbsp chopped unsalted peanuts	salt and pepper
1 tsp garam masala	600 ml/1 pint/2½ cups water	salad leaves and fresh herbs, to serve
	1 egg, beaten	
	3 tbsp plain (all-purpose) flour	

1 Put the lentils in a large saucepan with the (bell) pepper, onion, garlic, garam masala, chilli powder, ground cumin, lemon juice and peanuts.

2 Add the water and bring to the boil. Reduce the heat and simmer for 30 minutes or until the liquid has been absorbed, stirring occasionally.

3 Remove the mixture from the heat and leave to cool slightly. Beat in the egg and season with salt and pepper to taste. Leave to cool completely.

4 With floured hands, form the mixture into eight oblong shapes.

5 Mix the flour, turmeric and chilli powder together on a small plate. Roll the croquettes in the spiced flour mixture to coat.

6 Heat the oil in a large frying pan (skillet) and cook the croquettes, in batches, for 10 minutes, turning once, until crisp on both sides. Serve the croquettes with salad leaves and fresh herbs.

COOK'S TIP

Other lentils could be used, but they will require soaking and precooking before use. Red lentils are used for speed and convenience.

Refried Beans with Tortillas

Serves 4

INGREDIENTS

BEANS:

2 tbsp olive oil
1 onion, finely chopped
3 garlic cloves, crushed
1 green chilli, chopped
400 g/14 oz can red kidney
    beans, drained
400 g/14 oz can pinto
    beans, drained

2 tbsp chopped coriander
    (cilantro)
150 ml/¼ pint/⅔ cup
    vegetable stock
8 wheat tortillas
25 g/1 oz/¼ cup vegetarian
    Cheddar cheese, grated
salt and pepper

RELISH:

4 spring onions (scallions),
    chopped
1 red onion, chopped
1 green chilli, chopped
1 tbsp garlic wine vinegar
1 tsp caster (superfine) sugar
1 tomato, chopped

1 Heat the oil for the beans in a large frying pan (skillet). Add the onion and sauté for 3–5 minutes. Add the garlic and chilli and cook for 1 minute.

2 Mash the beans with a potato masher and stir into the pan with the coriander (cilantro).

3 Stir in the stock and cook the beans, stirring, for 5 minutes until soft and pulpy.

4 Place the tortillas on a baking tray (cookie sheet) and heat through in a warm oven for 1–2 minutes.

5 Mix the relish ingredients together.

6 Spoon the beans into a serving dish and top with the cheese. Season well. Roll the tortillas and serve with the relish and beans.

COOK'S TIP

Add a little more liquid to the beans when they are cooking if they begin to catch on the bottom of the frying pan (skillet).

Brown Rice, Vegetable & Herb Gratin

Serves 4

INGREDIENTS

100 g/3¹/₂ oz/¹/₃ cup brown rice
2 tbsp butter or margarine
1 red onion, chopped
2 garlic cloves, crushed
1 carrot, cut into matchsticks

1 courgette (zucchini), sliced
75 g/2³/₄ oz baby corn cobs,
    halved lengthwise
2 tbsp sunflower seeds
3 tbsp chopped mixed herbs

100 g/3¹/₂ oz/1 cup grated
    Mozzarella cheese
2 tbsp wholemeal (whole wheat)
    breadcrumbs
salt and pepper

1 Cook the rice in a saucepan of boiling salted water for 20 minutes. Drain well.

2 Lightly grease a 900 ml / 1¹/₂ pint ovenproof dish.

3 Heat the butter in a frying pan (skillet). Add the onion and cook, stirring, for 2 minutes or until softened.

4 Add the garlic, carrot, courgette (zucchini)

and corn cobs and cook for a further 5 minutes, stirring.

5 Mix the rice with the sunflower seeds and mixed herbs and stir into the pan.

6 Stir in half of the Mozzarella cheese and season with salt and pepper to taste.

7 Spoon the mixture into the greased dish and top with the breadcrumbs and remaining cheese.

Cook in a preheated oven, 180°C/350°F/Gas Mark 4, for 25–30 minutes or until the cheese begins to turn golden. Serve.

VARIATION

Use an alternative rice, such as basmati, and flavour the dish with curry spices, if you prefer.

Green Lentil & Mixed Vegetable Pan-Fry

Serves 4

INGREDIENTS

150 g/5½ oz/3¾ cups
green lentils
4 tbsp butter or vegetarian
margarine
2 garlic cloves, crushed
2 tbsp olive oil
1 tbsp cider vinegar

1 red onion, cut into eight
50 g/1¾ oz baby corn cobs,
halved lengthwise
1 yellow (bell) pepper, cut into
strips
1 red (bell) pepper, cut into strips
50 g/1¾ oz French (green)

beans, halved
125 ml/4 fl oz/6 tbsp /½ cup
vegetable stock
2 tbsp clear honey
salt and pepper
crusty bread, to serve

1 Soak the lentils in a large saucepan of cold water for 25 minutes. Bring to the boil, reduce the heat and simmer for 20 minutes. Drain thoroughly.

2 Add 1 tablespoon of the butter or margarine, 1 garlic clove, 1 tablespoon of oil and the vinegar to the lentils and mix well.

3 Melt the remaining butter, garlic and oil in a frying pan (skillet) and stir-fry the onion, corn cobs, (bell) peppers and beans for 3–4 minutes.

4 Add the vegetable stock and bring to the boil for about 10 minutes or until the liquid has evaporated.

5 Add the honey and season with salt and pepper to taste. Stir in the lentil mixture and cook for 1 minute to heat through. Spoon on to warmed serving plates and serve with crusty bread.

VARIATION

This pan-fry is very versatile – you can use a mixture of your favourite vegetables, if you prefer. Try courgettes (zucchini), carrots or mangetout (snow peas).

Falafel

Serves 4

INGREDIENTS

650 g/1 lb 7 oz/6 cups canned
    chickpeas (garbanzo beans),
    drained
1 red onion, chopped
3 garlic cloves, crushed
100 g/3¹/₂ oz wholemeal
    (whole wheat) bread

2 small red chillies
1 tsp ground cumin
1 tsp ground coriander
¹/₂ tsp turmeric
1 tbsp chopped coriander
    (cilantro), plus extra to garnish
1 egg, beaten

100 g/3¹/₂ oz/1 cup wholemeal
    (whole wheat) breadcrumbs
vegetable oil, for deep-frying
salt and pepper
tomato and cucumber salad and
    lemon wedges, to serve

1 Put the chickpeas (garbanzo beans), onion, garlic, bread, chillies, spices and coriander (cilantro) in a food processor and blend for 30 seconds. Stir and season well.

2 Remove the mixture from the food processor and shape into walnut-sized balls.

3 Place the beaten egg in a shallow bowl and place the wholemeal

(wholewheat) breadcrumbs on a plate. Dip the balls into the egg to coat and then roll them in the breadcrumbs, shaking off any excess.

4 Heat the oil for deep-frying to 180°C/350°F or until a cube of bread browns in 30 seconds. Fry the falafel, in batches, for 2–3 minutes until crisp and browned. Remove from the oil with a slotted spoon and dry on absorbent paper towels. Garnish with

coriander (cilantro) and serve with a tomato and cucumber salad and lemon wedges.

COOK'S TIP

Serve the falafel with a coriander (cilantro) and yogurt sauce. Mix 150 ml/¼ pint/⅔ cup natural (unsweetened) yogurt with 2 tbsp chopped coriander (cilantro) and 1 crushed garlic clove.

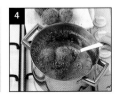

Cabbage & Walnut Stir-Fry

Serves 4

INGREDIENTS

350 g/12 oz white cabbage	8 spring onions (scallions),	100 g/3½ oz walnut halves
350 g/12 oz red cabbage	trimmed	2 tsp Dijon mustard
4 tbsp peanut oil	225 g/8 oz firm tofu (bean curd),	2 tsp poppy seeds
1 tbsp walnut oil	cubed	salt and pepper
2 garlic cloves, crushed	2 tbsp lemon juice	

1 Using a sharp knife, shred the white and red cabbages thinly and set aside until required.

2 Heat the peanut and walnut oils in a preheated wok. Add the garlic, cabbage, spring onions (scallions) and tofu (bean curd) and cook for 5 minutes, stirring.

3 Add the lemon juice, walnuts and mustard, season with salt and pepper and cook for a further 5 minutes or until the cabbage is tender.

4 Transfer the stir-fry to a warm serving bowl, sprinkle with poppy seeds and serve.

COOK'S TIP

As well as adding protein, vitamins and useful fats to the diet, nuts and seeds add flavour and texture to vegetarian meals. Keep a good supply of them in your store-cupboard as they can be used in a great variety of dishes – salads, bakes, stir-fries to name but a few.

VARIATION

Sesame seeds could be used instead of the poppy seeds and drizzle 1 teaspoon of sesame oil over the dish just before serving, if you wish.

Spinach Frittata

Serves 4

INGREDIENTS

450 g/1 lb spinach
2 tsp water
4 eggs, beaten
2 tbsp single (light) cream
2 garlic cloves, crushed
50 g/1¾ oz/¾ cup canned
    sweetcorn, drained
1 celery stick, chopped

1 red chilli, chopped
2 tomatoes, seeded and diced
2 tbsp olive oil
2 tbsp butter
25 g/1 oz/¼ cup pecan
    nut halves
2 tbsp grated Pecorino cheese

25 g/1 oz/¼ cup Fontina
    cheese, cubed
a pinch of paprika

1 Cook the spinach in 2 teaspoons of water in a covered pan for 5 minutes. Drain thoroughly and pat dry on absorbent paper towels.

2 Beat the eggs in a bowl and stir in the spinach, single (light) cream, garlic, sweetcorn, celery, chilli and tomatoes until the ingredients are well mixed.

3 Heat the oil and butter in a 20 cm/8 inch heavy-based frying pan (skillet).

4 Spoon the egg mixture into the frying pan (skillet) and sprinkle with the pecan nut halves, Pecorino and Fontina cheeses and paprika. Cook without stirring over a medium heat for 5–7 minutes or until the underside of the frittata is brown.

5 Put a large plate over the pan and invert to turn out the frittata. Slide it back into the frying pan (skillet) and cook the other side for a further 2–3 minutes. Serve the frittata straight from the frying pan (skillet) or transfer to a serving plate.

Marinated Grilled (Broiled) Fennel

Serves 4

INGREDIENTS

2 fennel bulbs
1 red (bell) pepper, cut into large
  cubes
1 lime, cut into eight wedges

MARINADE:
2 tbsp lime juice
4 tbsp olive oil
2 garlic cloves, crushed
1 tsp wholegrain mustard

1 tbsp chopped thyme
fennel fronds, to garnish
crisp salad, to serve

1 Cut each of the fennel bulbs into eight pieces and place in a shallow dish. Mix in the (bell) peppers.

2 To make the marinade, combine the lime juice, oil, garlic, mustard and thyme. Pour the marinade over the fennel and (bell) peppers and leave to marinate for 1 hour.

3 Thread the fennel and (bell) peppers on to wooden skewers with the lime wedges. Preheat a grill (broiler) to medium and grill (broil) the kebabs (kabobs) for 10 minutes, turning and basting with the marinade.

4 Transfer to serving plates, garnish with fennel fronds and serve with a crisp salad.

VARIATION

Substitute 2 tbsp orange juice for the lime juice and add 1 tbsp honey, if you prefer.

COOK'S TIP

Soak the skewers in water for 20 minutes before using to prevent them from burning during cooking.

Ciabatta Rolls

Serves 4

INGREDIENTS

4 ciabatta rolls
2 tbsp olive oil
1 garlic clove crushed

FILLING:
1 red (bell) pepper
1 green (bell) pepper
1 yellow (bell) pepper
4 radishes, sliced

1 bunch watercress
100 g/3½ oz/8 tbsp cream
cheese

1 Slice the ciabatta rolls in half. Heat the olive oil and crushed garlic in a saucepan. Pour the garlic and oil mixture over the cut surfaces of the rolls and leave to stand.

2 Halve the (bell) peppers and place, skin side uppermost, on a grill (broiler) rack. Cook under a hot grill (broiler) for 8–10 minutes until just beginning to char. Remove the (bell) peppers from the grill (broiler), peel and slice thinly.

3 Arrange the radish slices on one half of each roll with a few watercress leaves. Spoon the cream cheese on top. Pile the (bell) peppers on top of the cream cheese and top with the other half of the roll. Serve.

COOK'S TIP

To peel (bell) peppers, wrap them in foil after grilling (broiling). This traps the steam, loosening the skins and making them easier to peel.

COOK'S TIP

Allow the (bell) peppers to cool slightly before filling the roll otherwise the cheese will melt.

Crispy Potato Skins

Serves 4

INGREDIENTS

4 large baking potatoes
2 tbsp vegetable oil
4 tsp salt
150 ml/¼ pint/⅔ cup soured
cream and 2 tbsp chopped
chives, to serve
snipped chives, to garnish

BEAN SPROUT SALAD:
50 g/1¾ oz/½ cup bean sprouts
1 celery stick, sliced
1 orange, peeled and segmented
1 red dessert (eating)
apple, chopped
½ red (bell) pepper, chopped
1 tbsp chopped parsley
1 tbsp light soy sauce
1 tbsp clear honey
1 small garlic clove, crushed

BEAN FILLING:
100 g/3½ oz/1½ cups canned,
mixed beans, drained
1 onion, halved and sliced
1 tomato, chopped
2 spring onions
(scallions), chopped
2 tsp lemon juice
salt and pepper

1 Scrub the potatoes and put on a baking tray (cookie sheet). Prick the potatoes all over with a fork and rub the oil and salt into the skin.

2 Cook in a preheated oven at 200°C/ 400°F/Gas Mark 6 for 1 hour or until soft.

3 Cut the potatoes in half lengthwise and scoop out the flesh, leaving a 1 cm/½ inch thick shell. Put the shells, skin side uppermost, in the oven for 10 minutes until crisp.

4 Mix the ingredients for the bean sprout salad in a bowl, tossing in the soy sauce, honey and garlic to coat.

5 Mix the ingredients for the bean filling in a bowl.

6 Mix the soured cream and chives in another bowl.

7 Serve the potato skins hot, with the two salad fillings, garnished with snipped chives, and the sour cream and chive sauce.

Tomato, Olive & Mozzarella Bruschetta

Serves 4

INGREDIENTS

4 muffins

4 garlic cloves, crushed

2 tbsp butter

1 tbsp chopped basil

4 large, ripe tomatoes

1 tbsp tomato purée (paste)

8 pitted black olives, halved

50 g/1¾ oz Mozzarella
  cheese, sliced

salt and pepper

fresh basil leaves, to garnish

DRESSING:

1 tbsp olive oil

2 tsp lemon juice

1 tsp clear honey

1 Cut the muffins in half to give eight thick pieces. Toast the muffin halves under a hot grill (broiler) for 2–3 minutes until golden.

2 Mix the garlic, butter and basil together and spread on to each muffin half.

3 Cut a cross shape at the base of each tomato. Plunge the tomatoes in a bowl of boiling water – this will make the skin easier to peel. After a few minutes, pick each tomato up with a fork and peel away the skin. Chop the tomato flesh and mix with the tomato purée (paste) and olives. Divide the mixture between the muffins.

4 Mix the dressing ingredients and drizzle over each muffin. Arrange the Mozzarella cheese on top and season.

5 Return the muffins to the grill (broiler) for 1–2 minutes until the cheese melts.

6 Garnish with fresh basil leaves and serve at once.

VARIATION

Use balsamic vinegar instead of the lemon juice for an authentic Mediterranean flavour.

Lentil Pâté

Serves 4

INGREDIENTS

1 tbsp vegetable oil, plus extra for greasing	½ tsp ground coriander (cilantro)	2 tbsp milk
1 onion, chopped	850 ml/1½ pints/1¼ cups vegetable stock	2 tbsp mango chutney
2 garlic cloves, crushed	175 g/6 oz/¾ cup red lentils	2 tbsp chopped parsley
1 tsp garam masala	1 small egg	plua extra to garnish
		salad leaves and warm toast, to serve

1 Heat the oil in a large saucepan and sauté the onion and garlic for 2–3 minutes, stirring. Add the spices and cook for a further 30 seconds.

2 Stir in the stock and lentils and bring the mixture to the boil. Reduce the heat and simmer for 20 minutes until the lentils are cooked and softened. Remove the pan from the heat and drain off any excess moisture.

3 Put the mixture in a food processor and add the egg, milk, mango chutney and parsley. Blend until smooth.

4 Grease and line the base of a 450 g/1 lb loaf tin (pan) and spoon the mixture into the tin (pan), levelling the surface. Cover and cook in a preheated oven at 200°C/400°F/Gas Mark 6 for 40–45 minutes or until firm to the touch.

5 Allow the pâté to cool in the tin (pan) for 20 minutes, then transfer to the refrigerator to cool completely.

6 Turn out the pâté on to a serving plate, slice and garnish with chopped parsley. Serve with salad leaves and warm toast.

VARIATION

Use other spices, such as chilli powder or Chinese five-spice powder, to flavour the pâté and add tomato relish or chilli relish instead of the mango chutney, if you prefer.

Roasted Vegetables on Muffins

Serves 4

INGREDIENTS

1 red onion, cut into eight
1 aubergine (eggplant), halved
    and sliced
1 yellow (bell) pepper, sliced
1 courgette (zucchini), sliced
4 tbsp olive oil
1 tbsp garlic vinegar
2 tbsp vermouth
2 garlic cloves, crushed

1 tbsp chopped thyme
2 tsp light brown sugar
4 muffins, halved
salt and pepper

SAUCE:
2 tbsp butter
1 tbsp flour
150 ml/¹/₄ pint/²/₃ cup milk
85 ml/3 fl oz vegetable stock
75 g/2³/₄ oz/³/₄ cup vegetarian
    Cheddar, grated
1 tsp wholegrain mustard
3 tbsp chopped mixed herbs

1 Arrange the vegetables in a shallow ovenproof dish. Mix together the oil, vinegar, vermouth, garlic, thyme and sugar and pour over the vegetables. Leave to marinate for 1 hour.

2 Transfer the vegetables to a baking tray (cookie sheet). Cook in a pre-heated oven at 200°C/400°F/Gas Mark 6 for 20–25 minutes or until the vegetables have softened.

3 Meanwhile, make the sauce. Melt the butter in a small pan and add the flour. Cook for 1 minute and remove from the heat. Stir in the milk and stock and return the pan to the heat. Bring to the boil, stirring, until thickened. Stir in the cheese, mustard and mixed herbs and season well.

4 Preheat the grill (broiler) to high. Cut the muffins in half

and grill for 2–3 minutes until golden brown, then remove and arrange on a serving plate.

5 Spoon the roasted vegetables on to the muffins and pour the sauce over the top. Serve immediately.

Hummus & Garlic Toasts

Serves 4

INGREDIENTS

HUMMUS:
400 g/14 oz can chickpeas
(garbanzo beans)
juice of 1 large lemon
6 tbsp tahini (sesame seed paste)
2 tbsp olive oil

2 garlic cloves, crushed
salt and pepper
chopped fresh coriander (cilantro)
and black olives, to garnish

TOASTS:
1 ciabatta loaf, sliced
2 garlic cloves, crushed
1 tbsp chopped fresh
coriander (cilantro)
4 tbsp olive oil

1 To make the hummus, firstly drain the chickpeas (garbanzo beans), reserving a little of the liquid. Put the chickpeas (garbanzo beans) and liquid in a food processor and blend, gradually adding the reserved liquid and lemon juice. Blend well after each addition until smooth.

2 Stir in the tahini (sesame seed paste) and all but 1 teaspoon of the olive oil. Add the garlic, season to taste and blend again until smooth.

3 Spoon the hummus into a serving dish. Drizzle the remaining olive oil over the top, garnish with chopped coriander (cilantro) and olives. Leave to chill in the refrigerator whilst preparing the toasts.

4 Lay the slices of ciabatta on a grill (broiler) rack in a single layer.

5 Mix the garlic, coriander (cilantro) and olive oil together and drizzle over the bread slices. Cook under a hot grill

(broiler) for 2–3 minutes until golden brown, turning once. Serve hot with the hummus.

COOK'S TIP

Make the hummus 1 day in advance, and chill, covered, in the refrigerator until required. Garnish and serve.

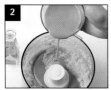

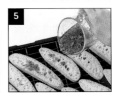

Mixed Bean Pâté

Serves 4

INGREDIENTS

400 g/14 oz can mixed beans,
drained
2 tbsp olive oil
juice of 1 lemon
2 garlic cloves, crushed

1 tbsp chopped fresh
coriander (cilantro)
2 spring onions (scallions),
chopped
salt and pepper

shredded spring onions
(scallions), to garnish

1 Rinse the beans thoroughly under cold running water and drain well.

2 Transfer the beans to a food processor or blender and process until smooth. Alternatively, place the beans in a bowl and mash with a fork or potato masher.

3 Add the olive oil, lemon juice, garlic, coriander (cilantro) and spring onions (scallions) and blend until fairly smooth. Season with salt and pepper to taste.

4 Transfer the pâté to a serving bowl and chill for at least 30 minutes. Garnish with shredded spring onions (scallions) and serve.

COOK'S TIP

Use canned beans which have no salt or sugar added and always rinse thoroughly before use.

COOK'S TIP

Serve the pâté with warm pitta bread or granary toast.

Vegetable Fritters with Sweet & Sour Sauce

Serves 4

INGREDIENTS

100 g/3^1/2 oz/^{3}/4 cup wholemeal
    (whole wheat) flour
pinch of salt
pinch of cayenne pepper
4 tsp olive oil
12 tbsp cold water
100 g/3^1/2 oz broccoli florets
100 g/3^1/2 oz cauliflower florets
50 g/1^3/4 oz mangetout
    (snow peas)

1 large carrot, cut into batons
1 red (bell) pepper, sliced
2 egg whites, beaten
oil, for deep-frying

SAUCE:
150 ml/^{1}/4 pint/^{2}/3 cup
    pineapple juice
150 ml/ ^{1}/4 pint/^{2}/3 cup
    vegetable stock
2 tbsp wine vinegar
2 tbsp light brown sugar
2 tsp cornflour (cornstarch)
2 spring onions (scallions),
    chopped

1 Sieve the flour and salt into a mixing bowl and add the cayenne pepper. Make a well in the centre and gradually beat in the oil and cold water to make a smooth batter.

2 Cook the vegetables in boiling water for 5 minutes and drain well.

3 Whisk the egg whites until peaking and fold them into the flour batter.

4 Dip the vegetables into the batter, turning to coat well. Drain off any excess batter. Heat the oil for deep-frying in a deep fat fryer to 180°C/350°F or until a cube of bread browns in 30 seconds. Fry

the vegetables for 1–2 minutes, in batches, until golden. Remove from the oil with a slotted spoon and drain on paper towels.

5 Place all of the sauce ingredients in a pan and bring to the boil, stirring, until thickened and clear. Serve with the fritters.

Mixed Bhajis

Serves 4

INGREDIENTS

BAHJIS:

175 g/6 oz/1¼ cups gram flour
1 tsp bicarbonate of soda
2 tsp ground coriander (cilantro)
1 tsp garam masala
1½ tsp turmeric
1½ tsp chilli powder

2 tbsp chopped
   coriander (cilantro)
1 small onion, halved and sliced
1 small leek, sliced
100 g/3½ oz cooked cauliflower
9-12 tbsp cold water
salt and pepper
vegetable oil, for deep-frying

SAUCE:

150 ml/¼ pint/⅔ cup natural
   (unsweetened) yogurt
2 tbsp chopped mint
½ tsp turmeric
1 garlic clove, crushed
fresh mint sprigs, to garnish

1 Sieve the flour, bicarbonate of soda and salt to taste into a mixing bowl and add the spices and fresh coriander (cilantro). Mix well until the ingredients are thoroughly combined.

2 Divide the mixture into 3 and place in separate bowls. Stir the onion into one bowl, the leek into another and the cauliflower into the third bowl. Add 3–4 tbsp of water to each bowl and mix each to form a smooth paste.

3 Heat the oil for deep frying in a deep fat fryer to 180°C/350°F or until a cube of bread browns in 30 seconds. Using 2 dessert spoons, form the mixture into rounds and cook each in the oil for 3–4 minutes until browned. Remove with a slotted spoon and drain on absorbent paper towels. Keep the bhajis warm in the oven whilst cooking the remainder.

4 Mix all of the sauce ingredients together and pour into a serving bowl. Garnish with mint sprigs and serve with the warm bhajis.

Mushroom & Garlic Soufflés

Serves 4

INGREDIENTS

50 g/1¾ oz/4 tbsp butter
75 g/2¾oz/1 cup flat
    mushrooms, chopped
2 tsp lime juice

2 garlic cloves, crushed
2 tbsp chopped marjoram
25 g/1 oz/3 tbsp plain (all-
    purpose) flour

225 ml/8 fl oz/1 cup milk
salt and pepper
2 eggs, separated

1 Lightly grease the inside of four 150 ml/¼ pint individual soufflé dishes with a little butter.

2 Melt 25 g/1 oz/2 tbsp of the butter in a frying pan (skillet). Add the mushrooms, lime juice and garlic and sauté for 2–3 minutes. Remove the mushroom mixture from the frying pan (skillet) with a slotted spoon and transfer to a mixing bowl. Stir in the marjoram.

3 Melt the remaining butter in a pan. Add the flour and cook for 1 minute, then remove from the heat. Stir in the milk and return to the heat. Bring to the boil, stirring until thickened.

4 Add the sauce to the mushroom mixture, mixing well and beat in the egg yolks.

5 Whisk the egg whites until peaking and fold into the mushroom mixture until fully incorporated.

6 Divide the mixture between the soufflé dishes. Place the dishes on a baking tray (cookie sheet) and cook in a preheated oven, 200°C/400°F/Gas Mark 6, for 8–10 minutes or until the soufflés have risen and are cooked through. Serve immediately.

COOK'S TIP

Insert a skewer into the centre of the soufflés to test if they are cooked through – it should come out clean. If not, cook for a few minutes longer, but do not overcook otherwise they will become rubbery.

Carrot, Fennel & Potato Medley

Serves 4

INGREDIENTS

2 tbsp olive oil
1 potato, cut into thin strips
1 fennel bulb, cut into thin strips
2 carrots, grated
1 red onion, cut into thin strips
chopped chives and fennel
    fronds, to garnish

DRESSING:
3 tbsp olive oil
1 tbsp garlic wine vinegar
1 garlic clove, crushed
1 tsp Dijon mustard
2 tsp clear honey
salt and pepper

1 Heat the olive oil in a frying pan (skillet), add the potato and fennel slices and cook for 2–3 minutes until beginning to brown. Remove from the frying pan (skillet) with a slotted spoon and drain on paper towels.

2 Arrange the carrot, red onion, potato and fennel in separate piles on a serving platter.

3 Mix the dressing ingredients together and pour over the vegetables. Toss well and sprinkle with chopped chives and fennel fronds. Serve immediately or leave in the refrigerator until required.

COOK'S TIP

Fennel is an aromatic plant which has a delicate, aniseed flavour. It can be eaten raw in salads, or boiled, braised, sautéed or grilled (broiled). For this salad, if fennel is unavailable, substitute 350 g/12 oz sliced leeks.

Onions à la Grecque

Serves 4

INGREDIENTS

450 g/1 lb shallots
3 tbsp olive oil
3 tbsp clear honey
2 tbsp garlic wine vinegar

3 tbsp dry white wine
1 tbsp tomato purée (paste)
2 celery stalks, sliced
2 tomatoes, seeded and chopped

salt and pepper
chopped celery leaves, to garnish

1 Peel the shallots. Heat the oil in a large saucepan, add the shallots and cook, stirring, for 3–5 minutes or until they begin to brown.

2 Add the honey and cook for a further 30 seconds over a high heat, then add the garlic wine vinegar and dry white wine, stirring well.

3 Stir in the tomato purée (paste), celery and tomatoes and bring the mixture to the boil. Cook over a high heat for 5–6 minutes. Season to taste and leave to cool slightly.

4 Garnish with chopped celery leaves and serve warm or cold from the refrigerator.

COOK'S TIP

This dish, served warm, can make an ideal light starter, or, served with another recipe, a great main-course side-dish.

VARIATION

Use button mushrooms instead of the shallots and fennel instead of the celery for another great starter.

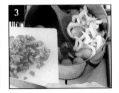

Aubergine (Eggplant) Timbale

Serves 4

INGREDIENTS

1 large aubergine (eggplant)
50 g/1¾ oz/½ cup macaroni
1 tbsp vegetable oil
1 onion, chopped
2 garlic cloves, crushed
2 tbsp drained canned sweetcorn
2 tbsp frozen peas, thawed
100 g/3½ oz spinach

25 g/1 oz/¼ cup vegetarian
   Cheddar, grated
1 egg, beaten
225 g/8 oz/3 cups canned,
   chopped tomatoes
1 tbsp chopped basil
salt and pepper

SAUCE:
4 tbsp olive oil
2 tbsp white wine vinegar
2 garlic cloves, crushed
3 tbsp chopped basil
1 tbsp caster (superfine) sugar

1 Cut the aubergine (eggplant) lengthwise into thin strips, using a potato peeler. Place in a bowl of salted boiling water and leave to stand for 3–4 minutes. Drain well.

2 Lightly grease four 150 ml/¼ pint individual ramekin dishes and use the aubergine (eggplant) slices to line the dishes, leaving 2.5 cm/1 inch of aubergine (eggplant) overlapping.

3 Cook the pasta in a pan of boiling water for 8–10 minutes until 'al dente'. Drain. Heat the oil in a pan and sauté the onion and garlic for 2–3 minutes. Stir in the sweetcorn and peas and remove from the heat.

4 Blanch the spinach, drain well, chop and reserve. Add the pasta to the onion mixture with the cheese, egg, tomatoes and basil. Season and mix. Half-fill each ramekin with some

of the pasta. Spoon the spinach on top and then the remaining pasta mixture. Fold the aubergine (eggplant) over the pasta filling to cover. Put the ramekins in a roasting tin (pan) half-filled with boiling water, cover and cook in a preheated oven, 180°C/350°F/Gas Mark 4, for 20–25 minutes or until set. Meanwhile, heat the sauce ingredients in a pan. Turn out the ramekins and serve with the sauce.

Puff Potato Pie

Serves 6

INGREDIENTS

750 g/1 lb 9 oz potatoes, peeled
and sliced thinly
2 spring onions (scallions),
chopped finely

1 red onion, chopped finely
150 ml/¼ pint/⅔ cup double
(heavy) cream

500 g/1 lb 2 oz fresh ready-made
puff pastry (pie dough)
2 eggs, beaten
salt and pepper

1 Lightly grease a baking tray (cookie sheet). Bring a saucepan of water to the boil, add the sliced potatoes, bring back to the boil and then simmer for a few minutes. Drain the potato slices and leave to cool. Dry off any excess moisture with paper towels.

2 In a bowl, mix together the spring onions (scallions), red onion and the cooled potato slices. Stir in 2 tbsp of the cream and plenty of seasoning.

3 Divide the pastry (pie dough) in half and roll out one piece to a 23 cm/9 inch round. Roll the remaining pastry (pie dough) to a 25 cm/ 10 inch round.

4 Place the smaller circle on to the baking tray (cookie sheet) and top with the potato mixture, leaving a 2.5 cm/1 inch border. Brush this border with a little of the beaten egg.

5 Top with the larger circle of pastry (pie dough), seal well and crimp the edges of the pastry (pie dough). Cut a steam vent in the middle of the pastry (pie dough) and, using the back of a knife, mark with a pattern. Brush with the beaten egg and bake in a preheated oven, 200°C/ 400°F/Gas Mark 6, for 30 minutes.

6 Mix the remaining beaten egg with the rest of the cream and pour into the pie through the steam vent. Return to the oven for 15 minutes, then leave to cool for 30 minutes. Serve warm or cold.

Spinach Cheese Moulds (Molds)

Serves 4

INGREDIENTS

100 g/3½ oz fresh spinach
  leaves
300 g/10½ oz skimmed milk soft
  cheese
2 garlic cloves, crushed

sprigs of fresh parsley, tarragon
  and chives, finely chopped
salt and pepper

TO SERVE:
salad leaves and fresh herbs
pitta bread

1 Trim the stalks from the spinach leaves. Rinse the leaves under running water. Pack the leaves into a saucepan while still wet, cover and cook for 3–4 minutes until wilted – they will cook in the steam from the wet leaves (do not overcook). Drain well and pat dry with absorbent kitchen paper.

2 Base-line 4 small pudding basins or individual ramekin dishes with baking parchment. Line the basins or ramekins with spinach leaves so that the leaves overhang the edges if they are large enough to do so.

3 Place the cheese in a bowl and add the garlic and herbs. Mix together thoroughly and season to taste.

4 Spoon the cheese and herb mixture into the basins or ramekins and pull over the overlapping spinach to cover the cheese, or lay extra leaves to cover the top. Place a greaseproof (waxed) paper circle on top of each dish and weigh down with a 100 g/3½ oz weight. Leave to chill in the refrigerator for 1 hour.

5 Remove the weights and peel off the paper. Loosen the moulds (molds) gently by running a small palette knife (spatula) around the edges of each dish and turn them out on to individual serving plates. Serve with a mixture of salad leaves and fresh herbs, and warm pitta bread.

Soufflé Omelette

Serves 4

INGREDIENTS

175 g/6 oz cherry tomatoes
225 g/8 oz mixed mushrooms
(such as button, chestnut,
shiitake, oyster and wild
mushrooms)

4 tbsp fresh vegetable stock
small bunch fresh thyme
4 medium eggs, separated
4 medium egg whites
4 tsp olive oil

25 g/1 oz rocket (arugula) leaves
salt and pepper
fresh thyme sprigs, to garnish

1 Halve the tomatoes and place them in a pan. Wipe the mushrooms with kitchen paper, trim if necessary and slice if large. Place in the pan.

2 Add the stock and thyme to the pan, and season to taste with salt and pepper. Bring to the boil, cover and simmer for 5–6 minutes until tender. Drain, remove the thyme and discard, and keep the mixture warm.

3 Meanwhile, whisk the egg yolks with 8 tablespoons of water until frothy. In a clean, grease-free bowl, mix the 8 egg whites until stiff and dry.

4 Spoon the egg yolk mixture into the egg whites and, using a metal spoon, fold the whites and yolks into each other until well mixed. Take care not to knock out too much of the air.

5 For each omelette, brush a small omelette pan with 1 teaspoon of oil and heat until hot. Pour in a quarter of the egg mixture and cook for 4–5 minutes or until the mixture has set.

6 Preheat the grill (broiler) to medium and finish cooking the omelette for 2–3 minutes.

7 Transfer the omelette to a warm serving plate. Fill the omelette with a few rocket (arugula) leaves, and a quarter of the mushroom and tomato mixture. Flip over the top of the omelette, garnish with sprigs of thyme and serve.

Side Dishes

If you are running short of ideas for interesting side dishes to serve with your main meals, these recipes will be a welcome inspiration. When the potato is thought of as a component of a meal, it is inevitably associated with meat and vegetables, and is served either roasted or boiled. In fact, the potato is so versatile in its ability to combine with other flavourings and be cooked in so many different ways that it is the perfect base for a whole variety of delicious side dishes. This chapter demonstrates that versatility with a wide range of tantalising recipes.

An ideal accompaniment complements the main dish, both visually and nutritionally. Main dishes are rich in protein so the vegetable side dishes in this chapter have been created to be a little lighter in texture, but still packed full of colour and flavour. They have been cooked in many different ways – there are baked, fried, steamed and braised dishes, all perfect complements to main meals for every occasion.

Colcannon

Serves 4

INGREDIENTS

225 g/8 oz green cabbage, shredded

85 ml/3 fl oz/⅓ cup milk

25 g/8 oz floury (mealy) potatoes, diced

1 large leek, chopped

pinch of grated nutmeg

15 g/½ oz/1 tbsp butter, melted

salt and pepper

1 Cook the shredded cabbage in a saucepan of boiling salted water for 7–10 minutes. Drain thoroughly and set aside.

2 Meanwhile, in a separate saucepan, bring the milk to the boil and add the potatoes and leek. Reduce the heat and simmer for 15–20 minutes or until they are cooked through.

3 Stir in the grated nutmeg and mash the potatoes and leeks together.

4 Add the drained cabbage to the potatoes and mix well.

5 Spoon the potato and cabbage mixture into a serving dish, making a hollow in the centre with the back of a spoon.

6 Pour the melted butter into the hollow and serve the dish immediately.

VARIATION

Add diced cooked bacon to the recipe for extra flavour, adding it with the leeks and cabbage.

COOK'S TIP

There are many different varieties of cabbage, which produce hearts at varying times of year, so you can be sure of being able to make this delicious cabbage dish all year round.

Candied Sweet Potatoes

Serves 4

INGREDIENTS

675 g/1½ lb sweet potatoes, sliced
40 g/1½ oz/3 tbsp butter

1 tbsp lime juice
75 g/2¾ oz/½ cup soft dark brown sugar

1 tbsp brandy
grated rind of 1 lime
lime wedges, to garnish

1 Cook the sweet potatoes in a saucepan of boiling water for 5 minutes. Test the potatoes have softened by pricking with a fork. Remove the sweet potatoes with a perforated spoon and drain thoroughly.

2 Melt the butter in a large frying pan (skillet). Add the lime juice and brown sugar and heat gently to dissolve the sugar.

3 Stir the sweet potatoes and the brandy into the sugar and lime juice mixture. Cook over a low heat for 10 minutes until the potato slices are cooked through.

4 Sprinkle the lime rind over the top of the sweet potatoes and mix well.

5 Transfer the candied sweet potatoes to a serving plate. Garnish with lime wedges and serve at once.

VARIATION

Serve this dish with spicy meats to complement the sweetness of the potatoes, if you prefer.

COOK'S TIP

Sweet potatoes have a pinkish skin and either white, yellow or orange flesh. It doesn't matter which type is used for this dish.

VARIATION

This dish may be prepared with waxy potatoes instead of sweet potatoes, if you prefer. Cook the potatoes for 10 minutes in step 1, instead of 5 minutes. Follow the same cooking method.

Potatoes with Onion & Herbs

Serves 4

INGREDIENTS

900 g/2 lb waxy potatoes, cut
  into cubes
125 g/4¹/₂ oz/¹/₂ cup butter

1 red onion, cut into 8
2 garlic cloves, crushed
1 tsp lemon juice

2 tbsp chopped fresh thyme
salt and pepper

1 Cook the cubed potatoes in a saucepan of boiling water for 10 minutes. Drain thoroughly.

2 Melt the butter in a large, heavy-based frying pan (skillet) and add the red onion wedges, garlic and lemon juice. Cook for 2–3 minutes, stirring.

3 Add the potatoes to the pan and mix well to coat in the butter mixture.

4 Reduce the heat, cover the frying pan (skillet) and cook for 25–30 minutes or until the potatoes are golden and tender.

5 Sprinkle the chopped thyme over the top of the potatoes and season with salt and pepper to taste.

6 Serve immediately as a side dish to accompany grilled meats or fish.

COOK'S TIP

Keep checking the potatoes and stirring throughout the cooking time to ensure that they do not burn or stick to the bottom of the frying pan (skillet).

COOK'S TIP

Onions are used in a multitude of dishes to which they add their pungent flavour. The beautifully coloured purple-red onions used here have a mild, slightly sweet flavour as well as looking extremely attractive. Because of their mild taste, they are equally good eaten raw in salads.

Caramelised New Potatoes

Serves 4

INGREDIENTS

675 g/1¹/₂ lb new potatoes,
  scrubbed
4 tbsp soft dark brown sugar
60 g/2 oz/¹/₂ cup butter

1 tbsp orange juice
1 tbsp chopped fresh parsley or
  coriander (cilantro)
60 g/2 oz/¹/₂ cup butter

salt and pepper
orange rind curls, to garnish

1 Cook the new potatoes in a saucepan of boiling water for 10 minutes or until almost tender. Drain thoroughly.

2 Melt the sugar in a large, heavy-based frying pan (skillet) over a low heat, stirring.

3 Add the butter and orange juice to the pan, stirring the mixture as the butter melts.

4 Add the potatoes to the orange and butter mixture and continue to cook, turning the potatoes frequently until they are completely coated in the caramel.

5 Sprinkle the chopped parsley or coriander (cilantro) over the potatoes and season to taste with salt and pepper.

6 Transfer the caramelised new potatoes to a serving dish and garnish with the orange rind. Serve immediately.

VARIATION

Lemon or lime juices may be used instead of the orange juce, if preferred. In addition, garnish the finished dish with pared lemon or lime rind, if preferred.

COOK'S TIP

Heat the sugar and butter gently, stirring constantly, to make sure that the mixture doesn't burn or stick to the bottom of the frying pan (skillet).

Spanish Potatoes

Serves 4

INGREDIENTS

2 tbsp olive oil

450 g/1 lb small new potatoes, halved

1 onion, halved and sliced

1 green (bell) pepper, cut into strips

1 tsp chilli powder

1 tsp prepared mustard

300 ml/$\frac{1}{2}$ pint/1$\frac{1}{4}$ cups passata

300 ml/$\frac{1}{2}$ pint/1$\frac{1}{4}$ cups vegetable stock

salt and pepper

chopped fresh parsley, to garnish

1 Heat the olive oil in a frying pan (skillet) and add the halved new potatoes and the sliced onion. Cook for 4–5 minutes, stirring frequently, until the onion slices have just softened.

2 Add the green (bell) pepper strips, chilli powder and mustard to the pan and cook for a further 2–3 minutes.

3 Stir the passata and the vegetable stock into the pan and bring to the boil. Reduce the heat and

cook the mixture for about 25 minutes or until the potatoes are tender.

4 Transfer the potatoes to a serving dish. Sprinkle the parsley over the top of the potatoes and serve hot. Alternatively, leave the Spanish potatoes to cool completely and serve cold.

COOK'S TIP

In Spain, tapas are traditionally served with a glass of chilled sherry or some other aperitif.

COOK'S TIP

The array of little appetizer snacks known as tapas are a traditional Spanish social custom. Spaniards often visit several bars throughout the evening eating different tapas, ranging from stuffed olives and salted almonds, to slices of ham and deep-fried squid rings.

Spicy Indian Potatoes with Spinach

Serves 4

INGREDIENTS

½ tsp coriander seeds
1 tsp cumin seeds
4 tbsp vegetable oil
2 cardamon pods
1 cm/½ inch piece ginger
   root, grated

1 red chilli, chopped
1 onion, chopped
2 garlic cloves, crushed
450 g/1 lb new potatoes,
   quartered
675 g/1½ lb spinach, chopped

150 ml/¼ pint/⅔ cup vegetable
   stock
4 tbsp natural yogurt
salt

1 Grind the coriander and cumin seeds using a pestle and mortar.

2 Heat the oil in a frying pan (skillet). Add the ground coriander and cumin seeds to the pan together with the cardamom pods and ginger and cook for about 2 minutes.

3 Add the chopped chilli, onion and garlic to the pan. Cook for a further 2 minutes, stirring frequently

4 Add the potatoes to the pan together with the vegetable stock. Cook gently for 30 minutes or until the potatoes are cooked through, stirring occasionally.

5 Add the spinach to the pan and cook for a further 5 minutes.

6 Remove the pan from the heat and stir in the yogurt. Season with salt and pepper to taste. Transfer the potatoes and spinach to a serving dish and serve.

COOK'S TIP

This spicy dish is ideal served with a meat curry or alternatively, as part of a vegetarian meal.

VARIATION

Use frozen spinach instead of fresh spinach, if you prefer. Defrost the frozen spinach and drain it thoroughly before adding it to the dish, otherwise it will turn soggy.

Potatoes & Mushrooms in Red Wine

Serves 4

INGREDIENTS

125 g/4¹⁄₂ oz/¹⁄₂ cup butter
450 g/1 lb new potatoes, halved
200 ml/7 fl oz/³⁄₄ cup red wine
85 ml/3 fl oz/¹⁄₃ cup beef stock

8 shallots, halved
125 g/4¹⁄₂ oz oyster mushrooms
1 tbsp chopped fresh sage or
    coriander (cilantro)

salt and pepper
sage leaves or coriander
    (cilantro) sprigs, to garnish

1 Melt the butter in a
heavy-based frying pan
(skillet) and add the halved
potatoes. Cook gently for 5
minutes, stirring constantly.

2 Add the red wine, beef
stock and halved
shallots. Season to taste with
salt and pepper and then
simmer for 30 minutes.

3 Stir in the mushrooms
and chopped sage or
coriander (cilantro) and
cook for 5 minutes.

4 Turn the potatoes and
mushrooms into a
warm serving dish. Garnish
with sage leaves or coriander
(cilantro) sprigs and serve
at once.

VARIATION

*If oyster mushrooms are
unavailable, other
mushrooms, such as large
open cap mushrooms, can be
used instead.*

COOK'S TIP

*Oyster mushrooms may be
grey, yellow or red in colour.
They have a soft, melting
texture and mild flavour. As
they cook, they emit a lot of
liquid and shrink to about
half their original size. They
require little cooking before
they start to turn mushy, so
add them at the end of the
cooking time.*

Gingered Potatoes

Serves 4

INGREDIENTS

675 g/1¹/₂ lb waxy potatoes,
    cubed
2 tbsp vegetable oil
5 cm/2 inch piece ginger root,
    grated

1 green chilli, chopped
1 celery stick, chopped
25 g/1 oz cashew nuts
few strands of saffron
3 tbsp boiling water

60 g/2 oz/¹/₄ cup butter
celery leaves, to garnish

1 Cook the potatoes in a saucepan of boiling water for 10 minutes. Drain thoroughly.

2 Heat the oil in a heavy-based frying pan (skillet) and add the potatoes. Cook for 3–4 minutes, stirring constantly.

3 Add the grated ginger, chilli, celery and cashew nuts and cook for 1 minute.

4 Meanwhile, place the saffron strands in a small bowl. Add the boiling water and leave to soak.

5 Add the butter to the pan and stir in the saffron mixture. Cook gently for 10 minutes or until the potatoes are tender.

6 Garnish the gingered potatoes with the celery leaves and serve at once.

COOK'S TIP

Use a non-stick, heavy-based frying pan (skillet) as the potato mixture is fairly dry and may stick to an ordinary pan.

VARIATION

If you prefer a less spicy dish, deseed the chopped green chilli or omit the chilli altogether.

Thai Potato Stir-Fry

Serves 4

INGREDIENTS

4 waxy potatoes, diced
2 tbsp vegetable oil
1 yellow (bell) pepper, diced
1 red (bell) pepper, diced
1 carrot, cut into matchstick
    strips

1 courgette (zucchini), cut into
    matchstick strips
2 garlic cloves, crushed
1 red chilli, sliced
1 bunch spring onions (scallions),
    halved lengthways

8 tbsp coconut milk
1 tsp chopped lemon grass
2 tsp lime juice
finely grated rind of 1 lime
1 tbsp chopped fresh coriander
    (cilantro)

1 Cook the diced potatoes in a saucepan of boiling water for 5 minutes. Drain thoroughly.

2 Heat the oil in a wok or large frying pan (skillet) and add the potatoes, diced (bell) peppers, carrot, courgette (zucchini), garlic and chilli. Stir-fry the vegetables for 2–3 minutes.

3 Stir in the spring onions, (scallions), coconut milk, chopped lemon grass and lime juice and stir-fry the mixture for a further 5 minutes.

4 Add the lime rind and coriander (cilantro) and stir-fry for 1 minute. Serve hot.

COOK'S TIP

Check that the potatoes are not overcooked in step 1, otherwise the potato pieces will disintegrate when they are stir-fried in the wok.

VARIATION

Almost any combination of vegetables is suitable for this dish; the yellow and red (bell) peppers, for example, can be replaced with crisp green beans or mangetout (snow peas).

Cheese & Potato Slices

Serves 4

INGREDIENTS

3 large waxy potatoes, unpeeled and thickly sliced	8 tbsp grated Parmesan cheese	oil, for deep frying
16 tbsp fresh white breadcrumbs	1½ tsp chilli powder	chilli powder, for dusting (optional)
	2 eggs, beaten	

1 Cook the sliced potatoes in a saucepan of boiling water for 10–15 minutes or until the potatoes are just tender. Drain thoroughly.

2 Mix the breadcrumbs, cheese and chilli powder together in a bowl then transfer to a shallow dish. Pour the beaten eggs into a separate shallow dish.

3 Dip the potato slices in egg and then roll them in the breadcrumbs to coat completely.

4 Heat the oil in a large saucepan or deep fat fryer to 180°C–190°C/350°F-375°F, or until a cube of bread browns in 30 seconds. Cook the cheese and potato slices, in several batches, for 4–5 minutes or until a golden brown colour.

5 Remove the cheese and potato slices with a perforated spoon and leave to drain thoroughly on paper towels. Keep the cheese and potato slices warm while you cook the remaining batches.

6 Transfer the cheese and potato slices to warm serving plates. Dust with chilli powder, if using, and serve immediately.

VARIATION

For a healthy alternative, use fresh wholemeal (whole wheat) breadcrumbs instead of the white ones used here, if you prefer.

COOK'S TIP

The cheese and potato slices may be coated in the breadcrumb mixture in advance and then stored in the refrigerator until ready to use.

Grilled Potatoes with Lime Mayonnaise

Serves 4

INGREDIENTS

450 g/1 lb potatoes, unpeeled
   and scrubbed
40 g/1¹⁄₂ oz/3 tbsp butter, melted
2 tbsp chopped fresh thyme
paprika, for dusting

LIME MAYONNAISE:
150 ml/¹⁄₄ pint/²⁄₃ cup
   mayonnaise
2 tsp lime juice
finely grated rind of 1 lime

1 garlic clove, crushed
pinch of paprika
salt and pepper

1 Cut the potatoes into 1 cm/¹⁄₂ inch thick slices.

2 Cook the potatoes in a saucepan of boiling water for 5–7 minutes – they should still be quite firm. Remove the potatoes with a perforated spoon and drain thoroughly.

3 Line a grill (broiler) pan with kitchen foil. Place the potato slices on top of the foil.

4 Brush the potatoes with the melted butter and sprinkle the chopped thyme on top. Season to taste with salt and pepper.

5 Cook the potatoes under a preheated medium heat for 10 minutes, turning once.

6 Meanwhile, make the lime mayonnaise. Combine the mayonnaise, lime juice, lime rind, garlic, paprika and salt and pepper to taste in a bowl.

7 Dust the hot potato slices with a little paprika and serve with the lime mayonnaise.

COOK'S TIP

For an impressive side dish, thread the potato slices on to skewers and cook over medium hot barbecue coals.

VARIATION

The lime mayonnaise may be spooned over the grilled (broiled) potatoes to coat them just before serving, if you prefer.

Trio of Potato Purées

Serves 4

INGREDIENTS

300 g/10½ oz floury (mealy) potatoes, chopped	1 tbsp milk	½ tsp ground cinnamon
125 g/4½ oz swede, chopped	15 g/½ oz/1 tbsp butter	1 tbsp orange juice
1 carrot, chopped	25 g/1 oz/¼ cup plain (all purpose) flour	¼ tsp grated nutmeg
450 g/1 lb spinach	1 egg	salt and pepper
		carrot matchsticks, to garnish

1 Lightly grease four 150 ml/¼ pint/⅔ cup ramekins or mini pudding basins.

2 Cook the potatoes in a saucepan of boiling water for 10 minutes. Meanwhile, in separate pans cook the swede and carrot in boiling water for 10 minutes. Blanch the spinach in a little boiling water for 5 minutes. Drain all of the vegetables.

3 Add the milk and butter to the potatoes and mash until smooth. Stir in the flour and egg.

4 Divide the potato mixture into 3 equal portions and place in 3 separate bowls. Spoon the swede into one bowl and mix well. Spoon the carrot into the second bowl and mix well. Spoon the spinach into the third bowl and mix well.

5 Add the cinnamon to the swede and potato mixture and season with salt and pepper to taste. Stir the orange juice into the carrot and potato mixture. Stir the nutmeg into the spinach and potato mixture.

6 Spoon a layer of the swede and potato mixture into each of the ramekins or basins and smooth over the top. Cover each with a layer of spinach and potato mixture, then top with the carrot and potato mixture. Cover the ramekins with foil and place in a roasting tin (pan). Half fill the tin (pan) with boiling water and cook in a preheated oven, 180°C/350°F/Gas Mark 4, for 40 minutes or until set.

7 Turn out on to serving plates, garnish with the carrot matchsticks and serve at once.

Spicy Potato Fries

Serves 4

INGREDIENTS

4 large waxy potatoes	50 g/1³/₄ oz/4 tbsp butter, melted	1 tsp garam masala
2 sweet potatoes	¹/₂ tsp chilli powder	salt

1 Cut the potatoes and sweet potatoes into slices about 1 cm/¹/₂ inch thick, then cut them into chip shapes.

2 Place the potatoes in a large bowl of cold salted water. Leave to soak for 20 minutes.

3 Remove the potato slices with a perforated spoon and drain thoroughly. Pat with paper towels until completely dry.

4 Pour the melted butter on to a baking (cookie) sheet. Transfer the potato slices to the baking (cookie)

sheet. Sprinkle with the chilli powder and garam masala, turning the potato slices to coat them with the mixture.

5 Cook the chips in a preheated oven, 200°C/ 400°F/Gas Mark 6, for 40 minutes, turning frequently until browned and cooked through.

6 Drain the chips on paper towels to remove the excess oil and serve at once.

COOK'S TIP

Rinsing the potatoes in cold water before cooking removes the starch, thus preventing them from sticking together. Soaking the potatoes in a bowl of cold salted water actually makes the cooked chips crisper.

VARIATION

For added flavour, sprinkle the chips with fennel seeds or cumin seeds, before serving.

Italian Potato Wedges

Serves 4

INGREDIENTS

2 large waxy potatoes, unpeeled	2 tbsp tomato purée (paste)	1 tbsp chopped fresh basil
4 large ripe tomatoes, peeled and seeded	1 small yellow (bell) pepper, cut into strips	50 g/1³/4 oz cheese, grated
150 ml/¹/4 pint/²/3 cup vegetable stock	125 g/4¹/2 oz button mushrooms, quartered	salt and pepper

1 Cut each of the potatoes into 8 equal wedges. Parboil the potatoes in a pan of boiling water for 15 minutes. Drain well and place in a shallow ovenproof dish.

2 Chop the tomatoes and add to the dish. Mix together the vegetable stock and tomato purée (paste), then pour the mixture over the potatoes and tomatoes.

3 Add the yellow (bell) pepper strips, quartered mushrooms and chopped basil. Season well with salt and pepper.

4 Sprinkle the grated cheese over the top and cook in a preheated oven, 190°C/375°F/Gas Mark 5, for 15–20 minutes until the topping is golden brown. Serve at once.

COOK'S TIP

For the topping, use any cheese that melts well, such as Mozzarella, the traditional pizza cheese. Alternatively, you could use either Gruyère or Emmental cheese, if you prefer.

VARIATION

These potato wedges can also be served as a light supper dish, accompanied by chunks of crusty, fresh brown or white bread.

Saffron-Flavoured Potatoes with Mustard

Serves 4

INGREDIENTS

1 tsp saffron strands	1 red onion, cut into 8 wedges	5 tbsp vegetable stock
6 tbsp boiling water	2 garlic cloves, crushed	5 tbsp dry white wine
675 g/1¹/₂ lb waxy potatoes, unpeeled and cut into wedges	1 tbsp white wine vinegar	2 tsp chopped fresh rosemary
	2 tbsp olive oil	salt and pepper
	1 tbsp wholegrain mustard	

1 Place the saffron strands in a small bowl and pour over the boiling water. Leave to soak for about 10 minutes.

2 Place the potatoes in a roasting tin (pan) together with the red onion wedges and crushed garlic.

3 Add the vinegar, oil, mustard, vegetable stock, white wine, rosemary and saffron water to the potatoes and onion in the tin (pan). Season to taste with salt and pepper.

4 Cover the roasting tin (pan) with kitchen foil and bake in a preheated oven, 200°C/400°F/Gas Mark 6, for 30 minutes.

5 Remove the foil and cook the potatoes for a further 10 minutes until crisp, browned and cooked through. Serve hot.

VARIATION

If preferred, use only wine to flavour the potatoes rather than a mixture of wine and stock.

COOK'S TIP

Turmeric may be used instead of saffron to provide the yellow colour in this recipe. However, it is worth using saffron, if possible, for the lovely nutty flavour it gives a dish.

Chilli Roast Potatoes

Serves 4

INGREDIENTS

450 g/1 lb small new potatoes,
   scrubbed
150 ml/¹/₄ pint/²/₃ cup vegetable
   oil

1 tsp chilli powder
¹/₂ tsp caraway seeds

1 tsp salt
1 tbsp chopped fresh basil

1 Cook the potatoes in a saucepan of boiling water for 10 minutes. Drain thoroughly.

2 Pour a little of the oil into a shallow roasting tin (pan) to coat the bottom of the tin (pan). Heat the oil in a preheated oven, 200°C/400°F/Gas Mark 6, for 10 minutes. Add the potatoes to the tin (pan) and brush them with the hot oil.

3 In a small bowl, mix together the chilli powder, caraway seeds and salt. Sprinkle the mixture over the potatoes, turning to coat them all over.

4 Add the remaining oil to the tin (pan) and roast in the oven for about 15 minutes or until the potatoes are cooked through.

5 Using a perforated spoon, remove the potatoes from the the oil, and transfer them to a warm serving dish. Sprinkle the chopped basil over the top and serve immediately.

COOK'S TIP

These spicy potatoes are ideal for serving with plain meat dishes, such as roasted or grilled lamb, pork or chicken.

VARIATION

Use any other spice of your choice, such as curry powder or paprika, for a variation in flavour.

Parmesan Potatoes

Serves 4

INGREDIENTS

6 potatoes
50 g/1¾ oz Parmesan cheese,
    grated

pinch of grated nutmeg
4 smoked bacon slices, cut into
    strips

1 tbsp chopped fresh parsley
oil, for roasting
salt

1 Cut the potatoes in half lengthways and cook them in a saucepan of boiling salted water for 10 minutes. Drain thoroughly.

2 Mix the grated Parmesan cheese, nutmeg and parsley together in a shallow bowl.

3 Roll the potato pieces in the cheese mixture to coat them completely. Shake off any excess.

4 Pour a little oil into a roasting tin (pan) and heat it in a preheated oven, 200°C/400°F/Gas Mark 6,

for 10 minutes. Remove from the oven and place the potatoes into the tin (pan). Return the tin (pan) to the oven and cook for 30 minutes, turning once.

5 Remove from the oven and sprinkle the bacon on top of the potatoes. Return to the oven for 15 minutes or until the potatoes and bacon are cooked. Drain off any excess fat and serve.

COOK'S TIP

Parmesan cheese has been used for its distinctive flavour, but any finely grated hard cheese would be suitable for this dish.

VARIATION

If you prefer, use slices of salami or Parma ham instead of the bacon, adding it to the dish 5 minutes before the end of the cooking time.

Potatoes Dauphinois

Serves 4

INGREDIENTS

15 g/¹/₂ oz/1 tbsp butter
675 g/1¹/₂ lb waxy potatoes,
    sliced

2 garlic cloves, crushed
1 red onion, sliced
75 g/3 oz Gruyère cheese, grated

300 ml/¹/₂ pint/1¹/₄ cups double
    (heavy) cream
salt and pepper

1 Lightly grease a 1 litre/1³/₄ pint/4 cup shallow ovenproof dish with a little butter.

2 Arrange a single layer of potato slices in the base of the prepared dish.

3 Top the potato slices with a little of the garlic, sliced red onion and grated Gruyère cheese. Season to taste with a little salt and pepper.

4 Repeat the layers in exactly the same order, finishing with a layer of potatoes topped with cheese.

5 Pour the cream over the top of the potatoes and cook in a preheated oven, 180°C/350°F/Gas Mark 4, for 1¹/₂ hours or until the potatoes are cooked through, browned and crispy. Serve at once.

COOK'S TIP

Add a layer of chopped bacon or ham to this dish, if you prefer, and serve with a crisp green salad for a light supper.

VARIATION

There are many versions of this classic potato dish, but the different recipes always contain double (heavy) cream, making it a rich and very filling side dish or accompaniment. This recipe must be cooked in a shallow dish to ensure there is plenty of crispy topping.

Pommes Anna

Serves 4

INGREDIENTS

60 g/2 oz/¼ cup butter, melted	4 tbsp chopped mixed fresh	salt and pepper
675 g/1½ lb waxy potatoes	herbs	chopped fresh herbs, to garnish

1 Brush a shallow 1 litre/1¾ pint/4 cup ovenproof dish with a little of the melted butter.

2 Slice the potatoes thinly and pat dry with paper towels.

3 Arrange a layer of potato slices in the prepared dish until the base is covered. Brush with a little butter and sprinkle with a quarter of the chopped mixed herbs. Season to taste.

4 Continue layering the potato slices, brushing each layer with melted butter and sprinkling with herbs, until all of the potato slices are used up.

5 Brush the top layer of potato slices with butter, cover the dish and cook in a preheated oven, 190°C/375°F/Gas Mark 5, for 1½ hours.

6 Turn out on to a warm ovenproof platter and return to the oven for a further 25–30 minutes until golden brown. Serve at once, garnished with herbs.

COOK'S TIP

Make sure that the potatoes are sliced very thinly until they are almost transparent, in order that they cook thoroughly.

COOK'S TIP

The butter holds the potato slices together so that the cooked dish can be turned out. Therefore, it is important that the potato slices are dried thoroughly with paper towels before layering them in the dish, otherwise the butter will not be able to stick to them.

Potatoes with Almonds & Cream

Serves 4

INGREDIENTS

2 large potatoes, unpeeled and sliced	50 g/1³/₄ oz almond flakes	1 garlic clove, crushed
1 tbsp vegetable oil	¹/₂ tsp turmeric	125 g/4¹/₂ oz rocket (arugula)
1 red onion, halved and sliced	300ml/¹/₂ pint/1¹/₄ cups double (heavy) cream	salt and pepper

1 Cook the sliced potatoes in a saucepan of boiling water for 10 minutes. Drain thoroughly.

2 Heat the vegetable oil in a frying pan (skillet) and cook the onion and garlic for 3–4 minutes, stirring frequently.

3 Add the almonds, turmeric and potato slices to the frying pan (skillet) and cook for 2–3 minutes, stirring constantly. Stir in the rocket (arugula).

4 Transfer the potato and almond mixture to a shallow ovenproof dish. Pour the double (heavy) cream over the top and season with salt and pepper.

5 Cook in a preheated oven, 190°C/375°F/ Gas Mark 5, for 20 minutes or until the potatoes are cooked through. Serve as an accompaniment to grilled (broiled) meat or fish dishes.

VARIATION

You could use other nuts, such as unsalted peanuts or cashews, instead of the almond flakes, if you prefer.

VARIATION

If rocket (arugula) is unavailable, use the same quantity of trimmed baby spinach instead.

Casseroled Potatoes

Serves 4

INGREDIENTS

675 g/1¹/₂ lb waxy potatoes, cut
    into chunks
15 g/¹/₂ oz/1 tbsp butter
2 leeks, sliced
150 ml/¹/₄ pint/²/₃ cup dry white
    wine

150 ml/¹/₄ pint/²/₃ cup vegetable
    stock
1 tbsp lemon juice
2 tbsp chopped mixed fresh
    herbs
salt and pepper

TO GARNISH:
grated lemon rind
mixed fresh herbs (optional)

1 Cook the potato chunks in a saucepan of boiling water for 5 minutes. Drain thoroughly.

2 Meanwhile, melt the butter in a frying pan (skillet) and sauté the leeks for 5 minutes or until they have softened.

3 Spoon the partly cooked potatoes and leeks into the base of an ovenproof dish.

4 In a measuring jug, mix together the wine, vegetable stock, lemon juice and chopped mixed herbs. Season to taste with salt and pepper, then pour the mixture over the potatoes.

5 Cook in a preheated oven, 190°C/375°F/ Gas Mark 5, for 35 minutes or until the potatoes are tender.

6 Garnish the potato casserole with lemon rind and fresh herbs, if using, and serve as an accompaniment to meat casseroles or roast meat.

COOK'S TIP

Cover the ovenproof dish halfway through cooking if the leeks start to brown on the top.

Cheese Crumble-Topped Mash

Serves 4

INGREDIENTS

900 g/2 lb floury (mealy)
   potatoes, diced
25 g/1 oz/2 tbsp butter
2 tbsp milk
50 g/1³/₄ oz mature (sharp)
   cheese or blue cheese, grated

CRUMBLE TOPPING:
40 g/1¹/₂ oz/3 tbsp butter
1 onion, cut into chunks
1 garlic clove, crushed
1 tbsp wholegrain mustard

175 g/ 6 oz/3 cups fresh
   wholemeal (whole wheat)
   breadcrumbs
2 tbsp chopped fresh parsley
salt and pepper

1 Cook the potatoes in a pan of boiling water for 10 minutes or until cooked through.

2 Meanwhile, make the crumble topping. Melt the butter in a frying pan (skillet). Add the onion, garlic and mustard and fry gently for 5 minutes until the onion chunks have softened, stirring constantly.

3 Put the breadcrumbs in a mixing bowl and stir in the fried onion. Season to taste with salt and pepper.

4 Drain the potatoes thoroughly and place them in a mixing bowl. Add the butter and milk, then mash until smooth. Stir in the grated cheese while the potato is still hot.

5 Spoon the mashed potato into a shallow ovenproof dish and sprinkle with the crumble topping.

6 Cook in a preheated oven, 200°C/400°F/ Gas Mark 6, for 10–15 minutes until the crumble topping is golden brown and crunchy. Serve immediately.

COOK'S TIP

For extra crunch, add freshly cooked vegetables, such as celery and (bell) peppers, to the mashed potato in step 4.

Carrot & Potato Soufflé

Serves 4

INGREDIENTS

25 g/1 oz/2 tbsp butter, melted
4 tbsp fresh wholemeal (whole
    wheat) breadcrumbs

675 g/1½ lb floury (mealy)
    potatoes, baked in their skins
2 carrots, grated
2 eggs, separated
2 tbsp orange juice

¼ tsp grated nutmeg
salt and pepper
carrot curls, to garnish

1 Brush the inside of a 900 ml/1½ pint/3¾ cup soufflé dish with butter. Sprinkle three quarters of the breadcrumbs over the base and sides of the dish.

2 Cut the baked potatoes in half and scoop the flesh into a mixing bowl.

3 Add the carrot, egg yolks, orange juice and nutmeg to the potato flesh. Season to taste with salt and pepper.

4 In a separate bowl, whisk the egg whites until they stand in soft peaks, then gently fold into the potato mixture with a metal spoon until well incorporated.

5 Gently spoon the potato and carrot mixture into the prepared soufflé dish. Sprinkle the remaining breadcrumbs over the top of the mixture.

6 Cook in a preheated oven, 200°C/400°F/ Gas Mark 6, for 40 minutes until risen and golden. Do not open the oven door during the cooking time,

otherwise the soufflé will sink. Serve at once, garnished with carrot curls.

COOK'S TIP

To bake the potatoes, prick the skins and cook in a preheated oven, 190°C/375°F/Gas Mark 5, for about 1 hour.

Steamed Potatoes en Papillotes

Serves 4

INGREDIENTS

16 small new potatoes	75 g/2³/₄ oz French (green) beans	4 rosemary sprigs
1 carrot, cut into matchstick strips	1 yellow (bell) pepper, cut into strips	salt and pepper
1 fennel bulb, sliced	16 tbsp dry white wine	rosemary sprigs, to garnish

1 Cut 4 squares of greaseproof (waxed) paper measuring about 25 cm/10 inches in size.

2 Divide the vegetables equally between the 4 paper squares, placing them in the centre.

3 Bring the edges of the paper together and scrunch them together to encase the vegetables, leaving the top open.

4 Place the parcels in a shallow roasting tin (pan) and spoon 4 tbsp of white wine into each parcel.

Add a rosemary sprig and season with salt and pepper

5 Fold the top of each parcel over to seal it. Cook in a preheated oven, 190°C/375°F/Gas Mark 5, for 30–35 minutes or until the vegetables are tender.

6 Transfer the sealed parcels to 4 individual serving plates and garnish with rosemary sprigs. The parcels should be opened at the table in order for the full aroma of the vegetables to be appreciated.

COOK'S TIP

These parcels may be cooked in a steamer, if preferred.

VARIATION

If small new potatoes are unavailable, use larger potatoes which have been halved or quartered to ensure that they cook through in the specified cooking time.

Cheese & Potato Layer Bake

Serves 4

INGREDIENTS

450 g/1 lb potatoes
1 leek, sliced
3 garlic cloves, crushed
50 g/1³/4 oz/¹/2 cup vegetarian
    Cheddar, grated

50 g/1³/4 oz/¹/2 cup
    Mozzarella, grated
25 g/1 oz/¹/4 cup Parmesan
    cheese, grated
2 tbsp chopped parsley

150 ml/¹/4 pint/²/3 cup single
    (light) cream
150 ml/¹/4 pint/²/3 cup milk
salt and pepper
freshly chopped flat-leaf parsley,
    to garnish

1 Cook the potatoes in a saucepan of boiling salted water for 10 minutes. Drain well.

2 Cut the potatoes into thin slices. Arrange a layer of potatoes in the base of an ovenproof dish. Layer with a little of the leek, garlic, cheeses and parsley. Season well.

3 Repeat the layers until all of the ingredients have been used, finishing with a layer of cheese on top.

4 Mix the cream and milk together, season with salt and pepper to taste and pour over the potato layers.

5 Cook in a preheated oven, 160°C/325°F/ Gas Mark 3, for 1–1¹/4 hours or until the cheese is golden brown and bubbling and the potatoes are cooked through.

6 Garnish with freshly chopped flat-leaf parsley and serve immediately.

COOK'S TIP

There is an Italian Parmesan called Grano Padano which is usually vegetarian. As Parmesan quickly loses its 'bite', it is best to buy it in small quantities and grate only as much as you need. Wrap the rest in foil and store in the refrigerator.

Cauliflower & Broccoli with Herb Sauce

Serves 4

INGREDIENTS

2 baby cauliflowers	SAUCE:	5 tbsp chopped coriander
225 g/8 oz broccoli	8 tbsp olive oil	(cilantro)
salt and pepper	4 tbsp butter or vegetarian	5 tbsp grated Cheddar
	margarine	
	2 tsp grated root ginger	
	juice and rind of 2 lemons	

1 Using a sharp knife, cut the cauliflowers in half and the broccoli into very large florets.

2 Cook the cauliflower and broccoli in a saucepan of boiling salted water for 10 minutes. Drain well, transfer to a shallow ovenproof dish and keep warm until required.

3 To make the sauce, put the oil and butter or vegetarian margarine in a pan and heat gently until the butter melts. Add the grated root ginger, lemon juice, lemon rind and coriander (cilantro) and simmer for 2–3 minutes, stirring occasionally.

4 Season the sauce with salt and pepper to taste, then pour over the vegetables in the dish and sprinkle the cheese on top.

5 Cook under a preheated hot grill (broiler) for 2–3 minutes or until the cheese is bubbling and golden. Leave to cool for 1–2 minutes and then serve.

VARIATION

Lime or orange could be used instead of the lemon for a fruity and refreshing sauce.

Steamed Vegetables with Vermouth

Serves 4

INGREDIENTS

1 carrot, cut into batons	4 small onions, halved	4 sprigs tarragon
1 fennel bulb, sliced	8 tbsp vermouth	salt and pepper
100 g/3¹/₂ oz courgettes (zucchini), sliced	4 tbsp lime juice	fresh tarragon sprigs, to garnish
1 red (bell) pepper, sliced	zest of 1 lime	
	pinch of paprika	

1 Place all of the vegetables in a large bowl and mix well.

2 Cut 4 large squares of baking parchment and place a quarter of the vegetables in the centre of each. Bring the sides of the paper up and pinch together to make an open parcel.

3 Mix together the vermouth, lime juice, lime zest and paprika and pour a quarter of the mixture into each parcel. Season with salt and pepper and add a tarragon sprig to each. Pinch the tops of the parcels together to seal.

4 Place the parcels in a steamer, cover and cook for 15–20 minutes or until the vegetables are tender. Garnish and serve.

COOKS TIP

Vermouth is a fortified white wine flavoured with various herbs and spices. It its available in both sweet and dry forms.

COOK'S TIP

Seal the parcels well to prevent them opening during cooking and causing the juices to evaporate.

Spicy Peas & Spinach

Serves 4

INGREDIENTS

225 g/8 oz/1 ¼ cups green split peas	1 tsp grated root ginger	300 ml/½ pint/1¼ cups vegetable stock
900 g/2 lb spinach	1 tsp ground cumin	salt and pepper
4 tbsp vegetable oil	½ tsp chilli powder	fresh coriander (cilantro) sprigs
1 onion, halved and sliced	½ tsp ground coriander (cilantro)	and lime wedges, to garnish
	2 garlic cloves, crushed	

1 Rinse the peas under cold running water. Transfer to a mixing bowl, cover with cold water and leave to soak for 2 hours. Drain well.

2 Meanwhile, cook the spinach in a large saucepan for 5 minutes until wilted. Drain well and roughly chop.

3 Heat the oil in a large saucepan and sauté the onion, spices and garlic. Sauté for 2–3 minutes, stirring well.

4 Add the peas and spinach and stir in the stock. Cover and simmer for 10–15 minutes or until the peas are cooked and the liquid has been absorbed. Season with salt and pepper to taste, garnish and serve.

VARIATION

If you do not have time to soak the green peas, canned lentils are a good substitute but remember to drain and rinse them first.

COOK'S TIP

Once the peas have been added, stir occasionally to prevent them from sticking to the pan.

Beans in Lemon & Herb Sauce

Serves 4

INGREDIENTS

900 g/2 lb mixed green beans,
such as broad (fava) beans,
French (green) beans,
runner beans
65 g/2 ¹/₂ oz/¹/₂ cup butter or

vegetarian margarine
4 tsp plain (all-purpose) flour
300 ml/¹/₂ pint/1 ¹/₄ cups
vegetable stock
85 ml/3 fl oz dry white wine

6 tbsp single (light) cream
3 tbsp chopped mixed herbs
2 tbsp lemon juice
rind of 1 lemon
salt and pepper

1 Cook the beans in a saucepan of boiling salted water for 10 minutes or until tender. Drain and place in a warm serving dish.

2 Meanwhile, melt the butter in a saucepan. Add the flour and cook for 1 minute. Remove the pan from the heat and gradually stir in the stock and wine. Return the pan to the heat and bring to the boil.

3 Remove the pan from the heat once again and stir in the single (light) cream, mixed herbs, lemon juice and zest. Season with salt and pepper to taste. Pour the sauce over the beans, mixing well. Serve immediately.

COOK'S TIP

Use a wide variety of herbs for flavour, such as rosemary, thyme, tarragon and sage.

VARIATION

Use lime rind and juice instead of lemon for an alternative citrus flavour. Replace the single (light) cream with natural (unsweetened) yogurt for a healthier version of this dish.

Curried Cauliflower & Spinach

Serves 4

INGREDIENTS

1 medium cauliflower
6 tbsp vegetable oil
1 tsp mustard seeds
1 tsp ground cumin
1 tsp garam masala
1 tsp turmeric
2 garlic cloves, crushed

1 onion, halved and sliced
1 green chilli, sliced
450 g/1 lb spinach
85 ml/3 fl oz/6 tbsp
    vegetable stock
1 tbsp chopped coriander
    (cilantro)

salt and pepper
coriander (cilantro) sprigs,
    to garnish

1 Break the cauliflower into small florets.

2 Heat the oil in a deep flameproof casserole dish. Add the mustard seeds and cook until they begin to pop.

3 Stir in the remaining spices, the garlic, onion and chilli and cook for 2–3 minutes, stirring.

4 Add the cauliflower, spinach, vegetable stock, coriander (cilantro) and seasoning and cook over a gentle heat for 15 minutes or until the cauliflower is tender. Uncover the dish and boil for 1 minute to thicken the juices. Garnish and serve.

COOK'S TIP

Mustard seeds are used throughout India and are particularly popular in southern vegetarian cooking. They are fried in oil first to bring out their flavour before the other ingredients are added.

Aubergine (Eggplant) & Courgette (Zucchini) Galette

Serves 4

INGREDIENTS

2 large aubergines (eggplants), sliced	2 tbsp tomato purée (paste)	olive oil, for frying
4 courgettes (zucchini)	2 garlic cloves, crushed	225 g/8 oz Mozzarella cheese, sliced
2 x 400 g/14 oz cans chopped tomatoes, drained	50 ml½ fl oz/4 tbsp olive oil	salt and pepper
	1 tsp caster (superfine) sugar	fresh basil leaves, to garnish
	2 tbsp chopped basil	

1 Put the aubergine (eggplant) slices in a colander and sprinkle with salt. Leave to stand for 30 minutes, then rinse well under cold water and drain. Thinly slice the courgettes (zucchini).

2 Meanwhile, put the tomatoes, tomato purée (paste), garlic, olive oil, sugar and chopped basil into a pan and simmer for 20 minutes or until reduced by half. Season well.

3 Heat 2 tablespoons of olive oil in a large frying pan (skillet) and cook the aubergine (eggplant) slices for 2–3 minutes until just beginning to brown. Remove from the pan.

4 Add a further 2 tablespoons of oil to the pan and fry the courgette (zucchini) slices until browned.

5 Lay half of the aubergine (eggplant) slices in the base of an ovenproof dish. Top with half of the tomato sauce and the courgettes (zucchini) and then half of the Mozzarella.

6 Repeat the layers and bake in a preheated oven, 180°C/350°F/Gas Mark 4, for 45–50 minutes or until the vegetables are tender. Garnish with basil leaves and serve.

Baked Celery with Cream & Pecans

Serves 4

INGREDIENTS

1 head of celery
½ tsp ground cumin
½ tsp ground coriander (cilantro)
1 garlic clove, crushed
1 red onion, thinly sliced

50 g/1¾ oz/½ cup pecan
   nut halves
150 ml/¼ pint/⅔ cup
   vegetable stock
150 ml/¼ pint/⅔ cup single
   (light) cream

50 g/1¾ oz fresh wholemeal
   (whole wheat) breadcrumbs
25 g/1 oz/¼ cup Parmesan
   cheese, grated
salt and pepper
celery leaves, to garnish

1 Trim the celery and cut into matchsticks. Place the celery in an ovenproof dish with the ground cumin, coriander (cilantro), garlic, onion and pecan nuts.

2 Mix the stock and cream together and pour over the vegetables. Season with salt and pepper to taste.

3 Mix the breadcrumbs and cheese together and sprinkle over the top to cover the vegetables.

4 Cook in a preheated oven, 200°C/400°F/Gas Mark 6, for 40 minutes or until the vegetables are tender and the top crispy. Garnish with celery leaves and serve at once.

COOK'S TIP

Once grated, Parmesan cheese quickly loses its 'bite' so it is best to grate only the amount you need for the recipe. Wrap the rest tightly in foil and it will keep for several months in the refrigerator.

VARIATION

You could use carrots or courgettes (zucchini) instead of the celery, if you prefer.

Pepperonata

Serves 4

INGREDIENTS

4 tbsp olive oil

1 onion, halved and finely sliced

2 red (bell) peppers, cut
into strips

2 green (bell) peppers, cut
into strips

2 yellow (bell) peppers, cut
into strips

2 garlic cloves, crushed

2 x 400 g/14 oz cans chopped
tomatoes, drained

2 tbsp chopped coriander
(cilantro)

2 tbsp chopped pitted
black olives

salt and pepper

1 Heat the oil in a large frying pan (skillet). Add the onion and sauté for 5 minutes, stirring until just beginning to colour.

2 Add the (bell) peppers and garlic to the pan and cook for a further 3–4 minutes.

3 Stir in the tomatoes and coriander (cilantro) and season with salt and pepper. Cover the pan and cook the vegetables gently for about 30 minutes or until the mixture is dry.

4 Stir in the pitted black olives and serve the pepperonata immediately.

VARIATION

If you don't like the distinctive flavour of fresh coriander (cilantro), you can substitute it with 2 tbsp chopped fresh flat-leaf parsley. Use green olives instead of black ones, if you prefer.

COOK'S TIP

Stir the vegetables occasionally during the 30 minutes cooking time to prevent them sticking to the bottom of the pan. If the liquid has not evaporated by the end of the cooking time, remove the lid and boil rapidly until the dish is dry.

Souffléd Cheesy Potato Fries

Serves 4

INGREDIENTS

900 g/2 lb potatoes, cut into chunks	cheese, grated	chopped flat-leaf parsley and grated vegetarian cheese, to garnish
150 ml/¼ pint/⅔ cup double (heavy) cream	pinch of cayenne pepper	
75 g/2¾ oz/¾ cup Gruyère	2 egg whites	
	oil, for deep-frying	
	salt and pepper	

1 Cook the potatoes in a saucepan of boiling salted water for 10 minutes. Drain well and pat dry with absorbent paper towels. Set aside until required.

2 Mix the double (heavy) cream and Gruyère cheese in a large bowl. Stir in the cayenne pepper and season with salt and pepper to taste.

3 Whisk the egg whites until stiff peaks form. Fold into the cheese mixture until fully incorporated.

4 Add the cooked potatoes, turning to coat thoroughly in the mixture.

5 Heat the oil for deep-frying to 180°C/350°F or until a cube of bread browns in 30 seconds. Remove the potatoes from the cheese mixture with a slotted spoon and cook in the oil, in batches, for 3–4 minutes or until golden.

6 Transfer the potatoes to a serving dish and garnish with parsley and grated cheese. Serve.

VARIATION

Add other flavourings, such as grated nutmeg or curry powder, to the cream and cheese.

Bulgur Pilau

Serves 4

INGREDIENTS

75 g/2³/₄ oz/6 tbsp butter or
    vegetarian margarine
1 red onion, halved and sliced
2 garlic cloves, crushed
350 g/12 oz/2 cups bulgur wheat
175 g/6 oz tomatoes, seeded
    and chopped
50 g/1³/₄ oz baby corn cobs,

halved lengthwise
75 g/2³/₄ oz small
    broccoli florets
850 ml/1¹/₂ pints/3³/₄ cups
    vegetable stock
2 tbsp clear honey
50 g/1³/₄ oz/¹/₃ cup sultanas
    (golden raisins)

50 g/1³/₄ oz/¹/₃ cup pine
    kernels (nuts)
¹/₂ tsp ground cinnamon
¹/₂ tsp ground cumin
salt and pepper
sliced spring onions (scallions),
    to garnish

1 Melt the butter or margarine in a large flameproof casserole dish.

2 Add the onion and garlic and sauté for 2–3 minutes, stirring occasionally.

3 Add the bulgur wheat, tomatoes, corn cobs, broccoli and stock and bring to the boil. Reduce the heat, cover and cook for 15–20 minutes, stirring occasionally

4 Stir in the honey, sultanas (golden raisins), pine kernels (nuts), ground cinnamon, cumin and salt and pepper to taste, mixing well. Remove the casserole from the heat, cover and leave for 10 minutes.

5 Spoon the bulgur pilau into a warm serving dish.

6 Garnish the bulgur pilau with sliced spring onions (scallions) and serve immediately.

COOK'S TIP

The dish is left to stand for 10 minutes in order for the bulgur to finish cooking and the flavours to mingle.

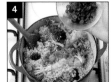

Carrot, Orange & Poppy Seed Bake

Serves 4

INGREDIENTS

675 g/1½ lb carrots, cut
   into thin strips
1 leek, sliced
300 ml/½ pint/1¼ cups fresh
   orange juice

2 tbsp clear honey
1 garlic clove, crushed
1 tsp mixed spice
2 tsp chopped thyme
1 tbsp poppy seeds

salt and pepper
fresh thyme sprigs and orange
   rind, to garnish

1 Cook the carrots and leek in a saucepan of boiling salted water for 5–6 minutes. Drain well and transfer to a shallow baking dish until required.

2 Mix together the orange juice, honey, garlic, mixed spice and thyme and pour the mixture over the vegetables. Add salt and pepper to taste.

3 Cover the baking dish and cook in a preheated oven, 180°C/ 350°F/ Gas Mark 4, for 30 minutes or until the vegetables are tender.

4 Remove the lid and sprinkle with poppy seeds. Garnish with fresh thyme sprigs and orange rind and serve.

COOK'S TIP

Lemon or lime juice could be used instead of the orange juice if you prefer. Garnish with lemon or lime rind.

VARIATION

If you prefer, use 2 tsp cumin instead of the mixed spice and omit the thyme, as cumin works particularly well with carrots.

Greek Green Beans

Serves 4

INGREDIENTS

400 g/14 oz can haricot (navy)
    beans, drained
1 tbsp olive oil
3 garlic cloves, crushed
425 ml/³⁄₄ pint/2 cups

vegetable stock
1 bay leaf
2 sprigs oregano
1 tbsp tomato purée (paste)
juice of 1 lemon

1 small red onion, chopped
25 g/1 oz /1¹⁄₄ cup pitted black
    olives, halved
salt and pepper

1 Put the haricot (navy) beans in a flameproof casserole dish.

2 Add the olive oil and crushed garlic and cook over a gentle heat, stirring occasionally, for 4–5 minutes.

3 Add the stock, bay leaf, oregano, tomato purée (paste), lemon juice and red onion, cover and simmer for about 1 hour or until the sauce has thickened.

4 Stir in the olives, season with salt and pepper to taste and serve.

COOK'S TIP

This dish may be made in advance and served cold with crusty bread, if preferred.

VARIATION

You can substitute other canned beans for the haricot (navy) beans – try cannellini or black-eyed beans (peas), or chick peas (garbanzo beans) instead. Remember to drain and rinse them thoroughly before use as canned beans often have sugar or salt added.

Sweet & Sour Aubergine (Eggplant)

Serves 4

INGREDIENTS

2 large aubergines (eggplant)	seeded and chopped	2 tbsp red wine vinegar
6 tbsp olive oil	3 tbsp chopped mint	1 tsp chilli flakes
4 garlic cloves, crushed	150 ml/ ¼ pint/²/₃ cup	salt and pepper
1 onion, cut into eight	vegetable stock	fresh mint sprigs, to garnish
4 large tomatoes,	4 tsp brown sugar	

1 Using a sharp knife, cut the aubergines (eggplant) into cubes. Put them in a colander, sprinkle with salt and leave to stand for 30 minutes. Rinse thoroughly under cold running water and drain well. This process removes all the bitter juices from the aubergines (eggplant). Pat dry with absorbent paper towels.

2 Heat the oil in a large frying pan (skillet) and sauté the aubergine (eggplant), stirring constantly for 1–2 minutes.

3 Stir in the garlic and onion and cook for a further 2–3 minutes.

4 Stir in the tomatoes, mint and stock, cover and cook for 15–20 minutes or until the vegetables are tender.

5 Stir in the brown sugar, red wine vinegar and chilli flakes, season with salt and pepper to taste and cook for 2–3 minutes. Garnish the aubergines with fresh mint sprigs and serve.

COOK'S TIP

Mint is a popular herb in Middle Eastern cooking. It is a useful herb to grow yourself as it can be added to a variety of dishes, particularly salads and vegetable dishes. It can be grown easily in a garden or window box.

Mini Vegetable Puff Pastry Cases

Serves 4

INGREDIENTS

450 g/1 lb puff pastry	spears	1 tsp lime juice
1 egg, beaten	2 tbsp butter or vegetarian	1 tsp chopped thyme
	margarine	pinch of dried mustard
FILLING:	1 leek, sliced	salt and pepper
225 g/8 oz sweet potato, cubed	2 small open-cap mushrooms,	
100 g/3½ oz baby asparagus	sliced	

1 Cut the pastry into 4 equal pieces. Roll each piece out on a lightly floured surface to form a 12.5 cm/5 inch square. Place on a dampened baking tray (cookie sheet) and score a smaller 7.5 cm/2.5 inch square inside.

2 Brush with beaten egg and cook in a preheated oven, 200°C/400°F/Gas Mark 6, for 20 minutes or until risen and golden brown.

3 Remove the pastry squares from the oven, then carefully cut out the central square of pastry, lift out and reserve.

4 To make the filling, cook the sweet potato in a saucepan of boiling water for 15 minutes, then drain well. Blanch the asparagus in a saucepan of boiling water for 10 minutes or until tender. Drain and reserve.

5 Melt the butter or margarine in a saucepan and sauté the leek and mushrooms for 2–3 minutes. Add the lime juice, thyme and mustard, season well and stir in the sweet potatoes and asparagus. Spoon into the pastry cases, top with the reserved pastry squares and serve immediately.

COOK'S TIP

Use a colourful selection of any vegetables you have at hand for this recipe.

Main Meals

This chapter contains a wide selection of delicious main-meal dishes which are more substantial than the snacks and light meal section and generally require more preparation and cooking. The potato is the main ingredient in many of the recipes in this chapter, but it also includes ideas for cooking with vegetables and for vegetarian dishes – so that there is sure to be something for everyone.

Some of the recipes included here contain meat, but many are purely vegetarian. There are recipes from all over the world as well as many traditional hearty bakes and roasts. They all make exciting eating at any time of the year and on any occasion. There are ideas for mid-week meals and for entertaining. There is no reason why you cannot experiment by substituting ingredients or adding your own imaginative touches to these meals.

Potato, Beef & Peanut Pot

Serves 4

INGREDIENTS

1 tbsp vegetable oil	2 large waxy potatoes, cubed	50 g/1³/₄ oz sugar snap peas
60 g/2 oz/¹/₄ cup butter	¹/₂ tsp paprika	1 red (bell) pepper, cut into strips
450 g/1 lb lean beef steak, cut	4 tbsp crunchy peanut butter	parsley sprigs, to garnish
into thin strips	600 ml/1 pint/2¹/₂ cups beef stock	(optional)
1 onion, halved and sliced	25 g/1 oz unsalted peanuts	
2 garlic cloves, crushed	2 tsp light soy sauce	

1 Heat the oil and butter in a flameproof casserole dish.

2 Add the beef strips and fry them gently for 3–4 minutes, stirring and turning the meat until it is sealed on all sides.

3 Add the onion and garlic and cook for a further 2 minutes, stirring constantly.

4 Add the potato cubes and cook for 3–4 minutes or until they begin to brown slightly.

5 Stir in the paprika and peanut butter, then gradually blend in the beef stock. Bring the mixture to the boil, stirring frequently.

6 Finally, add the peanuts, soy sauce, sugar snap peas and red (bell) pepper.

7 Cover and cook over a low heat for 45 minutes or until the beef is cooked through.

8 Garnish the dish with parsley sprigs, if wished, and serve.

COOK'S TIP

Serve this dish with plain boiled rice or noodles, if you wish.

VARIATION

Add a chopped green chilli to the sauce for extra spice, if you prefer.

Potato Ravioli

Serves 4

INGREDIENTS

FILLING:
1 tbsp vegetable oil
125 g/4¹/₂ oz ground beef
1 shallot, diced
1 garlic clove, crushed
1 tbsp plain (all-purpose) flour
1 tbsp tomato purée (paste)
150 ml/¹/₄ pint/²/₃ cup beef stock

1 celery stick, chopped
2 tomatoes, peeled and diced
2 tsp chopped fresh basil
salt and pepper

RAVIOLI:
450 g/1 lb floury (mealy)
    potatoes, diced

3 small egg yolks
3 tbsp olive oil
175 g/6 oz/1¹/₂ cups plain
    (all-purpose) flour
60 g/2 oz/¹/₄ cup butter, for frying
shredded basil leaves, to garnish

1 To make the filling, heat the oil in a pan and fry the beef for 3–4 minutes, breaking it up with a spoon. Add the shallot and garlic and cook for 2–3 minutes until the shallot has softened.

2 Stir in the flour and tomato purée (paste) and cook for 1 minute. Stir in the beef stock, celery, tomatoes and chopped fresh basil. Season to taste with salt and pepper.

3 Cook the mixture over a low heat for 20 minutes. Remove from the heat and leave to cool.

4 To make the ravioli, cook the potatoes in a pan of boiling water for 10 minutes until cooked.

5 Mash the potatoes and place them in a mixing bowl. Blend in the egg yolks and oil. Season with salt and pepper, then stir in the flour and mix to form a dough.

6 On a lightly floured surface, divide the dough into 24 pieces and shape into flat rounds. Spoon the filling on to one half of each round and fold the dough over to encase the filling, pressing down to seal the edges.

7 Melt the butter in a frying pan (skillet) and cook the ravioli for 6–8 minutes, turning once, until golden. Serve hot, garnished with shredded basil leaves.

Veal Italienne

Serves 4

INGREDIENTS

60 g/2 oz/¼ cup butter
1 tbsp olive oil
675 g/1½ lb potatoes, cubed
4 veal escalopes, weighing about
    175 g/6 oz each
1 onion, cut into 8 wedges
2 garlic cloves, crushed

2 tbsp plain (all-purpose) flour
2 tbsp tomato purée (paste)
150 ml/¼ pint/⅔ cup red wine
300 ml/½ pint/1¼ cups chicken
    stock
8 ripe tomatoes, peeled, seeded
    and diced

25 g/1 oz stoned (pitted) black
    olives, halved
2 tbsp chopped fresh basil
salt and pepper
fresh basil leaves, to garnish

1 Heat the butter and oil in a large frying pan (skillet). Add the potato cubes and cook for 5–7 minutes, stirring frequently, until they begin to brown.

2 Remove the potatoes from the pan (skillet) with a perforated spoon and set aside.

3 Place the veal in the frying pan (skillet) and cook for 2-3 minutes on each side until sealed. Remove from the pan and set aside.

4 Stir the onion and garlic into the pan (skillet) and cook for 2–3 minutes.

5 Add the flour and tomato purée (paste) and cook for 1 minute, stirring. Gradually blend in the red wine and chicken stock, stirring to make a smooth sauce.

6 Return the potatoes and veal to the pan (skillet). Stir in the tomatoes, olives and chopped basil and season with salt and pepper.

7 Transfer to a casserole dish and cook in a preheated oven, 180°C/350°F/Gas Mark 4, for 1 hour or until the potatoes and veal are cooked through. Garnish with basil leaves and serve.

COOK'S TIP

For a quicker cooking time and really tender meat, pound the meat with a meat mallet to flatten it slightly before cooking.

Lamb Hotpot

Serves 4

INGREDIENTS

675 g/1¹/₂ lb best end of lamb
    neck cutlets
2 lamb's kidneys
1 large onion, sliced thinly

675 g/1¹/₂ lb waxy potatoes,
    scrubbed and sliced thinly
2 tbsp chopped fresh thyme
150 ml/¹/₄ pint/²/₃ cup lamb stock

25 g/1 oz/2 tbsp butter, melted
salt and pepper
fresh thyme sprigs, to garnish

1 Remove any excess fat from the lamb. Skin and core the kidneys and cut them into slices.

2 Arrange a layer of potatoes in the base of a 1.8 litre/3 pint/3¹/₂ cup ovenproof dish.

3 Arrange the lamb neck cutlets on top of the potatoes and cover with the sliced kidneys, onion and chopped fresh thyme.

4 Pour the lamb stock over the meat and season to taste with salt and pepper.

5 Layer the remaining potato slices on top, overlapping to completely cover the meat and sliced onion.

6 Brush the potato slices with the butter, cover the dish and cook in a preheated oven, 180°C/ 350°F/ Gas Mark 4, for 1¹/₂ hours.

7 Remove the lid and cook for a further 30 minutes until golden brown on top.

8 Garnish with fresh thyme sprigs and serve hot.

COOK'S TIP

Although this is a classic recipe, extra ingredients of your choice, such as celery or carrots, can be added to the dish for variety and colour.

VARIATION

Traditionally, oysters are also included in this tasty hotpot. Add them to the layers along with the kidneys, if wished.

Potato & Lamb Kofta

Serves 4

INGREDIENTS

450 g/1 lb floury (mealy)
potatoes, diced
25 g/1 oz/2 tbsp butter
225 g/8 oz minced lamb
1 onion, chopped
2 garlic cloves, crushed

$\frac{1}{2}$ tsp ground coriander
(cilantro)
2 eggs, beaten
oil, for deep-frying
mint sprigs, to garnish

SAUCE:
150 ml/$\frac{1}{4}$ pint/$\frac{2}{3}$ cup natural
yogurt
50 g/2 oz cucumber, finely chopped
1 tbsp chopped mint
1 garlic clove, crushed

1 Cook the diced potatoes in a saucepan of boiling water for 10 minutes until cooked through. Drain, mash until smooth and transfer to a mixing bowl.

2 Melt the butter in a frying pan (skillet), add the lamb, onion, garlic and coriander (cilantro) and fry for 15 minutes, stirring.

3 Drain off the liquid from the pan, then stir the meat mixture into the mashed potatoes. Stir in the eggs and season.

4 To make the sauce, combine the yogurt, cucumber, mint and garlic in a bowl and set aside.

5 Heat the oil in a large saucepan or a deep fat fryer to 180°C–190°C/ 350°F–375°F, or until a cube of bread browns in 30 seconds. Drop spoonfuls of the potato mixture into the hot oil and cook in batches for 4–5 minutes or until golden brown.

6 Remove the kofta with a perforated spoon, drain thoroughly on

paper towels, set aside and keep warm. Garnish with fresh mint sprigs and serve with the sauce.

COOK'S TIP

These kofta can be made with any sort of minced meat, such as turkey, chicken or pork, and flavoured with appropriate fresh herbs, such as sage or coriander (cilantro).

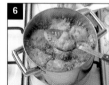

Spanish Potato Bake

Serves 4

INGREDIENTS

675 g/1¹/₂ lb waxy potatoes, diced
3 tbsp olive oil
1 onion, halved and sliced
2 garlic cloves, crushed

400 g/14 oz can plum tomatoes,
   chopped
75 g/2³/₄ oz chorizo sausage, sliced
1 green (bell) pepper, cut into strips
¹/₂ tsp paprika

25 g/1 oz stoned (pitted) black
   olives, halved
8 eggs
1 tbsp chopped fresh parsley
salt and pepper

1 Cook the diced potatoes in a saucepan of boiling water for 10 minutes or until softened. Drain and set aside.

2 Heat the olive oil in a large frying pan (skillet), add the sliced onion and garlic and fry gently for 2–3 minutes until the onion softens.

3 Add the chopped canned tomatoes and cook over a low heat for about 10 minutes until the mixture has reduced slightly.

4 Stir the potatoes into the pan with the chorizo, green (bell) pepper, paprika and olives. Cook for 5 minutes, stirring. Transfer to a shallow ovenproof dish.

5 Make 8 small hollows in the top of the mixture and break an egg into each hollow.

6 Cook in a preheated oven, 225°C/425°F/ Gas Mark 7, for 5–6 minutes or until the eggs are just cooked. Sprinkle with parsley and serve with crusty bread.

VARIATION

Add a little spice to the dish by incorporating 1 tsp chilli powder in step 4, if wished.

Potato & Pepperoni Pizza

Makes 1 large pizza

INGREDIENTS

900 g/2 lb floury (mealy) potatoes, diced	85 ml/3 fl oz/¹/₃ cup passata	2 large open cap mushrooms, sliced
15 g/¹/₂ oz/1 tbsp butter	2 tbsp tomato purée (paste)	25 g/1 oz stoned (pitted) black
2 garlic cloves, crushed	50 g/1³/₄ oz pepperoni slices	olives, quartered
2 tbsp mixed chopped fresh herbs	1 green (bell) pepper, cut into strips	125 g/4¹/₂ oz Mozzarella cheese,
1 egg, beaten	1 yellow (bell) pepper, cut into strips	sliced

1 Grease and flour a 23 cm/9 inch pizza tin (pan).

2 Cook the diced potatoes in a saucepan of boiling water for 10 minutes or until cooked through. Drain and mash until smooth. Transfer the mashed potato to a mixing bowl and stir in the butter, garlic, herbs and egg.

3 Spread the mixture into the prepared pizza pan. Cook in a preheated oven, 225°C/425°F/Gas Mark 7, for 7–10 minutes or until the pizza base begins to set.

4 Mix the passata and tomato purée (paste) together and spoon it over the pizza base, to within 1 cm/¹/₂ inch of the edge of the base.

5 Arrange the pepperoni, (bell) peppers, mushrooms and olives on top of the passata.

6 Scatter the Mozzarella cheese on top of the pizza. Cook in the oven for 20 minutes or until the base is cooked through and the cheese has melted on top. Serve hot with a mixed salad.

COOK'S TIP

This pizza base is softer in texture than a normal bread dough and is ideal served from the tin (pan). Top with any of your favourite pizza ingredients that you have to hand.

Potato & Sausage Pan-Fry

Serves 4

INGREDIENTS

675 g/1½ lb waxy potatoes, cubed	1 onion, quartered	vegetable stock
25 g/1 oz/2 tbsp butter	1 courgette (zucchini), sliced	1 tsp Worcestershire sauce
8 large herb sausages	150 ml/¼ pint/²⁄₃ cup dry white wine	2 tbsp chopped mixed fresh herbs
4 smoked bacon slices	300 ml/½ pint/1¼ cups	salt and pepper
		chopped fresh herbs, to garnish

1 Cook the cubed potatoes in a saucepan of boiling water for 10 minutes or until softened. Drain thoroughly and set aside.

2 Meanwhile, melt the butter in a large frying pan (skillet). Add the herb sausages and cook for 5 minutes, turning them frequently to ensure that they brown on all sides.

3 Add the bacon slices, onion, courgette (zucchini) and potatoes to the pan. Cook the mixture

for a further 10 minutes, stirring the mixture and turning the sausages frequently.

4 Stir in the white wine, stock, Worcestershire sauce and chopped mixed herbs. Season with salt and pepper to taste and cook the mixture over a gentle heat for 10 minutes. Season with a little more salt and pepper, if necessary.

5 Transfer the potato and sausage panfry to warm serving plates, garnish with chopped fresh herbs and

COOK'S TIP

Use different flavours of sausage to vary the dish – there are many different varieties available, such as leek and mustard.

VARIATION

For an attractive colour, use a red onion cut into quarters rather than a white onion.

Potato, Tomato & Sausage Pan-Fry

Serves 4

INGREDIENTS

2 large potatoes, sliced	150 ml/¼ pint/⅔ cup red wine	2 tbsp chopped fresh basil
1 tbsp vegetable oil	150 ml/¼ pint/⅔ cup passata	salt and pepper
8 flavoured sausages	2 large tomatoes, each cut into 8	shredded fresh basil, to garnish
1 red onion, cut into 8	175 g/6 oz broccoli florets,	
1 tbsp tomato purée (paste)	blanched	

1 Cook the sliced potatoes in a saucepan of boiling water for 7 minutes. Drain thoroughly and set aside.

2 Meanwhile, heat the oil in a large frying pan (skillet). Add the sausages and cook for 5 minutes, turning the sausages frequently to ensure that they are browned on all sides.

3 Add the onion pieces to the pan and continue to cook for a further 5 minutes, stirring the mixture frequently.

4 Stir in the tomato purée (paste), red wine and the passata and mix together well. Add the tomato wedges, broccoli florets and chopped basil to the panfry and mix carefully.

5 Add the parboiled potato slices to the pan. Cook the mixture for about 10 minutes or until the sausages are completely cooked through. Season to taste with salt and pepper.

6 Garnish the panfry with fresh shredded basil and serve hot.

COOK'S TIP

Omit the passata from this recipe and use canned plum tomatoes or chopped tomatoes for convenience.

VARIATION

Broccoli is particularly good in this dish as it adds a splash of colour, but other vegetables of your choice can be used instead, if preferred.

Potato, Chicken & Banana Cakes

Serves 4

INGREDIENTS

450 g/1 lb floury (mealy)
   potatoes, diced
225 g/8 oz minced chicken
1 large banana
2 tbsp plain (all purpose) flour
1 tsp lemon juice

1 onion, finely chopped
2 tbsp chopped fresh sage
25 g/1 oz/2 tbsp butter
2 tbsp vegetable oil
150 ml/¼ pint/⅔ cup single
   (light) cream

150 ml/¼ pint/⅔ cup chicken
   stock
salt and pepper
fresh sage leaves, to garnish

1 Cook the diced potatoes in a saucepan of boiling water for 10 minutes until cooked through. Drain and mash the potatoes until smooth. Stir in the chicken.

2 Mash the banana and add it to the potato with the flour, lemon juice, onion and half of the chopped sage. Season well and stir the mixture together.

3 Divide the mixture into 8 equal portions. With lightly floured hands,
shape each portion into a round patty.

4 Heat the butter and oil in a frying pan (skillet), add the potato cakes and cook for 12–15 minutes or until cooked through, turning once. Remove from the pan (skillet) and keep warm.

5 Stir the cream and stock into the pan (skillet) with the remaining chopped sage. Cook over a low heat for 2–3 minutes.

6 Arrange the potato cakes on a serving plate, garnish with fresh sage leaves and serve with the cream and sage sauce.

COOK'S TIP

Do not boil the sauce once the cream has been added as it will curdle. Cook it gently over a very low heat.

Creamy Chicken & Potato Casserole

Serves 4

INGREDIENTS

2 tbsp vegetable oil
60 g/2 oz/$^1/_4$ cup butter
4 chicken portions, about 225
   g/8 oz each
2 leeks, sliced
1 garlic clove, crushed
4 tbsp plain (all-purpose) flour

900 ml/1$^1/_2$ pints/3$^3/_4$ cups
   chicken stock
300 ml/$^1/_2$ pint/1$^1/_4$ cups dry
   white wine
125 g/4$^1/_2$ oz baby carrots, halved
   lengthways
125 g/4$^1/_2$ oz baby sweetcorn

cobs (baby corn), halved
   lengthways
450 g/1 lb small new potatoes
1 bouquet garni
150 ml/$^1/_4$ pint/$^2/_3$ cup double
   (heavy) cream
salt and pepper

1 Heat the oil in a large frying pan (skillet). Cook the chicken for 10 minutes, turning until browned all over. Transfer the chicken to a casserole dish using a perforated spoon.

2 Add the leek and garlic to the frying pan (skillet) and cook for 2–3 minutes, stirring. Stir in the flour and cook for a further 1 minute. Remove the frying pan (skillet) from the heat and stir in the stock and wine. Season well.

3 Return the pan to the heat and bring the mixture to the boil. Stir in the carrots, sweetcorn, potatoes and bouquet garni.

4 Transfer the mixture to the casserole dish. Cover and cook in a preheated oven, 180°C/350°F/Gas Mark 4, for about 1 hour.

5 Remove the casserole from the oven and stir in the cream. Return the casserole to the oven, uncovered, and cook for a further 15 minutes.

Remove the bouquet garni and discard. Taste and adjust the seasoning, if necessary. Serve the casserole with plain rice or fresh vegetables, such as broccoli.

COOK'S TIP

Use turkey fillets instead of the chicken, if preferred, and vary the vegetables according to those you have to hand.

Potato-Topped Cod

Serves 4

INGREDIENTS

60 g/2 oz/¼ cup butter
4 waxy potatoes, sliced
1 large onion, finely chopped
1 tsp wholegrain mustard
1 tsp garam masala

pinch of chilli powder
1 tbsp chopped fresh dill
75 g/2¾ oz/1¼ cups fresh
    breadcrumbs
4 cod fillets, about 175 g/6 oz each

50 g/1¾ oz Gruyère cheese,
    grated
salt and pepper
fresh dill sprigs, to garnish

1 Melt half of the butter in a frying pan (skillet). Add the potatoes and fry for 5 minutes, turning until they are browned all over. Remove the potatoes from the pan with a perforated spoon.

2 Add the remaining butter to the frying pan (skillet) and stir in the onion, mustard, garam masala, chilli powder, chopped dill and breadcrumbs. Cook for 1–2 minutes, stirring and mixing well.

3 Layer half of the potatoes in the base of an ovenproof dish and place the cod fillets on top. Cover the cod fillets with the rest of the potato slices. Season to taste with salt and pepper.

4 Spoon the spicy mixture from the frying pan (skillet) over the potato and sprinkle with the grated cheese.

5 Cook in a preheated oven, 200°C/400°F/ Gas Mark 6, for 20–25 minutes or until the topping is golden and crisp and the fish is cooked through. Garnish with fresh dill sprigs and serve at once.

COOK'S TIP

This dish is ideal served with baked vegetables which can be cooked in the oven at the same time.

VARIATION

You can use any fish for this recipe: for special occasions use salmon steaks or fillets.

Potato Curry

Serves 4

INGREDIENTS

4 tbsp vegetable oil	½ tsp ground cumin	75 g/2¾ oz frozen peas
675 g/1½ lb waxy potatoes, cut into large chunks	½ tsp ground coriander (cilantro)	2 tbsp chopped fresh coriander (cilantro)
2 onions, quartered	2.5 cm/1 inch piece ginger root, grated	300 ml/½ pint/1¼ cups vegetable stock
3 garlic cloves, crushed	1 red chilli, chopped	shredded fresh coriander (cilantro), to garnish
1 tsp garam masala	225 g/8 oz cauliflower florets	
½ tsp turmeric	4 tomatoes, peeled and quartered	

1 Heat the vegetable oil in a large heavy-based saucepan or frying pan (skillet). Add the potato chunks, onion and garlic and fry gently for 2–3 minutes, stirring the mixture frequently.

2 Add the garam masala, turmeric, ground cumin, ground coriander (cilantro), grated ginger and chopped chilli to the pan, mixing the spices into the vegetables. Fry for 1 minute, stirring constantly.

3 Add the cauliflower florets, tomatoes, peas, chopped coriander (cilantro) and vegetable stock to the curry mixture.

4 Cook the potato curry over a low heat for 30–40 minutes or until the potatoes are completely cooked through.

5 Garnish the potato curry with fresh coriander (cilantro) and serve with plain boiled rice or warm Indian bread.

COOK'S TIP

Use a large heavy-based saucepan or frying pan (skillet) for this recipe to ensure that the potatoes are cooked thoroughly.

Potato & Spinach Gnocchi

Serves 4

INGREDIENTS

300 g/10¹/₂ oz floury (mealy)
potatoes, diced
175 g/6 oz spinach
125 g/4¹/₂ oz/1 cup plain
(all-purpose) flour
1 egg yolk

1 tsp olive oil
salt and pepper
spinach leaves, to garnish

SAUCE:
1 tbsp olive oil
2 shallots, chopped
1 garlic clove, crushed
300 ml/¹/₂ pint/1¹/₄ cups passata
2 tsp soft light brown sugar

1 Cook the diced potatoes in a saucepan of boiling water for 10 minutes until cooked through. Drain and mash the potatoes.

2 Meanwhile, in a separate pan, blanch the spinach in a little boiling water for 1–2 minutes. Drain well and shred the leaves.

3 Transfer the mashed potato to a lightly floured chopping board and make a well in the centre.

Add the egg yolk, olive oil, spinach and a little of the flour and quickly mix the ingredients into the potato, adding more flour as you go, until you have a firm dough. Divide the mixture into very small dumplings.

4 Cook the gnocchi in batches in a saucepan of boiling salted water for about 5 minutes or until they rise to the top of the pan.

5 Meanwhile, make the sauce. Put the oil, shallots, garlic, passata and

sugar into a saucepan and cook over a low heat for 10–15 minutes or until the sauce has thickened.

6 Drain the gnocchi using a perforated spoon and transfer to warm serving dishes. Spoon the sauce over the gnocchi and garnish with the fresh spinach leaves.

VARIATION

Add chopped fresh herbs and cheese to the gnocchi dough instead of the spinach, if you prefer.

Potato-Topped Vegetables in Wine

Serves 4

INGREDIENTS

1 carrot, diced
175 g/6 oz cauliflower florets
175 g/6 oz broccoli florets
1 fennel bulb, sliced
75 g/2³⁄₄ oz green beans, halved
25 g/1 oz/2 tbsp butter
25 g/1 oz/¹⁄₄ cup plain
  (all-purpose) flour

150 ml/¹⁄₄ pint/²⁄₃ cup vegetable
  stock
150 ml/¹⁄₄ pint/²⁄₃ cup dry white
  wine
150 ml/¹⁄₄ pint/²⁄₃ cup milk
2 tbsp chopped fresh sage
175 g/6 oz chestnut mushrooms,
  quartered

TOPPING:
4 floury (mealy) potatoes, diced
25 g/1 oz/2 tbsp butter
4 tbsp natural yogurt
4 tbsp grated Parmesan cheese
1 tsp fennel seeds
salt and pepper

1 Cook the carrot, cauliflower, broccoli, fennel and beans in a saucepan of boiling water for 10 minutes. Drain the vegetables thoroughly and set aside.

2 Melt the butter in a saucepan and stir in the flour. Cook for 1 minute, then remove from the heat. Stir in the stock, wine and milk and bring to the boil, stirring until thickened. Stir in the reserved vegetables and mushrooms.

3 Meanwhile, make the topping. Cook the diced potatoes in a separate pan of boiling water for 10–15 minutes or until cooked through. Drain the potatoes and mash with the butter, yogurt and half of the cheese. Stir in the fennel seeds.

4 Spoon the vegetable mixture into a 1 litre/1³⁄₄ pint /4 cup pie dish. Spoon or pipe the potato over the top, covering the filling completely. Sprinkle the remaining cheese on

top. Cook in a preheated oven, 190°C/375°F/Gas Mark 5, for 30–35 minutes or until the topping is golden. Serve hot.

COOK'S TIP

Any combination of vegetables may be used in this dish, and frozen mixed vegetables can be defrosted and used for convenience and speed.

Potato & Three-Cheese Soufflé

Serves 4

INGREDIENTS

25 g/1 oz/2 tbsp butter
2 tsp plain (all-purpose) flour
900 g/2 lb floury (mealy)
   potatoes

8 eggs, separated
25 g/1 oz Gruyère cheese, grated
25 g/1 oz mature (sharp) cheese,
   grated

25 g/1 oz blue cheese, crumbled
salt and pepper

1 Butter a 2.4 litre/4 pint/ 10 cup soufflé dish and dust with the flour. Set aside.

2 Cook the potatoes in a saucepan of boiling water until cooked through. Mash until very smooth and transfer to a mixing bowl to cool.

3 Whisk the egg yolks into the potato and stir in the 3 different cheeses. Season well with salt and pepper.

4 In a clean bowl, whisk the egg whites until standing in peaks, then gently fold them into the potato mixture with a metal spoon until fully incorporated.

5 Spoon the potato mixture into the prepared soufflé dish.

6 Cook in a preheated oven, 220°C/425°F/ Gas Mark 7, for 35–40 minutes until risen and set. Serve immediately.

COOK'S TIP

Insert a fine skewer into the centre of the soufflé; it should come out clean when the soufflé is fully cooked through.

VARIATION

You can add chopped cooked bacon to the soufflé for extra flavour, if wished.

Nutty Harvest Loaf

Serves 4

INGREDIENTS

450 g/1 lb floury (mealy)
potatoes, diced
25 g/1 oz/2 tbsp butter
1 onion, chopped
2 garlic cloves, crushed
125 g/4¹/₂ oz unsalted peanuts
75 g/2³/₄ oz fresh white
breadcrumbs
1 egg, beaten

2 tbsp chopped fresh coriander
(cilantro)
150 ml/¹/₄ pint/²/₃ cup vegetable
stock
75 g/2³/₄ oz closed cap
mushrooms, sliced
50 g/1³/₄ oz sun-dried tomatoes,
sliced
salt and pepper

SAUCE:
150 ml/¹/₄ pint/²/₃ cup crème
fraîche
2 tsp tomato purée (paste)
2 tsp clear honey
2 tbsp chopped fresh coriander
(cilantro)

1 Grease a 450 g/1 lb loaf tin (pan). Cook the potatoes in a saucepan of boiling water for 10 minutes until cooked through. Drain well, mash and set aside.

2 Melt half of the butter in a frying pan (skillet). Add the onion and garlic and fry gently for 2–3 minutes until soft. Finely chop the nuts or blend them in a food processor for 30 seconds with the breadcrumbs.

3 Mix the chopped nuts and breadcrumbs into the potatoes with the egg, coriander (cilantro) and vegetable stock. Stir in the onion and garlic and mix well.

4 Melt the remaining butter in the frying pan (skillet), add the sliced mushrooms and cook for 2–3 minutes.

5 Press half of the potato mixture into the base of the loaf tin (pan). Spoon the mushrooms on top and sprinkle with the sun-dried tomatoes. Spoon the remaining potato mixture on top and smooth the surface. Cover with foil and bake in a preheated oven, 190°C/350°F/ Gas Mark 5, for 1 hour or until firm to the touch.

6 Meanwhile, mix the sauce ingredients together. Cut the nutty harvest loaf into slices and serve with the sauce.

Vegetable Cake

Serves 4

INGREDIENTS

BASE:

2 tbsp vegetable oil

4 large waxy potatoes, sliced thinly

TOPPING:

1 tbsp vegetable oil

1 leek, chopped

1 courgette (zucchini), grated

1 red (bell) pepper, diced

1 green (bell) pepper, diced

1 carrot, grated

2 tsp chopped fresh parsley

225 g/8 oz full fat soft cheese

25 g/1 oz mature (sharp) cheese, grated

2 eggs, beaten

salt and pepper

shredded cooked leek, to garnish

1 Grease a 20 cm/8 inch springform cake tin (pan).

2 To make the base, heat the oil in a frying pan (skillet). Cook the potato slices in batches over a medium heat until softened and browned. Drain thoroughly on paper towels and arrange the slices in the base of the tin (pan).

3 To make the topping, heat the oil in a separate frying pan (skillet) and fry the leek over a low heat for 3–4 minutes until softened.

4 Add the courgette (zucchini), (bell) peppers, carrot and parsley to the pan and cook over a low heat for 5–7 minutes or until the vegetables have softened.

5 Meanwhile, beat the cheeses and eggs together in a bowl. Stir in the vegetables and season to taste with salt and pepper. Spoon the mixture on to the potato base.

6 Cook in a preheated oven, 190°C/375°F/ Gas Mark 5, for 20–25 minutes until the cake is set.

7 Remove the vegetable cake from the tin (pan), garnish with shredded leek and serve with a crisp salad.

COOK'S TIP

Add diced tofu (bean curd) or diced meat, such as pork or chicken, to the topping, if wished. Cook the meat with the vegetables in step 4.

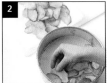

Bubble & Squeak

Serves 4

INGREDIENTS

450 g/1 lb floury (mealy)
  potatoes, diced
225 g/8 oz Savoy cabbage,
  shredded

5 tbsp vegetable oil
2 leeks, chopped
1 garlic clove, crushed

225 g/8 oz smoked tofu
  (bean curd), cubed
salt and pepper
shredded cooked leek, to garnish

1 Cook the diced potatoes in a saucepan of boiling water for 10 minutes until tender. Drain and mash the potatoes.

2 Meanwhile, in a separate saucepan blanch the cabbage in boiling water for 5 minutes. Drain and add to the potato.

3 Heat the oil in a heavy-based frying pan (skillet), add the leeks and garlic and fry gently for 2–3 minutes. Stir into the potato and cabbage mixture.

4 Add the smoked tofu (bean curd) and season well with salt and pepper. Cook over a moderate heat for 10 minutes.

5 Carefully turn the whole mixture over and continue to cook over a moderate heat for a further 5–7 minutes until crispy underneath. Serve immediately, garnished with shredded leek.

VARIATION

You can add cooked meats, such as beef or chicken, instead of the tofu (bean curd) for a more traditional recipe. Any gravy from the cooked meats can also be added, but ensure that the mixture is not too wet.

COOK'S TIP

This vegetarian recipe is a perfect main meal, as the smoked tofu (bean curd) cubes added to the basic bubble and squeak mixture make it very substantial.

Potato Hash

Serves 4

INGREDIENTS

25 g/1 oz/2 tbsp butter	3 large waxy potatoes, diced	salt and pepper
1 red onion, halved and sliced	2 tbsp plain (all purpose) flour	chopped fresh parsley, to garnish
1 carrot, diced	600 ml/1 pint/1¼ cups vegetable	
25 g/1 oz French (green) beans,	stock	
halved	225 g/8 oz tofu (bean curd), diced	

1 Melt the butter in a frying pan (skillet). Add the onion, carrot, French (green) beans and potatoes and fry gently, stirring, for 5–7 minutes or until the vegetables begin to brown.

2 Add the flour to the frying pan (skillet) and cook for 1 minute, stirring constantly. Gradually pour in the stock.

3 Reduce the heat and leave the mixture to simmer for 15 minutes or until the potatoes are tender.

4 Add the diced tofu (bean curd) to the mixture and cook for a further 5 minutes. Season to taste with salt and pepper.

5 Sprinkle the chopped parsley over the top of the potato hash to garnish, then serve hot straight from the pan (skillet).

VARIATION

Use cooked diced meat, such as beef or lamb, instead of the tofu (bean curd) for a non-vegetarian dish.

COOK'S TIP

Hash is an American term meaning to chop food into small pieces. Therefore a traditional hash dish is made from chopped fresh ingredients, such as roast beef or corned beef, (bell) peppers, onion and celery, often served with gravy.

Twice-Baked Potatoes with Pesto

Serves 4

INGREDIENTS

4 baking potatoes, about 225 g/
    8 oz each
150 ml/^{1}/$_4$ pint/^{2}/$_3$ cup double
    (heavy) cream
1 tbsp lemon juice

2 garlic cloves, crushed
85 ml/3 fl oz/^{1}/$_3$ cup
    vegetable stock
3 tbsp chopped fresh basil
2 tbsp pine kernels (nuts)

2 tbsp grated Parmesan cheese
salt and pepper

1 Scrub the potatoes and prick the skins with a fork. Rub a little salt into the skins and place on a baking (cookie) sheet.

2 Cook in a preheated oven, 190°C/375°F/ Gas Mark 5, for 1 hour or until the potatoes are cooked through and the skins crisp.

3 Remove the potatoes from the oven and cut them in half lengthways. Using a spoon, scoop the potato flesh into a mixing bowl, leaving a thin shell of

potato inside the skins. Mash the potato flesh with a fork.

4 Meanwhile, mix the cream and stock in a saucepan and simmer for 8–10 minutes or until reduced by half.

5 Stir in the lemon juice, garlic and chopped basil and season to taste with salt and pepper. Stir the mixture into the potato flesh with the pine kernels (nuts).

6 Spoon the mixture back into the potato

shells and sprinkle the Parmesan cheese on top. Return the potatoes to the oven for 10 minutes or until the cheese has browned. Serve with fresh salad.

VARIATION

Add full fat soft cheese or thinly sliced mushrooms to the mashed potato flesh in step 5, if you prefer.

Baked Potatoes with Guacamole & Salsa

Serves 4

INGREDIENTS

4 baking potatoes, about 225 g/
    8 oz each
1 large ripe avocado
175 g/6 oz smoked tofu
    (bean curd), diced
2 garlic cloves, crushed
1 onion, chopped finely

1 tomato, chopped finely
1 tsp lemon juice
125 g/4½ oz mixed salad leaves
fresh coriander (cilantro) sprigs,
    to garnish

SALSA:
2 ripe tomatoes, seeded and diced
1 tbsp chopped coriander
    (cilantro)
1 shallot, diced finely
1 green chilli, diced
1 tbsp lemon juice
salt and pepper

1 Scrub the potatoes and prick the skins with a fork. Rub a little salt into the skins and place them on a baking (cookie) sheet.

2 Cook in a preheated oven, 190°C/375°F/ Gas Mark 5, for 1 hour or until cooked through and the skins are crisp.

3 Cut the potatoes in half lengthways and scoop the flesh into a bowl, leaving a thin layer of potato inside the shells.

4 Halve and stone the avocado. Using a spoon, scoop out the avocado flesh and add to the bowl containing the potato. Stir in the lemon juice and mash the mixture together with a fork. Mix in the tofu (bean curd), garlic, onion and tomato. Spoon the mixture into one half of the potato shells.

5 Arrange the salad leaves on top of the guacamole mixture and place the other half of the potato shell on top.

6 To make the salsa, mix the tomatoes, coriander (cilantro), shallots, chilli, lemon juice and salt and pepper to taste in a bowl. Garnish the potatoes with sprigs of fresh coriander (cilantro) and serve with the salsa.

Pan Potato Cake

Serves 4

INGREDIENTS

675 g/1¹/₂ lb waxy potatoes,
  unpeeled and sliced
1 carrot, diced
225 g/8 oz small broccoli florets

60 g/2 oz/¹/₄ cup butter
2 tbsp vegetable oil
1 red onion, quartered
2 garlic cloves, crushed

175 g/6 oz tofu (bean curd), diced
2 tbsp chopped fresh sage
75 g/2³/₄ oz mature (sharp)
  cheese, grated

1 Cook the sliced potatoes in a saucepan of boiling water for 10 minutes. Drain thoroughly.

2 Meanwhile, cook the carrot and broccoli in a separate pan of boiling water for 5 minutes. Drain with a perforated spoon.

3 Heat the butter and oil in a 23 cm/9 inch frying pan (skillet), add the onion and garlic and fry gently for 2–3 minutes. Add half of the potatoes slices to the frying pan (skillet), covering the base of the pan (skillet).

4 Cover the potato slices with the carrot, broccoli and the tofu (bean curd). Sprinkle with half of the sage and cover with the remaining potato slices. Sprinkle the grated cheese over the top.

5 Cook over a moderate heat for 8–10 minutes, then heat under a preheated medium grill (broiler) for 2–3 minutes or until the cheese melts and browns.

6 Garnish with the remaining sage and serve straight from the pan (skillet).

COOK'S TIP

Make sure that the mixture fills the whole width of your frying pan (skillet) to enable the layers to remain intact.

Four-Cheese & Potato Layer Bake

Serves 4

INGREDIENTS

900 g/2 lb unpeeled waxy
    potatoes, cut into wedges
25 g/1 oz/2 tbsp butter
1 red onion, halved and sliced
2 garlic cloves, crushed
25 g/1 oz/¼ cup plain
    (all purpose) flour
600 ml/1 pint/2½ cups milk

397 g/14 oz can artichoke hearts
    in brine, drained and halved
150 g/5½ oz frozen mixed
    vegetables, thawed
125 g/4½ oz Gruyère cheese,
    grated
125 g/4½ oz mature (sharp)
    cheese, grated

50 g/1¾ oz Gorgonzola cheese,
    crumbled
25 g/1 oz Parmesan cheese, grated
225 g/8 oz tofu (bean curd), sliced
2 tbsp chopped fresh thyme
salt and pepper
thyme sprigs, to garnish

1 Cook the potato wedges in a saucepan of boiling water for 10 minutes. Drain thoroughly.

2 Meanwhile, melt the butter in a saucepan. Add the sliced onion and garlic and fry gently for 2–3 minutes.

3 Stir the flour into the pan and cook for 1 minute. Gradually add the milk and bring to the boil, stirring constantly.

4 Reduce the heat and add the artichoke hearts, mixed vegetables, half of each of the 4 cheeses and the tofu (bean curd) to the pan, mixing well. Stir in the chopped fresh thyme and season with salt and pepper to taste.

5 Arrange a layer of parboiled potato wedges in the base of a shallow ovenproof dish. Spoon the vegetable mixture over the top and cover with the remaining potato wedges. Sprinkle the rest of the 4 cheeses over the top.

6 Cook in a preheated oven, 200°C/400°F/ Gas Mark 6, for 30 minutes or until the potatoes are cooked and the top is golden brown. Serve the bake garnished with fresh thyme sprigs.

Potato & Aubergine (Eggplant) Gratin

Serves 4

INGREDIENTS

450 g/1/lb waxy potatoes, sliced
1 tbsp vegetable oil
1 onion, chopped
2 garlic cloves, crushed
450 g/1 lb tofu (bean curd), diced

2 tbsp tomato purée (paste)
2 tbsp plain (all-purpose) flour
300 ml/¹/₂ pint/1¹/₄ cups
    vegetable stock
2 large tomatoes, sliced

1 aubergine (eggplant), sliced
2 tbsp chopped fresh thyme
450 g/1 lb natural yogurt
2 eggs, beaten
salt and pepper

1 Cook the sliced potatoes in a saucepan of boiling water for 10 minutes until tender but not breaking up. Drain and set aside.

2 Heat the oil in a pan and fry the onion and garlic for 2–3 minutes.

3 Add the diced tofu (bean curd), tomato purée (paste) and flour and cook for 1 minute. Gradually stir in the vegetable stock and bring to the boil, stirring constantly. Reduce the heat and leave to simmer for 10 minutes.

4 Arrange a layer of the potato slices in the base of a deep ovenproof dish. Spoon the tofu (bean curd) mixture on top.

5 Layer the tomatoes, then the aubergine (eggplant) and then the remaining potato slices on top of the tofu mixture, making sure that it is completely covered.

6 Mix the yogurt and beaten eggs together in a bowl and season well with salt and pepper. Spoon the yogurt topping over the sliced potatoes.

7 Cook in a preheated oven, 190°C/375°F/ Gas Mark 5, for 35–45 minutes or until the topping is browned. Serve hot, with a crisp green salad.

VARIATION

You can use marinated or smoked tofu (bean curd) for extra flavour, if you wish.

Spicy Potato & Nut Terrine

Serves 4

INGREDIENTS

225 g/8 oz floury (mealy) potatoes, diced	2 tbsp chopped mixed herbs	SAUCE:
225 g/8 oz pecan nuts	1 tsp paprika	3 large tomatoes, peeled, seeded and chopped
225 g/8 oz unsalted cashew nuts	1 tsp ground cumin	
1 onion, chopped finely	1 tsp ground coriander (cilantro)	2 tbsp tomato purée (paste)
2 garlic cloves, crushed	4 eggs, beaten	85 ml/3 fl oz/¹⁄₃ cup red wine
125 g/4¹⁄₂ oz open cap mushrooms, diced	125 g/4¹⁄₂ oz full fat soft cheese	1 tbsp red wine vinegar
25 g/1 oz/2 tbsp butter	50 g/2 oz Parmesan cheese, grated	pinch of caster sugar
	salt and pepper	

1 Lightly grease a 1.1 kg/ 2 lb loaf tin (pan) and line with baking parchment.

2 Cook the potatoes in a pan of boiling water for 10 minutes or until cooked through. Drain and mash the potatoes.

3 Finely chop the pecan and cashew nuts or work in a food processor. Mix the nuts with the onion, garlic and mushrooms. Melt the butter in a frying pan (skillet) and cook the nut mixture for 5–7 minutes. Add the herbs and spices to the pan. Stir in the eggs, cheeses, potatoes and season.

4 Spoon the mixture into the prepared loaf tin (pan), pressing down firmly. Cook in a preheated oven, 190°C/375°F/Gas Mark 5, for 1 hour or until set.

5 To make the sauce, mix the tomatoes, tomato purée (paste), wine, wine vinegar and sugar in a pan and bring to the boil, stirring. Cook for 10 minutes or until the tomatoes have reduced. Pass the sauce through a sieve or blend in a food processor for 30 seconds. Turn the terrine out of the tin (pan) and cut into slices. Serve with a little of the tomato sauce.

Mushroom & Spinach Puff Pastry

Serves 4

INGREDIENTS

2 tbsp butter	175 g/6 oz baby spinach	salt and pepper
1 red onion, halved and sliced	pinch of nutmeg	2 tsp poppy seeds
2 garlic cloves, crushed	4 tbsp double (heavy) cream	
225 g/8 oz/3 cups open-cap	225 g/8 oz prepared puff pastry	
mushrooms, sliced	1 egg, beaten	

1 Melt the butter in a frying pan (skillet). Add the onion and garlic to the pan and sauté for 3–4 minutes, stirring well, until the onion has softened.

2 Add the mushrooms, spinach and nutmeg and cook for a further 2–3 minutes.

3 Stir in the double (heavy) cream, mixing well.

4 Season with salt and pepper to taste and remove the pan from the heat.

5 Roll the pastry out on a lightly floured surface and cut into four 15 cm/6 inch circles.

6 Spoon a quarter of the filling on to one half of each circle and fold the pastry over to encase the filling. Press down to seal the edges of the pastry and brush with the beaten egg. Sprinkle with the poppy seeds.

7 Place the parcels on to a dampened baking tray (cookie sheet) and cook in a preheated oven, 200°C/400°F/Gas Mark 6, for 20 minutes until risen and golden brown.

8 Transfer the mushroom and spinach puff pastry parcels to serving plates and serve immediately.

Chick Pea (Garbanzo Bean) Roast with Sherry Sauce

Serves 4

INGREDIENTS

450 g/1 lb can chickpeas
(garbanzo beans), drained
1 tsp marmite (yeast extract)
150 g/5¹/₂ oz/1¹/₄ cups chopped
walnuts
150 g/5¹/₂ oz/1¹/₄ cups fresh
white breadcrumbs
1 onion, finely chopped
100 g/3¹/₂ oz/1¹/₄ cups

mushrooms, sliced
50 g/1³/₄ oz canned sweetcorn,
drained
2 garlic cloves, crushed
2 tbsp dry sherry
2 tbsp vegetable stock
1 tbsp chopped coriander
(cilantro)
225 g/8 oz prepared puff pastry

1 egg, beaten
2 tbsp milk
salt and pepper
SAUCE:
1 tbsp vegetable oil
1 leek, thinly sliced
4 tbsp dry sherry
150 ml/¹/₄ pint/²/₃ cup
vegetable stock

1 Blend the chickpeas (garbanzo beans), marmite, nuts and breadcrumbs in a food processor for 30 seconds. In a frying pan (skillet) sauté the onion and mushrooms in their own juices for 3–4 minutes. Stir in the chick-pea mixture, corn and garlic. Add the sherry, stock, coriander (cilantro) and seasoning and bind the mixture together. Remove from the heat and allow to cool.

2 Roll the pastry out on to a lightly floured surface to form a 35.5 cm/14 inch x 30 cm/12 inch rectangle. Shape the chickpea (garbanzo bean) mixture into a loaf shape and wrap the pastry around it, sealing the edges. Place seam-side down on a dampened baking tray and score the top in a criss-cross pattern. Mix the egg and milk and brush over the pastry. Cook in a preheated oven, 200°C/400°F/Gas Mark 6, for 25–30 minutes. Heat the oil for the sauce in a pan and sauté the leek for 5 minutes. Add the sherry and stock, bring to the boil. Simmer for 5 minutes and serve with the roast.

Kidney Bean Kiev

Serves 4

INGREDIENTS

GARLIC BUTTER:
100 g/3½ oz/ 8 tbsp butter
3 garlic cloves, crushed
1 tbsp chopped parsley

BEAN PATTIES:
650 g/1 lb 7 oz canned red
   kidney beans
150 g/5½ oz/1¼ cups fresh
   white breadcrumbs
25 g/1 oz/2 tbsp butter

1 leek, chopped
1 celery stick, chopped
1 tbsp chopped parsley
1 egg, beaten
salt and pepper
vegetable oil, for shallow frying

1 To make the garlic butter, put the butter, garlic and parsley in a bowl and blend together with a wooden spoon. Place the garlic butter mixture on to a sheet of baking parchment, roll into a cigar shape and wrap in the baking parchment. Leave to chill in the refrigerator.

2 Using a potato masher, mash the red kidney beans in a mixing bowl and stir in 75g /2¾ oz/³⁄4 cup of the breadcrumbs until thoroughly blended.

3 Melt the butter in a frying pan (skillet) and sauté the leek and celery for 3–4 minutes, stirring.

4 Add the bean mixture to the pan together with the parsley, season with salt and pepper to taste and mix well. Remove from the heat and leave to cool slightly.

5 Shape the bean mixture into 4 equal sized ovals.

6 Slice the garlic butter into 4 and place a slice in the centre of each bean patty. Mould the bean mixture around the garlic butter to encase it completely.

7 Dip each bean patty into the beaten egg to coat and then roll in the remaining breadcrumbs.

8 Heat a little oil in a frying pan (skillet) and fry the patties, turning once, for 7–10 minutes or until golden. Serve.

Cashew Nut Paella

Serves 4

INGREDIENTS

2 tbsp olive oil	1 green chilli, sliced	vegetable stock
1 tbsp butter	1 green (bell) pepper, diced	75 g/2³/₄ oz/³/₄ cup unsalted
1 red onion, chopped	1 red (bell) pepper, diced	cashew nuts
150 g/5¹/₂ oz/1 cup arborio rice	75 g/2³/₄ oz baby corn cobs,	25 g/1 oz/¹/₄ cup frozen peas
1 tsp ground turmeric	halved lengthwise	2 tbsp chopped parsley
1 tsp ground cumin	2 tbsp pitted black olives	pinch of cayenne pepper
¹/₂ tsp chilli powder	1 large tomato, seeded and diced	salt and pepper
3 garlic cloves, crushed	450 ml/³/₄ pint/2 cups	fresh herbs, to garnish

1 Heat the olive oil and butter in a large frying pan (skillet) or paella pan until the butter has melted.

2 Add the chopped onion to the pan and sauté for 2–3 minutes, stirring, until the onion has softened.

3 Stir in the rice, turmeric, cumin, chilli powder, garlic, chilli, (bell) peppers, corn cobs, olives and tomato and cook over a medium heat for 1–2 minutes, stirring occasionally.

4 Pour in the stock and bring the mixture to the boil. Reduce the heat and cook for 20 minutes, stirring.

5 Add the cashew nuts and peas to the mixture in the pan and cook for a further 5 minutes, stirring occasionally. Season to taste and sprinkle with parsley and cayenne pepper. Transfer to warm serving plates, garnish and serve immediately.

COOK'S TIP

For authenticity and flavour, use a few saffron strands soaked in a little boiling water instead of the turmeric. Saffron has a lovely, nutty flavour.

Vegetable & Tofu (Bean Curd) Strudels

Serves 4

INGREDIENTS

FILLING:
2 tbsp vegetable oil
2 tbsp butter or vegetarian
    margarine
150 g/5½ oz/⅓ cup potatoes
    finely diced
1 leek, shredded

2 garlic cloves, crushed
1 tsp garam masala
½ tsp chilli powder
½ tsp turmeric
50 g/1¾ oz okra, sliced
100 g/3½ oz/1¼ cups button
    mushrooms, sliced

2 tomatoes, diced
225 g/8 oz firm tofu
    (bean curd), diced
12 sheets filo pastry
2 tbsp butter or vegetarian
    margarine, melted
salt and pepper

1 To make the filling, heat the oil and butter in a frying pan (skillet). Add the potatoes and leek and cook for 2–3 minutes, stirring.

2 Add the garlic and spices, okra, mushrooms, tomatoes, tofu (bean curd) and seasoning and cook, stirring, for 5–7 minutes or until tender.

3 Lay the pastry out on a chopping board and brush each individual sheet with butter. Place 3 sheets

on top of one another; repeat to make 4 stacks.

4 Spoon a quarter of the filling along the centre of each stack and brush the edges with butter. Fold the short edges in and roll up lengthwise to form a cigar shape; brush the outside with butter. Place the strudels on a greased baking tray (cookie sheet).

5 Cook in a preheated oven, 190°C/375°F/Gas Mark 5,

and cook the strudels for 20 minutes or until golden brown. Serve immediately.

COOK'S TIP

Decorate the outside of the strudels with crumpled pastry trimmings before cooking for a really impressive effect.

Vegetable Lasagne

Serves 4

INGREDIENTS

1 aubergine (eggplant), sliced
3 tbsp olive oil
2 garlic cloves, crushed
1 red onion, halved and sliced
1 green (bell) pepper, diced
1 red (bell) pepper, diced
1 yellow (bell) pepper, diced
225 g/8 oz /3cups mixed
    mushrooms, sliced
2 celery sticks, sliced
1 courgette (zucchini), diced
$^1/_2$ tsp chilli powder

$^1/_2$ tsp ground cumin
2 tomatoes, chopped
300 ml/$^1/_2$ pint/1$^1/_4$ cups
    passata (sieved tomatoes)
2 tbsp chopped basil
8 no pre-cook lasagne verdi sheets
salt and pepper

CHEESE SAUCE:
2 tbsp butter or vegetarian
    margarine
1 tbsp flour
150 ml/ $^1/_4$ pint/ $^2/_3$ cup
    vegetable stock
300 ml/$^1/_2$ pint/1$^1/_4$ cups milk
75 g/23/4 oz/$^3/_4$ cup vegetarian
    Cheddar, grated
1 tsp Dijon mustard
1 tbsp chopped basil
1 egg, beaten

1 Place the aubergine (eggplant) slices in a colander, sprinkle with salt and leave for 20 minutes. Rinse under cold water, drain and reserve. Heat the oil in a pan and sauté the garlic and onion for 1–2 minutes. Add the (bell) peppers, mushrooms, celery and courgette (zucchini) and cook for 3–4 minutes, stirring. Stir in the spices and cook for 1 minute. Mix the tomatoes, passata (sieved tomatoes) and basil together and season well.

2 For the sauce, melt the butter in a pan, add the flour and cook for 1 minute. Remove from the heat and stir in the stock and milk. Return to the heat and add half of the cheese and the mustard. Boil, stirring, until thickened. Stir in the basil and season. Remove from the heat and stir in the egg. Place half of the lasagne sheets in an ovenproof dish. Top with half of the vegetables, then half of the tomato sauce. Cover with half the aubergines (eggplants). Repeat and spoon the cheese sauce on top. Sprinkle with cheese and cook in a preheated oven, 180°C/350°F/Gas 4, for 40 minutes.

Lentil & Rice Casserole

Serves 4

INGREDIENTS

225 g/8 oz/1¼ cups red
    split lentils
50 g/1¾ oz/⅓ cup long-grain
    white rice
1 litre/1¾ pints/5 cups vegetable
    stock
150 ml/¼ pint/⅔ cup dry
    white wine
1 leek, cut into chunks

3 garlic cloves, crushed
400 g/14 oz can
    chopped tomatoes
1 tsp ground cumin
1 tsp chilli powder
1 tsp garam masala
1 red (bell) pepper, sliced
100 g/3½ oz small
    broccoli florets

8 baby corn cobs,
    halved lengthwise
50 g/1¾ oz French (green)
    beans, halved
1 tbsp fresh basil, shredded
salt and pepper
fresh basil sprigs, to garnish

1 Place the lentils, rice, vegetable stock and white wine in a flameproof casserole dish and cook over a gentle heat for 20 minutes, stirring occasionally.

2 Add the leek, garlic, tomatoes, cumin, chilli powder, garam masala, (bell) pepper, broccoli, corn cobs and French (green) beans.

3 Bring the mixture to the boil, reduce the heat, cover and simmer for a further 10–15 minutes or until the vegetables are tender.

4 Add the shredded basil and season with salt and pepper to taste.

5 Garnish with fresh basil sprigs and serve immediately.

VARIATION

You can vary the rice in this recipe – use brown or wild rice, if you prefer.

Vegetable Hot Pot

Serves 4

INGREDIENTS

2 large potatoes, thinly sliced
2 tbsp vegetable oil
1 red onion, halved and sliced
1 leek, sliced
2 garlic cloves, crushed
1 carrot, cut into chunks
100 g/3½ oz broccoli florets

100 g/3½ oz cauliflower florets
2 small turnips, quartered
1 tbsp plain (all-purpose) flour
700 ml/1 ¼ pints/3½ cups
  vegetable stock
150 ml/¼ pint/⅔ cup dry cider
1 dessert (eating) apple, sliced

2 tbsp chopped sage
pinch of cayenne pepper
50 g/1¾ oz/½ cup vegetarian
  Cheddar cheese, grated
salt and pepper

1 Cook the potato slices in a saucepan of boiling water for 10 minutes. Drain thoroughly and reserve.

2 Heat the oil in a flameproof casserole dish and sauté the onion, leek and garlic for 2–3 minutes. Add the remaining vegetables and cook for a further 3–4 minutes, stirring.

3 Stir in the flour and cook for 1 minute. Gradually add the stock and cider and bring the mixture to the boil. Add the apple, sage and cayenne pepper and season well. Remove the dish from the heat. Transfer the vegetables to an ovenproof dish.

4 Arrange the potato slices on top of the vegetable mixture to cover.

5 Sprinkle the cheese on top of the potato slices and cook in a preheated oven, 190°C/375°F/Gas Mark 5, for 30–35 minutes or until the potato is golden brown and beginning to crispen slightly around the edges. Serve immediately.

COOK'S TIP

If the potato begins to brown too quickly, cover with foil for the last 10 minutes of cooking time to prevent the top from burning.

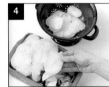

Vegetable Chop Suey

Serves 4

INGREDIENTS

2 tbsp peanut oil
1 onion, chopped
3 garlic cloves, chopped
1 green (bell) pepper, diced
1 red (bell) pepper, diced
75 g/2³/4 oz broccoli florets

1 courgette (zucchini), sliced
25 g/1 oz French (green) beans
1 carrot, cut into matchsticks
100 g/3¹/2 oz bean sprouts
2 tsp light brown sugar
2 tbsp light soy sauce

125 ml/4 fl oz/¹/2 cup
    vegetable stock
salt and pepper
noodles, to serve

1 Heat the oil in a preheated wok until almost smoking. Add the onion and garlic and stir-fry for 30 seconds.

2 Stir in the (bell) peppers, broccoli, courgette (zucchini), beans and carrot and stir-fry for a further 2–3 minutes.

3 Add the bean sprouts, light brown sugar, soy sauce and vegetable stock. Season with salt and pepper to taste and cook for about 2 minutes.

4 Transfer the vegetables to serving plates and serve immediately with noodles.

COOK'S TIP

The clever design of a wok, with its spherical base and high sloping sides, enables the food to be tossed so that it is cooked quickly and evenly. It is essential to heat the wok sufficiently before you add the ingredients to ensure quick and even cooking.

COOK'S TIP

Ensure that the vegetable pieces are of the same size in order that they all cook in the stated time.

VARIATION

Add 1 tbsp chilli oil for a hotter flavour and add cashew nuts for extra crunch.

Vegetable Toad-in-the-Hole

Serves 4

INGREDIENTS

BATTER:
100 g/3½ oz/¾ cup plain (all-
  purpose) flour
2 eggs, beaten
200 ml/7 fl oz/¾ cup milk
2 tbsp wholegrain mustard
2 tbsp vegetable oil

FILLING:
2 tbsp butter
2 garlic cloves, crushed
1 onion, cut into eight
75 g/2¾ oz baby carrots, halved
  lengthwise
50 g/1¾ oz French (green) beans

50 g/1¾ oz canned sweetcorn,
  drained
2 tomatoes, seeded and cut into
  chunks
1 tsp wholegrain mustard
1 tbsp chopped mixed herbs
salt and pepper

1 To make the batter, sieve the flour and a pinch of salt into a large bowl. Make a well in the centre and beat in the eggs and milk to make a batter. Stir in the mustard and leave to stand.

2 Pour the oil into a shallow ovenproof dish and heat in a preheated oven, 200°C/400°F/ Gas Mark 6, for 10 minutes.

3 To make the filling, melt the butter in a frying pan (skillet) and sauté the garlic and onion for 2 minutes, stirring. Cook the carrots and beans in a saucepan of boiling water for 7 minutes or until tender. Drain well.

4 Add the sweetcorn and tomato to the frying pan (skillet) with the mustard and herbs. Season well and add the carrots and beans.

5 Remove the dish from the oven and pour in the batter. Spoon the vegetables into the centre, return to the oven and cook for 30–35 minutes until the batter has risen and set. Serve the vegetable toad-in-the-hole immediately.

COOK'S TIP

It is important that the oil is hot before adding the batter so that the batter begins to cook and rise immediately.

Vegetable Jalousie

Serves 4

INGREDIENTS

450 g/1 lb prepared puff pastry
1 egg, beaten

FILLING:
2 tbsp butter or vegetarian
   margarine
1 leek, shredded

2 garlic cloves, crushed
1 red (bell) pepper, sliced
1 yellow (bell) pepper, sliced
50 g/1¾ oz mushrooms, sliced
75 g/2¾ oz small
   asparagus spears
2 tbsp flour

85 ml/3 fl oz/6 tbsp
   vegetable stock
85 ml/3 fl oz/6 tbsp milk
4 tbsp dry white wine
1 tbsp chopped oregano
salt and pepper

1 Melt the butter or margarine in a pan and sauté the leek and garlic for 2 minutes, stirring. Add the remaining vegetables and cook, stirring, for 3–4 minutes.

2 Add the flour and cook for 1 minute. Remove the pan from the heat and stir in the vegetable stock, milk and white wine. Return the pan to the heat and bring to the boil, stirring, until thickened. Stir in the oregano and season with salt and pepper to taste.

3 Roll half of the pastry out on a lightly floured surface to form a rectangle 42.5 cm/15 inches x 15 cm/6 inches.

4 Roll out the other half of the pastry to the same shape, but a little larger. Put the smaller rectangle on a baking tray (cookie sheet) lined with dampened baking parchment.

5 Spoon the filling on top of the smaller rectangle, leaving a 1.25 cm/½ inch clean edge.

6 Cut parallel slits across the larger rectangle to within 2.5 cm/1 inch of each edge.

7 Brush the edge of the smaller rectangle with egg and place the larger rectangle on top, sealing the edges well.

8 Brush the whole jalousie with egg and cook in a preheated oven, 200°C/400°F/Gas Mark 6, for 30–35 minutes until risen and golden. Serve immediately.

Cauliflower, Broccoli & Cheese Flan

Serves 8

INGREDIENTS

PASTRY:

175 g/6 oz/11/4 cups plain (all-
    purpose) flour

pinch of salt

1/2 tsp paprika

1 tsp dried thyme

75 g/2³/4 oz/6 tbsp vegetarian
    margarine

3 tbsp water

FILLING:

100 g/3¹/2 oz cauliflower florets

100 g/3¹/2 oz broccoli florets

1 onion, cut into eight

2 tbsp butter or vegetarian
    margarine

1 tbsp plain (all-purpose) flour

85 ml/3 fl oz/6 tbsp
    vegetable stock

125 ml/4 fl oz/8 tbsp milk

75 g/2³/4 oz/³/4 cup vegetarian
    Cheddar cheese, grated

salt and pepper

paprika and thyme, to garnish

1 To make the pastry, sieve the flour and salt into a bowl. Add the paprika and thyme and rub in the margarine. Stir in the water and bind to form a dough.

2 Roll the pastry out on a floured surface and use to line an 18cm/7 inch loose-bottomed flan tin (pan). Prick the base with a fork and line with baking parchment. Fill with ceramic baking beans and bake in a preheated oven, at 190°C/375°F/ Gas Mark 5, for 15 minutes. Remove the parchment and beans and return the pastry case to the oven for 5 minutes.

3 To make the filling, cook the vegetables in a pan of boiling water for 10–12 minutes until tender. Drain and reserve.

4 Melt the butter in a pan. Add the flour and cook, stirring, for 1 minute.

Remove from the heat, stir in the stock and milk and return to the heat. Bring to the boil, stirring, and add 50 g/ 1¹/4 oz/¹/2 cup of the cheese. Season.

5 Spoon the cauliflower, broccoli and onion into the pastry case. Pour over the sauce and sprinkle with the cheese. Return to the oven for 10 minutes until the cheese is bubbling. Dust with paprika, garnish and serve.

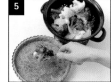

Roast (Bell) Pepper Tart

Serves 8

INGREDIENTS

PASTRY:

175 g/6 oz/1¼ cups plain (all-purpose) flour

pinch of salt

75 g/2¾ oz/6 tbsp butter or vegetarian margarine

2 tbsp green pitted olives, finely chopped

3 tbsp cold water

FILLING:

1 red (bell) pepper

1 green (bell) pepper

1 yellow (bell) pepper

2 garlic cloves, crushed

2 tbsp olive oil

100 g/3½ oz/1 cup Mozzarella cheese, grated

2 eggs

150 ml/5 fl oz/⅔ cup milk

1 tbsp chopped basil

salt and pepper

1 To make the pastry, sieve the flour and a pinch of salt into a bowl. Rub in the butter or margarine until the mixture resembles breadcrumbs. Add the olives and cold water, bringing the mixture together to form a dough.

2 Roll the dough out on to a floured surface and use to line a 20 cm/8 inch loose-bottomed flan tin (pan). Prick the base with a fork and leave to chill.

3 Cut the (bell) peppers in half lengthwise and lay skin-side uppermost on a baking tray (cookie sheet). Mix the garlic and oil and brush over the (bell) peppers. Cook in a preheated oven, 200°C/400°F/Gas Mark 6, for 20 minutes or until beginning to char slightly. Let the (bell) peppers cool slightly and thinly slice. Arrange in the base of the pastry case, layering with the Mozzarella cheese.

4 Beat the egg and milk and add the basil. Season and pour over the (bell) peppers. Put the tart on a baking tray (cookie sheet) and return to the oven for 20 minutes or until set. Serve hot or cold.

Vegetable Biryani

Serves 4

INGREDIENTS

1 large potato, cubed
100 g/3½ oz baby carrots
50 g/1¾ oz okra, thickly sliced
2 celery sticks, sliced
75 g/2¾ oz baby button
    mushrooms, halved
1 aubergine (eggplant), halved
    and sliced

300 ml/½ pint/1¼ cups natural
    (unsweetened) yogurt
1 tbsp grated root ginger
2 large onions, grated
4 garlic cloves, crushed
1 tsp turmeric
1 tbsp curry powder
2 tbsp butter

2 onions, sliced
225 g/8 oz/1¼ cups
    basmati rice
chopped coriander (cilantro),
    to garnish

1 Cook the potato cubes, carrots and okra in a pan of boiling salted water for 7–8 minutes. Drain well and place in a large bowl. Mix with the celery, mushrooms and aubergine (eggplant).

2 Mix the natural (unsweetened) yogurt, ginger, grated onions, garlic, turmeric and curry powder and spoon over the vegetables, tossing to coat thoroughly. Leave to marinate for at least 2 hours.

3 Heat the butter in a frying pan (skillet) and cook the sliced onions for 5–6 minutes until golden brown. Remove a few onions from the pan and reserve for garnishing.

4 Cook the rice in a pan of boiling water for 7 minutes. Drain well.

5 Add the marinated vegetables to the onions and cook for 10 minutes.

6 Put half of the rice in a 2 litre/3½ pint casserole dish. Spoon the vegetables on top and cover with the remaining rice. Cover and cook in a preheated oven, 190°C/375°F/Gas Mark 5, for 20–25 minutes or until the rice is tender.

7 Spoon the biryani on to a serving plate, garnish with the reserved onions and chopped coriander (cilantro) and serve immediately.

Baked Cheese & Tomato Macaroni

Serves 4

INGREDIENTS

225 g/8 oz/2 cups elbow
macaroni
175 g/6 oz/1½ cups grated
vegetarian cheese
100 g/3½ oz/1 cup grated
Parmesan cheese
4 tbsp fresh white breadcrumbs

1 tbsp chopped basil
1 tbsp butter or margarine

TOMATO SAUCE:
1 tbsp olive oil
1 shallot, finely chopped
2 garlic cloves, crushed

450 g/1 lb canned chopped
tomatoes
1 tbsp chopped basil
salt and pepper

1 To make the tomato sauce, heat the oil in a saucepan and sauté the shallots and garlic for 1 minute. Add the tomatoes, basil, salt and pepper to taste and cook over a medium heat, stirring, for 10 minutes.

2 Meanwhile, cook the macaroni in a pan of boiling salted water for 8 minutes or until just undercooked. Drain.

3 Mix both of the cheeses together.

4 Grease a deep, ovenproof dish. Spoon a third of the tomato sauce into the base of the dish, top with a third of the macaroni and then a third of the cheeses. Season with salt and pepper. Repeat the layers twice.

5 Combine the breadcrumbs and basil and sprinkle over the top. Dot with the butter or

margarine and cook in a preheated oven, 190°C/375°F/Gas Mark 5, for 25 minutes or until the dish is golden brown and bubbling. Serve.

COOK'S TIP

Use other pasta shapes, such as penne, if you have them to hand, instead of the macaroni.

Chickpea (Garbanzo Bean) & Vegetable Casserole

Serves 4

INGREDIENTS

1 tbsp olive oil
1 red onion, halved and sliced
3 garlic cloves, crushed
225 g/8 oz spinach
1 fennel bulb, cut into eight
1 red (bell) pepper, cubed
1 tbsp plain (all-purpose) flour

450 ml/³/₄ pint/3³/₄ cups
  vegetable stock
85 ml/3 fl oz/6 tbsp dry white
  wine
400 g/14 oz can chickpeas
  (garbanzo beans), drained
1 bay leaf

1 tsp ground coriander (cilantro)
¹/₂ tsp paprika
salt and pepper
fennel fronds, to garnish

1 Heat the olive oil in a large flameproof casserole dish and sauté the onion and garlic for 1 minute, stirring. Add the spinach and cook for 4 minutes or until wilted.

2 Add the fennel and (bell) pepper and cook for 2 minutes, stirring.

3 Stir in the flour and cook for 1 minute.

4 Add the stock, wine, chickpeas (garbanzo beans), bay leaf, coriander (cilantro) and paprika, cover and cook for 30 minutes. Season to taste, garnish with fennel fronds and serve immediately.

VARIATION

Replace the coriander (cilantro) with nutmeg, if you prefer, as it works well with spinach.

COOK'S TIP

Use other canned pulses or mixed beans instead of the chickpeas (garbanzo beans), if you prefer.

Sweet & Sour Vegetables & Tofu (Bean Curd)

Serves 4

INGREDIENTS

1 tbsp peanut oil
2 garlic cloves, crushed
1 tsp grated root ginger
50 g/1³/₄ oz baby corn cobs
50 g/1³/₄ oz mangetout
   (snow peas)
1 carrot, cut into matchsticks
1 green (bell) pepper, cut

into matchsticks
8 spring onions (scallions),
   trimmed
50 g/1³/₄ oz canned bamboo
   shoots
225 g/8 oz marinated firm tofu
   (bean curd), cubed
2 tbsp dry sherry

2 tbsp rice vinegar
2 tbsp clear honey
1 tbsp light soy sauce
150 ml/¹/₄ pint/ ²/₃ cup
   vegetable stock
1 tbsp cornflour (cornstarch)

1 Heat the oil in a preheated wok until almost smoking.

2 Add the garlic and grated root ginger and cook for 30 seconds, stirring frequently.

3 Add the baby corn cobs, mangetout (snow peas), carrot and (bell) pepper and stir-fry for about 5 minutes or until the vegetables are tender.

4 Add the spring onions (scallions), bamboo shoots and tofu (bean curd) and cook for a further 2 minutes.

5 Stir in the sherry, rice vinegar, honey, soy sauce, vegetable stock and cornflour (cornstarch) and bring to the boil. Reduce the heat and simmer for 2 minutes. Transfer to serving dishes and serve immediately.

VARIATION

You can replace any of the vegetables in this dish with others of your choice. For a colourful, attractive stir-fry, select vegetables with bright, contrasting colours.

Spicy Potato & Lemon Casserole

Serves 4

INGREDIENTS

100 ml/3½ fl oz/½ cup
   olive oil
2 red onions, cut into eight
3 garlic cloves, crushed
2 tsp ground cumin
2 tsp ground coriander

pinch of cayenne pepper
1 carrot, thickly sliced
2 small turnips, quartered
1 courgette (zucchini), sliced
450 g/1 lb potatoes, thickly sliced
juice and rind of 2 large lemons

300 ml/½ pint/1¼ cups
   vegetable stock
2 tbsp chopped
   coriander (cilantro)
salt and pepper

1 Heat the olive oil in a flameproof casserole.

2 Add the red onion and sauté for 3 minutes, stirring.

3 Add the garlic and cook for 30 seconds. Mix in the spices and cook for 1 minute, stirring.

4 Add the carrot, turnips, courgette (zucchini) and potatoes and stir to coat in the oil.

5 Add the lemon juice and rind, stock and salt and pepper to taste, cover and cook over a medium heat for 20–30 minutes, stirring occasionally.

6 Remove the lid, sprinkle in the coriander (cilantro) and stir well. Serve immediately.

COOK'S TIP

Check the vegetables whilst cooking as they may begin to stick to the pan. Add a little more boiling water or stock if necessary.

COOK'S TIP

A selection of spices and herbs is important for adding variety to your cooking – add to your range each time you try a new recipe.

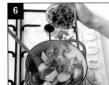

Vegetable Cannelloni

Serves 4

INGREDIENTS

1 aubergine (eggplant)	12 cannelloni tubes	2 x 400 g/14 oz cans
125 m/¼ fl oz/½ cup olive oil	salt and pepper	chopped tomatoes
225 g/8 oz spinach		1 tsp caster (superfine) sugar
2 garlic cloves, crushed	TOMATO SAUCE:	2 tbsp chopped basil
1 tsp ground cumin	1 tbsp olive oil	50 g/1¾ oz/½ cup
75 g/2¾ oz/1 cup	1 onion, chopped	Mozzarella, sliced
mushrooms, chopped	2 garlic cloves, crushed	

1 Cut the aubergine (eggplant) into small dice.

2 Heat the oil in a frying pan (skillet) and cook the aubergine (eggplant) for 2–3 minutes.

3 Add the spinach, garlic, cumin and mushrooms. Season and cook for 2–3 minutes, stirring. Spoon the mixture into the cannelloni tubes and place in an ovenproof dish in a single layer.

4 To make the sauce, heat the olive oil in a saucepan and sauté the onion and garlic for 1 minute. Add the tomatoes, caster (superfine) sugar and chopped basil and bring to the boil. Reduce the heat and simmer for about 5 minutes. Pour the sauce over the cannelloni tubes.

5 Arrange the sliced Mozzarella on top of the sauce and cook in a preheated oven, 190°C/ 375°F/ Gas Mark 5, for 30 minutes or until the cheese is bubbling and golden brown. Serve immediately.

COOK'S TIP

You can prepare the tomato sauce in advance and store it in the refrigerator for up to 24 hours.

Cauliflower Bake

Serves 4

INGREDIENTS

450 g/1 lb cauliflower, broken
    into florets
2 large potatoes, cubed
100 g/3½ oz cherry tomatoes

SAUCE:
25 g/1 oz/2 tbsp butter or
    vegetarian margarine
1 leek, sliced
1 garlic clove, crushed
25 g/1 oz/3 tbsp plain (all-
    purpose) flour
300 ml/½ pint/1¼ cups milk

75 g/2¾ oz/¾ cup mixed grated
    cheese, such as vegetarian
    Cheddar, Parmesan and
    Gruyère
½ tsp paprika
2 tbsp chopped flat-leaf parsley
salt and pepper
chopped fresh parsley, to garnish

1 Cook the cauliflower in a saucepan of boiling water for 10 minutes. Drain well and reserve. Meanwhile, cook the potatoes in a pan of boiling water for 10 minutes, drain and reserve.

2 To make the sauce, melt the butter or margarine in a saucepan and sauté the leek and garlic for 1 minute. Add the flour and cook for 1 minute. Remove the pan from the heat and gradually stir in the milk, 50 g/1¾ oz/ ½ cup of the cheese, the paprika and parsley. Return the pan to the heat and bring to the boil, stirring. Season with salt and pepper to taste.

3 Spoon the cauliflower into a deep ovenproof dish. Add the cherry tomatoes and top with the potatoes. Pour the sauce over the potatoes and sprinkle on the remaining cheese.

4 Cook in a preheated oven, 180°C/350°F/Gas Mark 4, for 20 minutes or until the vegetables are cooked through and the cheese is golden brown and bubbling. Garnish and serve immediately.

VARIATION

This dish could be made with broccoli instead of the cauliflower as an alternative.

Leek & Herb Soufflé

Serves 4

INGREDIENTS

350 g/12 oz baby leeks
1 tbsp olive oil
125 ml/4 fl oz/½ cup
   vegetable stock
50 g/1¾ oz/½ cup walnuts

2 eggs, separated
2 tbsp chopped mixed herbs
2 tbsp natural
   (unsweetened) yogurt
salt and pepper

1 Using a sharp knife, chop the leeks finely.

2 Heat the oil in a frying pan (skillet) and sauté the leeks for 2–3 minutes.

3 Add the stock to the pan and cook over a gentle heat for a further 5 minutes.

4 Place the walnuts in a food processor and blend until finely chopped.

5 Add the leek mixture to the nuts and blend to form a purée. Transfer to a mixing bowl.

6 Combine the egg yolks, herbs and yogurt and pour into the leek purée. Season with salt and pepper to taste and mix well.

7 In a separate mixing bowl, whisk the egg whites until firm peaks form.

8 Fold the egg whites into the leek mixture. Spoon the mixture into a lightly greased 900 ml/1½ pint ramekin dish and place on a warmed baking tray (cookie sheet).

9 Cook in a preheated oven, 180°C/350°F/ Gas Mark 4, for 35–40 minutes or until set. Serve the soufflé immediately.

Artichoke & Cheese Tart

Serves 8

INGREDIENTS

175 g/6 oz/1 ¼ cups wholemeal (whole wheat) flour	FILLING:	Cheddar, grated
2 garlic cloves, crushed	2 tbsp olive oil	50 g/1¾ oz/½ cup Gorgonzola
75 g/2¾ oz/6 tbsp butter or vegetarian margarine	1 red onion, halved and sliced	cheese, crumbled
salt and pepper	10 canned or fresh artichoke hearts	2 eggs, beaten
		1 tbsp chopped fresh rosemary
	100 g/3½ oz/1 cup vegetarian	150 ml/¼ pint/⅔ cup milk

1 To make the pastry, sieve the flour into a mixing bowl, add a pinch of salt and the garlic. Rub in the butter until the mixture resembles breadcrumbs. Stir in 3 tablespoons of water and bring the mixture together to form a dough.

2 Roll the pastry out on a lightly floured surface to fit a 20cm/8 inch flan tin (pan). Prick the pastry with a fork.

3 Heat the oil in a frying pan (skillet) and sauté the onion for 3 minutes. Add the artichoke hearts and cook for a further 2 minutes.

4 Mix the cheeses with the beaten eggs, rosemary and milk. Stir in the drained artichoke mixture and season to taste.

5 Spoon the artichoke and cheese mixture into the pastry case and cook in a preheated oven, 200°C/400°F/Gas Mark 6,

for 25 minutes or until cooked and set. Serve the flan hot or cold.

COOK'S TIP

Gently press the centre of the flan with your fingertip to test if it is cooked through. It should feel fairly firm, but not solid. If overcooked the flan will begin to 'weep'.

Tagliatelle with Courgette (Zucchini) Sauce

Serves 4

INGREDIENTS

650 g/1 lb 7 oz courgettes (zucchini)
6 tbsp olive oil
3 garlic cloves, crushed
3 tbsp chopped basil
2 red chillies, sliced

juice of 1 large lemon
5 tbsp single (light) cream
4 tbsp grated Parmesan cheese
225 g/8 oz tagliatelle
salt and pepper

1 Using a vegetable peeler, slice the courgettes (zucchini) into thin ribbons.

2 Heat the oil in a frying pan (skillet) and sauté the garlic for 30 seconds.

3 Add the courgettes (zucchini) and cook over a gentle heat, stirring, for 5–7 minutes.

4 Stir in the basil, chillies, lemon juice, single (light) cream and grated Parmesan cheese and season with salt and pepper to taste.

5 Meanwhile, cook the tagliatelle in a large pan of lightly salted boiling water for 10 minutes until 'al dente'. Drain the pasta thoroughly and put in a warm serving bowl.

6 Pile the courgette (zucchini) mixture on top of the pasta. Serve immediately.

VARIATION

Lime juice and zest could be used instead of the lemon as an alternative.

Olive, (Bell) Pepper & Cherry Tomato Pasta

Serves 4

INGREDIENTS

225 g/8 oz/2 cups penne
2 tbsp olive oil
2 tbsp butter
2 garlic cloves, crushed
1 green (bell) pepper,
    thinly sliced

1 yellow (bell) pepper,
    thinly sliced
16 cherry tomatoes, halved
1 tbsp chopped oregano
125 ml/4 fl oz/½ cup dry
    white wine

2 tbsp quartered, pitted
    black olives
75 g/2¾ oz rocket (arugula)
salt and pepper
fresh oregano sprigs, to garnish

1 Cook the pasta in a saucepan of boiling salted water for 8–10 minutes or until 'al dente'. Drain thoroughly.

2 Heat the oil and butter in a pan until the butter melts. Sauté the garlic for 30 seconds. Add the (bell) peppers and cook for 3–4 minutes, stirring.

3 Stir in the cherry tomatoes, oregano, wine and olives and cook for 3–4 minutes. Season well with salt and pepper and stir in the rocket until just wilted.

4 Transfer the pasta to a serving dish, spoon over the sauce and mix well. Garnish and serve.

COOK'S TIP

Ensure that the saucepan is large enough to prevent the pasta from sticking together during cooking.

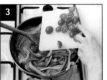

Spinach & Pine Kernel (Nut) Pasta

Serves 4

INGREDIENTS

225 g/8 oz pasta shapes
   or spaghetti
125 ml/4 fl oz/$^1/_2$ cup olive oil
2 garlic cloves, crushed
1 onion, quartered
   and sliced

3 large flat mushrooms, sliced
225 g/8 oz spinach
2 tbsp pine kernels (nuts)
85 ml/3 fl oz/6 tbsp dry
   white wine
salt and pepper

Parmesan shavings,
   to garnish

1 Cook the pasta in a saucepan of boiling salted water for 8–10 minutes or until 'al dente'. Drain well.

2 Meanwhile, heat the oil in a large saucepan and sauté the garlic and onion for 1 minute.

3 Add the sliced mushrooms and cook for 2 minutes, stirring occasionally.

4 Add the spinach and cook for 4–5 minutes or until the spinach has wilted.

5 Stir in the pine kernels (nuts) and wine, season well and cook for 1 minute.

6 Transfer the pasta to a warm serving bowl and toss the sauce into it, mixing well. Garnish with shavings of Parmesan cheese and serve.

COOK'S TIP

Freshly grate a little nutmeg over the dish for extra flavour as it is particularly good with spinach.

COOK'S TIP

'Al dente' means that the pasta should be tender but still have a bite to it.

Tofu (Bean Curd) & Vegetable Stir-Fry

Serves 4

INGREDIENTS

175 g/6 oz/1¼ cups
   potatoes, cubed
1 tbsp olive oil
1 red onion, sliced
225 g/8 oz firm tofu
   (bean curd), diced

2 courgettes (zucchini), diced
8 canned artichoke
   hearts, halved
150 ml/ ¼ pint/ ⅔ cup passata
   (sieved tomatoes)
1 tsp caster (superfine) sugar

2 tbsp chopped basil
salt and pepper

1 Cook the potatoes in a saucepan of boiling water for 10 minutes. Drain thoroughly and set aside until required.

2 Heat the oil in a large frying pan (skillet) and sauté the red onion for 2 minutes until the onion has softened, stirring.

3 Stir in the tofu (bean curd) and courgettes (zucchini) and cook for 3–4 minutes until they begin to brown slightly. Add the potatoes, stirring to mix.

4 Stir in the artichoke hearts, passata (sieved tomatoes), sugar and basil, season with salt and pepper and cook for a further 5 minutes, stirring well. Transfer the stir-fry to serving dishes and serve immediately.

COOK'S TIP

Canned artichoke hearts should be drained thoroughly and rinsed before use because they often have salt added.

VARIATION

Aubergines (eggplants) could be used instead of the courgettes (zucchini), if preferred.

Cantonese Garden Vegetable Stir-Fry

Serves 4

INGREDIENTS

2 tbsp peanut oil

1 tsp Chinese five-spice powder

75 g/2¾ oz baby carrots, halved

2 celery sticks, sliced

2 baby leeks, sliced

50 g/1¾ oz mangetout
(snow peas)

4 baby courgettes (zucchini),
halved lengthwise

8 baby corn cobs

225 g/8 oz firm marinated
tofu (bean curd), cubed

4 tbsp fresh orange juice

1 tbsp clear honey

celery leaves and orange zest,
to garnish

cooked rice or noodles, to serve

1 Heat the oil in a preheated wok until almost smoking. Add the Chinese five-spice powder, carrots, celery, leeks, mangetout (snow peas), courgettes (zucchini) and corn cobs and stir-fry for 3–4 minutes.

2 Add the tofu (bean curd) and cook for a further 2 minutes, stirring.

3 Stir in the orange juice and honey, reduce the heat and cook for 1–2 minutes.

4 Transfer the stir-fry to a serving dish, garnish with celery leaves and orange zest and serve with rice or noodles.

COOK'S TIP

Chinese five-spice powder is a mixture of fennel, star anise, cinnamon bark, cloves and Szechuan pepper. It is very pungent so should be used sparingly. If kept in an airtight container, it will keep indefinitely.

Risotto Verde

Serves 4

INGREDIENTS

1.75 litres/3 pints/7½ cups vegetable stock	225 g/8 oz/1¼ cups arborio rice	3 tbsp natural (unsweetened) yogurt
2 tbsp olive oil	300 ml/½ pint/1¼ cups dry white wine	salt and pepper
2 garlic cloves, crushed	4 tbsp chopped mixed herbs	shredded leek, to garnish
2 leeks, shredded	225 g/8 oz baby spinach	

1 Pour the stock into a large saucepan and bring to the boil. Reduce the heat to a simmer.

2 Meanwhile, heat the oil in a separate pan and sauté the garlic and leeks for 2–3 minutes until softened.

3 Stir in the rice and cook for 2 minutes, stirring until well coated.

4 Pour in half of the wine and a little of the hot stock. Cook over a gentle heat until all of the liquid has been absorbed. Add the remaining stock and wine and cook over a low heat for 25 minutes or until the rice is creamy.

5 Stir in the chopped mixed herbs and baby spinach, season well with salt and pepper and cook for 2 minutes.

6 Stir in the natural (unsweetened) yogurt, garnish with the shredded leek and serve immediately.

COOK'S TIP

Do not hurry the process of cooking the risotto as the rice must absorb the liquid slowly in order for it to reach the correct consistency.

Baked Pasta in Tomato Sauce

Serves 8

INGREDIENTS

100 g/3½ oz/1 cup pasta shapes,
    such as penne or casareccia
1 tbsp olive oil
1 leek, chopped
3 garlic cloves, crushed
1 green (bell) pepper, chopped
400 g/14 oz can
    chopped tomatoes
2 tbsp chopped, pitted

black olives
2 eggs, beaten
1 tbsp chopped basil

TOMATO SAUCE:
1 tbsp olive oil
1 onion, chopped
225 g/8 oz can

chopped tomatoes
1 tsp caster (superfine) sugar
2 tbsp tomato purée (paste)
150 ml/¼ pint/⅔ cup
    vegetable stock
salt and pepper

1 Cook the pasta in a saucepan of boiling salted water for 8 minutes. Drain thoroughly.

2 Meanwhile, heat the oil in a saucepan and sauté the leek and garlic for 2 minutes, stirring. Add the (bell) pepper, tomatoes and olives and cook for a further 5 minutes.

3 Remove the pan from the heat and stir in the pasta, beaten eggs and basil. Season well, and spoon into a lightly greased 1 litre/2 pint ovenproof pudding basin.

4 Place the pudding basin in a roasting tin (pan) and half-fill the tin (pan) with boiling water. Cover and cook in a preheated oven, 180°C/350°F/Gas Mark 6, for 40 minutes until set.

5 To make the sauce, heat the oil in a pan and sauté the onion for 2 minutes. Add the remaining ingredients and cook for 10 minutes. Put the sauce in a food processor or blender and blend until smooth. Return to a clean saucepan and heat until hot.

6 Turn the pasta out of the pudding basin on to a warm plate. Slice and serve with the tomato sauce.

Spaghetti with Pear & Walnut Sauce

Serves 4

INGREDIENTS

225 g/8 oz spaghetti
2 small ripe pears, peeled and sliced
150 ml/¼ pint/²⁄₃ cup vegetable stock
85 ml/3 fl oz/6 tbsp dry white wine

2 tbsp butter
1 tbsp olive oil
1 red onion, quartered and sliced
1 garlic clove, crushed
50 g/1³⁄₄ oz/½ cup walnut halves
2 tbsp chopped oregano

1 tbsp lemon juice
75 g/2³⁄₄ oz/³⁄₄ cup dolcelatte cheese
salt and pepper
fresh oregano sprigs, to garnish

1 Cook the pasta in a saucepan of boiling salted water for 8–10 minutes or until 'al dente'. Drain thoroughly and keep warm until required.

2 Meanwhile, place the pears in a pan and pour over the stock and wine. Poach the pears over a gentle heat for 10 minutes. Drain and reserve the cooking liquid and pears.

3 Heat the butter and oil in a saucepan until the butter melts, then sauté the onion and garlic for 2–3 minutes, stirring.

4 Add the walnuts, oregano and lemon juice, stirring.

5 Stir in the reserved pears with 4 tablespoons of the poaching liquid.

6 Crumble the dolcelatte cheese into the pan and cook over a gentle heat, stirring occasionally, for 1–2 minutes or until the cheese just begins to melt. Season the sauce with salt and pepper to taste.

7 Toss the pasta into the sauce, garnish and serve.

COOK'S TIP

You can use any good-flavoured blue cheese for this dish. Other varieties to try are Roquefort, which has a very strong flavour, Gorgonzola or Stilton.

Pies & Bakes

The following chapter includes a range of hearty savoury pies and bakes which are ideal for cold autumn (fall) and winter evenings. However, a few less robust meals are also included which are more suitable for a light spring or summer meal. Many of the recipes are adaptable, and you may like to substitute your favourite vegetables for the ones suggested in the recipe, or vary them according to seasonal availability.

There are both sweet and savoury recipes in this chapter, as the potato lends itself to sweeter dishes, mixed with fruit and spices. Also included are a few bread recipes, as the potato makes excellent bread; an assortment of fabulous pies using different pastries; and pastry bites. This chapter contains something for every occasion, illustrating how well potatoes and vegetables lend themselves to a wide variety of dishes.

Potato, Beef & Leek Pasties

Makes 4

INGREDIENTS

225 g/8 oz waxy potatoes, diced	1 leek, sliced	15 g/$\frac{1}{2}$ oz/1 tbsp butter
1 small carrot, diced	225 g/8 oz ready made	salt and pepper
225 g/8 oz beef steak, cubed	shortcrust pastry (pie dough)	1 egg, beaten

1 Lightly grease a baking (cookie) sheet.

2 Mix the potatoes, carrots, beef and leek in a large bowl. Season well with salt and pepper.

3 Divide the pastry (pie dough) into 4 equal portions. On a lightly floured surface, roll each portion into a 20 cm/8 inch round.

4 Spoon the potato mixture on to one half of each round, to within 1 cm/$\frac{1}{2}$ inch of the edge. Top the potato mixture with the butter, dividing it equally between the rounds. Brush the pastry (pie dough) edge with a little of the beaten egg.

5 Fold the pastry (pie dough) over to encase the filling and crimp the edges together.

6 Transfer the pasties to the prepared baking (cookie) sheet and brush them with the beaten egg.

7 Cook in a preheated oven, 200°C/400°F/Gas Mark 6, for 20 minutes. Reduce the oven temperature to 160°C/325°F/Gas Mark 3 and cook the pasties for a further 30 minutes until cooked.

8 Serve the pasties with a crisp salad or onion gravy.

COOK'S TIP

These pasties can be made in advance and frozen.

VARIATION

Use other types of meat, such as pork or chicken, in the pasties and add chunks of apple in step 2, if preferred.

Potato & Tomato Calzone

Makes 4

INGREDIENTS

DOUGH:
450 g/1 lb/4 cups white bread
  flour
1 tsp easy blend dried yeast
300 ml/½ pint/1¼ cups
  vegetable stock
1 tbsp clear honey

1 tsp caraway seeds
milk, for glazing

FILLING:
225 g/8 oz waxy potatoes, diced
1 tbsp vegetable oil
1 onion, halved and sliced

2 garlic cloves, crushed
40 g/1½ oz sun-dried tomatoes
2 tbsp chopped fresh basil
2 tbsp tomato purée (paste)
2 celery sticks, sliced
50 g/2 oz Mozzarella cheese,
  grated

1 To make the dough, sift the flour into a large mixing bowl and stir in the yeast. Make a well in the centre of the mixture.

2 Stir in the vegetable stock, honey and caraway seeds and bring the mixture together to form a dough.

3 Turn the dough out on to a lightly floured surface and knead for 8 minutes until smooth. Place the dough in a lightly oiled mixing bowl, cover and leave to rise in a warm place for 1 hour or until it has doubled in size.

4 Meanwhile, make the filling. Heat the oil in a frying pan (skillet) and add all the remaining ingredients except for the cheese. Cook for about 5 minutes, stirring.

5 Divide the risen dough into 4 pieces. On a lightly floured surface, roll them out to form four 18 cm/7 inch circles. Spoon equal amounts of the filling on to one half of each circle.

6 Sprinkle the cheese over the filling. Brush the edge of the dough with milk and fold the dough over to form 4 semi-circles, pressing to seal the edges.

7 Place on a non-stick baking (cookie) sheet and brush with milk. Cook in a preheated oven, 220°C/425°F/Gas Mark 7, for 30 minutes until golden and risen.

Potato & Meat Filo Parcels

Serves 4

INGREDIENTS

225 g/8 oz waxy potatoes, diced
    finely
1 tbsp vegetable oil
125 g/4½ oz ground beef
1 leek, sliced
1 small yellow (bell) pepper,

diced finely
125 g/4½ oz button mushrooms,
    sliced
1 tbsp plain (all-purpose) flour
1 tbsp tomato purée (paste)
85 ml/3 fl oz/⅓ cup red wine

85 ml/3 fl oz/⅓ cup beef stock
1 tbsp chopped fresh rosemary
225 g/8 oz filo pastry (pie
    dough), thawed if frozen
2 tbsp butter, melted
salt and pepper

1 Cook the diced potatoes in a saucepan of boiling water for 5 minutes. Drain and set aside.

2 Meanwhile, heat the oil in a saucepan and fry the ground beef, leek, yellow (bell) pepper and mushrooms over a low heat for 5 minutes.

3 Stir in the flour and tomato purée (paste) and cook for 1 minute. Gradually add the red wine and beef stock, stirring to thicken. Add the rosemary, season to taste with salt and pepper and leave to cool slightly.

4 Lay 4 sheets of filo pastry (pie dough) on a work surface (counter) or board. Brush each sheet with butter and lay a second layer of filo on top. Trim the sheets to make four 20 cm/8 inch squares.

5 Brush the edges of the pastry with a little butter. Spoon a quarter of the beef mixture into the centre of each square. Bring up the corners and the sides of the squares to form a

parcel, scrunching the edges together. Make sure that the parcels are well sealed by pressing the pastry (pie dough) together, otherwise the filling will leak.

6 Place the parcels on a baking (cookie) sheet and brush with butter. Bake in a preheated oven, 180°C/350°F/Gas Mark 4, for 20 minutes. Serve hot.

4

5

5

Carrot-Topped Beef Pie

Serves 4

INGREDIENTS

450 g/1 lb ground beef	2 tbsp tomato purée (paste)	2 large carrots, diced
1 onion, chopped	1 celery stick, chopped	25 g/1 oz/2 tbsp butter
1 garlic clove, crushed	3 tbsp chopped fresh parsley	3 tbsp milk
1 tbsp plain (all-purpose) flour	1 tbsp Worcestershire sauce	salt and pepper
300 ml/¹/₂ pint/1¹/₄ cups beef	675 g/1¹/₂ lb floury (mealy)	
stock	potatoes, diced	

1 Dry fry the beef in a large pan set over a high heat for 3–4 minutes or until sealed. Add the onion and garlic and cook for a further 5 minutes, stirring.

2 Add the flour and cook for 1 minute. Gradually blend in the beef stock and tomato purée (paste). Stir in the celery, 1 tbsp of the parsley and the Worcestershire sauce. Season to taste with salt and pepper.

3 Bring the mixture to the boil, then reduce the heat and simmer for 20–25 minutes. Spoon the beef mixture into a 1.1 litre/2 pint/5 cup pie dish.

4 Meanwhile, cook the potatoes and carrots in a saucepan of boiling water for 10 minutes. Drain and mash them together.

5 Stir the butter, milk and the remaining parsley into the potato and carrot mixture and season. Spoon the potato on top of the beef mixture to cover it completely; alternatively, pipe the potato with a piping (pastry) bag.

6 Cook the pie in a preheated oven, 190°C/375°F/Gas Mark 5, for 45 minutes or until cooked through. Serve hot.

VARIATION

You can use ground lamb, turkey or pork instead of the beef, adding appropriate herbs, such as rosemary and sage, for added flavour.

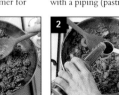

Potato, Beef & Kidney Pie

Serves 4

INGREDIENTS

225 g/8 oz waxy potatoes, cubed
25 g/1 oz/2 tbsp butter
450 g/1 lb lean steak, cubed
150 g/5½ oz ox kidney, cored
and chopped

12 shallots
25 g/1 oz/¼ cup plain
(all-purpose) flour
150 ml/¼ pint/⅔ cup beef stock
150 ml/¼ pint/⅔ cup stout

225 g/8 oz ready-made puff
pastry (pie dough)
1 egg, beaten
salt and pepper

1 Cook the cubed potatoes in a saucepan of boiling water for 10 minutes. Drain thoroughly.

2 Meanwhile, melt the butter in a saucepan and add the steak cubes and the kidney. Cook for 5 minutes, stirring until the meat is sealed on all sides.

3 Add the shallots and cook for a further 3–4 minutes. Stir in the flour and cook for 1 minute. Gradually stir in the beef stock and stout and bring to the boil, stirring constantly.

4 Stir the potatoes into the meat mixture and season with salt and pepper. Reduce the heat until the mixture is simmering. Cover the saucepan and cook for 1 hour, stirring occasionally.

5 Spoon the beef mixture into the base of a pie dish. Roll the pastry (pie dough) on a lightly floured surface until 1 cm/½ inch larger than the top of the dish.

6 Cut a strip of pastry (pie dough) long enough and wide enough to fit around the edge of the dish. Brush the edge of the dish with beaten egg and press the pastry (pie dough) strip around the edge. Brush with egg and place the pastry (pie dough) lid on top. Crimp to seal the edge and brush with beaten egg.

7 Cook in a preheated oven, 230°C/450°F/ Gas Mark 8, for 20–25 minutes or until the pastry has risen and is golden. Serve hot, straight from the dish.

Raised Potato, Pork & Apple Pie

Serves 8

INGREDIENTS

FILLING:

900 g/2 lb waxy potatoes, sliced

25 g/1 oz/2 tbsp butter

2 tbsp vegetable oil

450 g/1 lb lean pork, cubed

2 onions, sliced

4 garlic cloves, crushed

4 tbsp tomato purée (paste)

600 ml/1 pint/2½ cups stock

2 tbsp chopped fresh sage

2 dessert apples, peeled and sliced

salt and pepper

PASTRY (PIE DOUGH):

675 g/1½ lb/6 cups plain
   (all-purpose) flour

pinch of salt

50 g/1¾ oz/10 tsp butter

125 g/4½ oz/½ cup lard
   (shortening)

300 ml/½ pint/1¼ cups water

1 egg, beaten

1 tsp gelatine

1 Cook the potatoes in boiling water for 10 minutes. Drain and set aside. Heat the butter and oil in a flameproof casserole dish and fry the pork until browned, turning. Add the onion and garlic and cook for 5 minutes. Stir in the rest of the filling ingredients, except for the potatoes and the apples. Reduce the heat, cover and simmer for 1½ hours. Drain the stock from the casserole dish and reserve. Leave the pork to cool.

2 To make the pastry (pie dough), sieve the flour into a bowl. Add the salt and make a well in the centre. Melt the butter and lard in a pan with the water; then bring to the boil. Pour into the flour and mix to form a dough. Turn on to a floured surface and knead until smooth. Reserve a quarter of the dough and use the rest to line the base and sides of a large pie tin (pan) or deep 20 cm/8 inch loose-bottom cake tin (pan).

3 Layer the pork, potatoes and the apple in the base. Roll out the reserved pastry (pie dough) to make a lid. Dampen the edges and place the lid on top, sealing well. Brush with egg and make a hole in the top. Cook in a preheated oven, 200°C/400°F/Gas Mark 6, for 30 minutes, then at 160°C/325°F/Gas Mark 3 for 45 minutes. Dissolve the gelatine in the reserved stock and pour into the hole in the lid as the pie cools. Serve well chilled.

Potato, Sausage & Onion Pie

Serves 4

INGREDIENTS

2 large waxy potatoes, unpeeled
and sliced
25 g/1 oz/2 tbsp butter
4 thick pork and herb sausages
1 leek, sliced
2 garlic cloves, crushed

150 ml/¼ pint/⅔ cup vegetable
stock
150 ml/¼ pint/⅔ cup dry cider
or apple juice
2 tbsp chopped fresh sage
2 tbsp cornflour (cornstarch)

4 tbsp water
75 g/2¾ oz mature (sharp)
cheese, grated
salt and pepper

1 Cook the sliced potatoes in a saucepan of boiling water for 10 minutes. Drain and set aside.

2 Meanwhile, melt the butter in a frying pan (skillet) and cook the sausages for 8–10 minutes, turning them frequently so that they brown on all sides. Remove the sausages from the pan (skillet) and cut them into thick slices.

3 Add the leek, garlic and sausage slices to the pan (skillet) and cook for 2–3 minutes.

4 Add the vegetable stock, cider or apple juice and chopped sage. Season with salt and pepper. Blend the cornflour (cornstarch) with the water. Stir it into the pan (skillet) and bring to the boil, stirring until the sauce is thick and clear. Spoon the mixture into the base of a deep pie dish.

5 Layer the potato slices on top of the sausage mixture to cover it completely. Season with salt and pepper and sprinkle the grated cheese over the top.

6 Cook in a preheated oven, 190°C/375°F/ Gas Mark 5, for 25–30 minutes or until the potatoes are cooked and the cheese is golden brown. Serve the pie hot.

VARIATION

Other vegetables, such as broccoli or cauliflower, can be added to the filling. You can use white wine instead of the cider or apple juice, if you prefer.

Potato & Broccoli Pie

Serves 4

INGREDIENTS

450 g/1 lb waxy potatoes, cut
    into chunks
25 g/1 oz/2 tbsp butter
1 tbsp vegetable oil
175 g/6 oz lean pork, cubed
1 red onion, cut into 8

25 g/1 oz plain (all-purpose)
    flour
150 ml/¼ pint/⅔ cup vegetable
    stock
150 ml/¼ pint/⅔ cup milk
75 g/2¾ oz dolcelatte, crumbled

175 g/6 oz broccoli florets
25 g/1 oz walnuts
225 g/8 oz ready-made puff
    pastry (pie dough)
milk, for glazing
salt and pepper

1 Cook the potato chunks in a saucepan of boiling water for 5 minutes. Drain and set aside.

2 Meanwhile, heat the butter and oil in a heavy-based pan. Add the pork cubes and cook for 5 minutes, turning until browned.

3 Add the onion and cook for a further 2 minutes. Stir in the flour and cook for 1 minute, then gradually stir in the vegetable stock and milk. Bring to the boil, stirring constantly.

4 Add the cheese, broccoli, potatoes and walnuts to the pan and simmer for 5 minutes. Season with salt and pepper, then spoon the mixture into a pie dish.

5 On a floured surface, roll out the pastry (pie dough) until 2.5 cm/ 1 inch larger than the dish. Cut a 2.5 cm/1 inch wide strip from the pastry (pie dough). Dampen the edge of the dish and place the pastry (pie dough) strip around it. Brush with milk and put the pastry (pie dough) lid on top.

6 Seal and crimp the edges and make 2 small slits in the centre of the lid. Brush with milk and cook in a preheated oven, 200°C/400°F/Gas Mark 6, for 25 minutes or until the pastry has risen and is golden.

COOK'S TIP

Use a hard cheese such as mature (sharp) cheese instead of the dolcelatte, if you prefer.

Potato & Ham Pie

Serves 4

INGREDIENTS

225 g/8 oz waxy potatoes, cubed
25 g/1 oz/2 tbsp butter
8 shallots, halved
225 g/8 oz smoked ham, cubed
25 g/1 oz/¼ cup plain
 (all-purpose) flour
300 ml/½ pint/1¼ cups milk

2 tbsp wholegrain mustard
50 g/1¾ oz pineapple, cubed

PASTRY (PIE DOUGH):
225 g/8 oz/2 cups plain
 (all-purpose) flour
½ tsp dry mustard

pinch of salt
pinch of cayenne pepper
150 g/5½ oz/⅔ cup butter
125 g/4½ oz mature (sharp)
 cheese, grated
2 egg yolks, plus extra for brushing
4–6 tsp cold water

1 Cook the potato cubes in a saucepan of boiling water for 10 minutes. Drain and set aside.

2 Meanwhile, melt the butter in a saucepan, add the shallots and fry gently for 3–4 minutes until they begin to colour.

3 Add the ham and cook for 2–3 minutes. Stir in the flour and cook for 1 minute. Gradually stir in the milk. Add the mustard and pineapple and bring to the boil, stirring. Season

well with salt and pepper and add the potatoes.

4 Sieve the flour for the pastry (pie dough) into a bowl with the mustard, salt and cayenne. Rub the butter into the mixture until it resembles breadcrumbs. Add the cheese and mix to form a dough with the egg yolks and water.

5 On a floured surface, roll out half of the pastry and line a shallow pie dish; trim the edges.

6 Spoon the filling into the pie dish. Brush the edges of the pastry (pie dough) with water.

7 Roll out the remaining pastry (pie dough) to make a lid and press it on top of the pie, sealing the edges. Decorate the top of the pie with the pastry (pie dough) trimmings. Brush the pie with egg yolk and cook in a preheated oven, 190°C/375°F/Gas Mark 5, for 40–45 minutes or until the pastry is cooked and golden.

Potato & Turkey Pie

Serves 4

INGREDIENTS

300 g/10½ oz waxy potatoes, diced

25 g/1 oz/2 tbsp butter

1 tbsp vegetable oil

300 g/10½ oz lean turkey meat, cubed

1 red onion, halved and sliced

25 g/1 oz/¼ cup plain (all-purpose) flour

300 ml/½ pint/1¼ cups milk

150 ml/¼ pint/⅔ cup double (heavy) cream

2 celery sticks, sliced

75 g/2¾ oz dried apricots, chopped

25 g/1 oz walnut pieces

2 tbsp chopped fresh parsley

salt and pepper

225 g/8 oz ready made shortcrust pastry (pie dough)

beaten egg, for brushing

1 Cook the diced potatoes in a saucepan of boiling water for 10 minutes until tender. Drain and set aside.

2 Meanwhile, heat the butter and oil in a saucepan. Add the turkey and cook for 5 minutes, turning until browned.

3 Add the sliced onion and cook for 2–3 minutes. Stir in the flour and cook for 1 minute. Gradually stir in the milk and the double (heavy) cream. Bring to the boil, stirring, then reduce the heat until the mixture is simmering.

4 Stir in the celery, apricots, walnut pieces, parsley and potatoes. Season well with salt and pepper. Spoon the potato and turkey mixture into the base of a 1.1 litre/2 pint/5 cup pie dish.

5 On a lightly floured surface, roll out the pastry (pie dough) until it is 2.5 cm/1 inch larger than the dish. Trim a 2.5 cm/1 inch wide strip from the pastry (pie dough) and place the strip on the dampened rim of the dish. Brush with water and cover with the pastry (pie dough) lid, pressing to seal the edges.

6 Brush the top of the pie with beaten egg and cook in a preheated oven, 200°C/400°F/Gas Mark 6, for 25–30 minutes or until the pastry is cooked and golden brown. Serve at once.

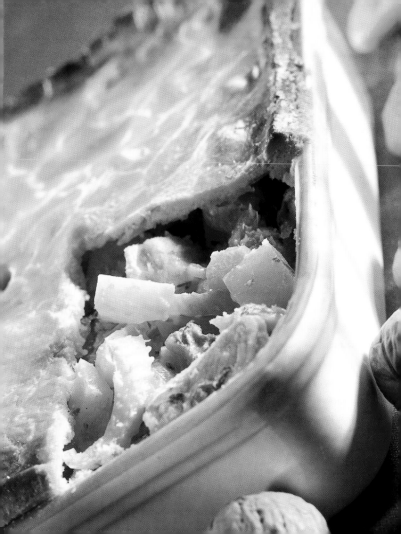

Potato Crisp Pie

Serves 4

INGREDIENTS

2 large waxy potatoes, sliced
60 g/2 oz/$\frac{1}{4}$ cup butter
1 skinned chicken breast fillet,
    about 175 g/6 oz
2 garlic cloves, crushed
4 spring onions (scallions), sliced

25 g/1 oz/$\frac{1}{4}$ cup plain
    (all-purpose) flour
150 ml/$\frac{1}{4}$ pint/$\frac{2}{3}$ cup dry white
    wine
150 ml/$\frac{1}{4}$ pint/$\frac{2}{3}$ cup double
    (heavy) cream

225 g/8 oz broccoli florets
4 large tomatoes, sliced
75 g/3 oz Gruyère cheese, sliced
225 ml/8 fl oz/1 cup natural yogurt
25 g/1 oz/$\frac{1}{3}$ cup rolled oats,
    toasted

1 Cook the potatoes in a saucepan of boiling water for 10 minutes. Drain and set aside.

2 Meanwhile, melt the butter in a frying pan (skillet). Cut the chicken into strips and cook for 5 minutes, turning. Add the garlic and spring onions (scallions) and cook for a further 2 minutes.

3 Stir in the flour and cook for 1 minute. Gradually add the wine and cream. Bring to the boil, stirring, then reduce the heat until the sauce is simmering, then cook for 5 minutes.

4 Meanwhile, blanch the broccoli in boiling water, drain and refresh in cold water.

5 Place half of the potatoes in the base of a pie dish and top with half of the tomatoes and half of the broccoli.

6 Spoon the chicken sauce on top and repeat the layers in the same order once more.

7 Arrange the Gruyère cheese on top and spoon over the yogurt. Sprinkle with the oats and cook in a preheated oven, 200°C/400°F/Gas Mark 6, for 25 minutes until the top is golden brown. Serve the pie immediately.

COOK'S TIP

Add chopped nuts, such as pine kernels (nuts), to the topping for extra crunch, if you prefer.

Potato, Leek & Chicken Pie

Serves 4

INGREDIENTS

225 g/8 oz waxy potatoes, cubed

60 g/2 oz/¼ cup butter

1 skinned chicken breast fillet, about 175 g/6 oz, cubed

150 g/5½ oz chestnut mushrooms, sliced

1 leek, sliced

25 g/1 oz/¼ cup plain (all purpose) flour

300 ml/½ pint/1¼ cups milk

1 tbsp Dijon mustard

2 tbsp chopped fresh sage

225 g/8 oz filo pastry (pie dough), thawed if frozen

40 g/1½ oz/3 tbsp butter, melted

salt and pepper

1 Cook the potato cubes in a saucepan of boiling water for 5 minutes. Drain and set aside.

2 Melt the butter in a frying pan (skillet) and cook the chicken cubes for 5 minutes or until browned all over.

3 Add the leek and mushrooms and cook for 3 minutes, stirring. Stir in the flour and cook for 1 minute. Gradually add the milk and bring to the boil. Add the mustard, chopped sage and potato cubes, then leave the mixture to simmer for 10 minutes.

4 Meanwhile, line a deep pie dish with half of the sheets of filo pastry (pie dough). Spoon the sauce into the dish and cover with one sheet of pastry (pie dough). Brush the pastry (pie dough) with butter and lay another sheet on top. Brush this sheet with butter.

5 Cut the remaining filo pastry (pie dough) into strips and fold them on to the top of the pie to create a ruffled effect. Brush the strips with the melted butter and cook in a preheated oven 180°C/350°F/Gas Mark 4 for 45 minutes or until golden brown and crisp. Serve hot.

COOK'S TIP

If the top of the pie starts to brown too quickly, cover it with foil halfway through the cooking time, to allow the pastry base to cook through without the top burning.

Layered Fish & Potato Pie

Serves 4

INGREDIENTS

900 g/2 lb waxy potatoes, sliced
60 g/2 oz/¼ cup butter
1 red onion, halved and sliced
50 g/1¾ oz/⅓ cup plain
    (all-purpose) flour
450 ml/¾ pint/2 cups milk

150 ml/¼ pint double (heavy)
    cream
225 g/8 oz smoked haddock
    fillet, cubed
225 g/8 oz cod fillet, cubed
1 red (bell) pepper, diced

125 g/4½ oz broccoli florets
50 g/1¾ oz Parmesan cheese,
    grated
salt and pepper

1 Cook the sliced potatoes in a saucepan of boiling water for 10 minutes. Drain and set aside.

2 Meanwhile, melt the butter in a saucepan, add the onion and fry gently for 3–4 minutes.

3 Add the flour and cook for 1 minute. Blend in the milk and cream and bring to the boil, stirring until the sauce has thickened.

4 Arrange half of the potato slices in the base of a shallow ovenproof dish.

5 Add the fish, diced (bell) pepper and broccoli to the sauce and cook over a low heat for 10 minutes. Season with salt and pepper, then spoon the mixture over the potatoes in the dish.

6 Arrange the remaining potato slices in a layer over the fish mixture. Sprinkle the Parmesan cheese over the top.

7 Cook in a preheated oven, 180°C/350°F Gas Mark 4, for 30 minutes or until the potatoes are cooked and the top is golden.

COOK'S TIP

Choose your favourite combination of fish, adding salmon or various shellfish for special occasions.

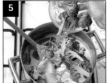

Potato-Topped Smoked Fish Pie

Serves 4

INGREDIENTS

450 g/1 lb floury (mealy)
potatoes, diced
225 g/8 oz swede, diced
60 g/2 oz/¼ cup butter
1 leek, sliced
50 g/1¾ oz baby sweetcorn
cobs, sliced
1 courgette (zucchini), halved

and sliced
50 g/1¾ oz/⅓ cup plain
(all-purpose) flour
300 ml/½ pint/1¼ cups milk
150 ml/¼ pint/⅔ cup fish stock
150 ml/¼ pint/⅔ cup double
(heavy) cream
450 g/1 lb smoked cod fillet, cut

into cubes
few drops of Tabasco sauce
125 g/4½ oz cooked peeled
prawns (shrimp)
2 tbsp chopped fresh parsley
2 tbsp grated Parmesan cheese
salt and pepper

1 Cook the potatoes and swede in a saucepan of boiling water for 20 minutes until very tender. Drain and mash until smooth.

2 Meanwhile, melt the butter in a saucepan, add the leeks, sweetcorn cobs and courgette (zucchini) and fry gently for 3–4 minutes, stirring.

3 Add the flour and cook for 1 minute. Gradually blend in the milk, fish stock and cream and bring to the boil, stirring until the mixture begins to thicken.

4 Stir in the fish, reduce the heat and cook for 5 minutes. Add the Tabasco sauce, prawns (shrimp), half of the parsley and season. Spoon the mixture into the base of an ovenproof dish.

5 Mix the remaining parsley into the potato and swede mixture, season and spoon or pipe on to the fish mixture, covering it completely. Sprinkle with the grated cheese and cook in a preheated oven, 180°C/350°F/Gas Mark 4, for 20 minutes. Serve the pie immediately.

VARIATION

Add cooked mashed parsnip to the potato instead of the swede.

Potato-Topped Lentil Bake

Serves 4

INGREDIENTS

TOPPING:
675 g/1^1/2 lb floury (mealy)
    potatoes, diced
25 g/1 oz/2 tbsp butter
1 tbsp milk
50 g/1^3/4 oz chopped pecan nuts

2 tbsp chopped fresh thyme
thyme sprigs, to garnish

FILLING:
225 g/8 oz/1 cup red lentils
60 g/2 oz/^{1}/4 cup butter
1 leek, sliced

2 garlic cloves, crushed
1 celery stick, chopped
125 g/4^1/2 oz broccoli florets
175 g/6 oz smoked tofu
    (bean curd), cubed
2 tsp tomato purée (paste)
salt and pepper

1 To make the topping, cook the potatoes in a saucepan of boiling water for 10–15 minutes or until cooked through. Drain well, add the butter and milk and mash thoroughly. Stir in the pecan nuts and chopped thyme and set aside.

2 Cook the lentils in boiling water for 20–30 minutes or until tender. Drain and set aside.

3 Melt the butter in a pan, add the leek, garlic, celery and broccoli.

Cook for 5 minutes, then add the tofu (bean curd) cubes.

4 Stir the lentils into the tofu (bean curd) and vegetable mixture with the tomato purée (paste). Season with salt and pepper to taste, then turn the mixture into the base of a shallow ovenproof dish.

5 Spoon the mashed potato on top of the lentil mixture to cover it completely.

6 Cook in a preheated oven, 200°C/400°F/ Gas Mark 6, for 30–35 minutes or until the topping is golden. Garnish with sprigs of fresh thyme and serve hot.

VARIATION

You can use any combination of vegetables in this dish. You can also add sliced cooked meat instead of the cubed tofu (bean curd) for a non-vegetarian dish.

Potato & Aubergine (Eggplant) Layer

Serves 4

INGREDIENTS

3 large waxy potatoes, sliced thinly

1 small aubergine (eggplant), sliced thinly

1 courgette (zucchini), sliced

2 tbsp vegetable oil

1 onion, diced

1 green (bell) pepper, diced

1 tsp cumin seeds

200 g/7 oz can chopped tomatoes

2 tbsp chopped fresh basil

175 g/6 oz Mozzarella cheese, sliced

225 g/8 oz tofu (bean curd), sliced

60 g/2 oz/1 cup fresh white breadcrumbs

2 tbsp grated Parmesan cheese

salt and pepper

fresh basil leaves, to garnish

1 Cook the sliced potatoes in a saucepan of boiling water for 5 minutes. Drain and set aside.

2 Lay the aubergine (eggplant) slices on a plate, sprinkle with salt and leave for 20 minutes. Blanch the courgette (zucchini) in boiling water for 2–3 minutes. Drain and set aside.

3 Meanwhile, heat 2 tbsp of the oil in a frying pan (skillet), add the onion and fry gently for 2–3 minutes until softened. Add the (bell) pepper, cumin seeds, basil and canned tomatoes. Season with salt and pepper. Leave the sauce to simmer for 30 minutes.

4 Rinse the aubergine (eggplant) slices and pat dry. Heat the remaining oil in a large frying pan (skillet) and fry the aubergine (eggplant) slices for 3–5 minutes, turning to brown both sides. Drain and set aside.

5 Arrange half of the potato slices in the base of 4 small loose-bottomed flan tins (pans). Cover with half of the courgette (zucchini) slices, half of the aubergine (eggplant) slices and half of the Mozzarella slices. Lay the tofu (bean curd) on top and spoon over the tomato sauce. Repeat the layers of vegetables and cheese.

6 Mix the breadcrumbs and Parmesan together and sprinkle over the top. Cook in a preheated oven, 190°C/375°F/Gas Mark 5, for 25–30 minutes or until golden. Garnish with basil leaves.

Sweet Potato Bread

Makes one loaf

INGREDIENTS

225 g/8 oz sweet potatoes, diced
150 ml/¼ pint/⅔ cup tepid
water
2 tbsp clear honey
2 tbsp vegetable oil

3 tbsp orange juice
75 g/2⅔ oz/generous ⅓ cup
semolina
225 g/8 oz/2 cups white bread
flour

7 g sachet easy blend dried yeast
1 tsp ground cinnamon
grated rind of 1 orange
60 g/2 oz/1 cup butter

1 Lightly grease a 675 g/
11/2 lb loaf tin (pan).

2 Cook the sweet
potatoes in a saucepan
of boiling water for 10
minutes or until soft. Drain
well and mash until smooth.

3 Meanwhile, mix the
water, honey, oil, and
orange juice together in a
large mixing bowl.

4 Add the mashed sweet
potatoes, semolina,
three quarters of the flour,
the yeast, cinnamon and

orange rind and mix well to
form a dough. Leave to
stand for about 10 minutes.

5 Cut the butter into
small pieces and knead
it into the dough with the
remaining flour. Knead for
about 5 minutes until the
dough is smooth.

6 Place the dough in the
prepared loaf tin (pan).
Cover and leave in a warm
place to rise for 1 hour or
until doubled in size.

7 Cook the loaf in a
preheated oven, 190°C/
375°F/Gas Mark 5, for
45–60 minutes or until the
base sounds hollow when
tapped. Serve the bread
warm, cut into slices.

COOK'S TIP

*If the baked loaf does not
sound hollow on the base
when it is tapped, remove it
from the tin (pan) and
return it to the oven for a few
extra minutes until
thoroughly cooked.*

Cheese & Potato Plait

Makes one loaf

INGREDIENTS

175 g/6 oz floury (mealy) potatoes, diced	675 g/1½ lb/6 cups white bread flour	2 tbsp chopped fresh rosemary
2 x 7 g sachets easy blend dried yeast	450 ml/¾ pint/2 cups vegetable stock	125 g/4½ oz Gruyère cheese, grated
	2 garlic cloves, crushed	1 tbsp vegetable oil
		1 tbsp salt

1 Lightly grease and flour a baking (cookie) sheet.

2 Cook the potatoes in a pan of boiling water for 10 minutes or until soft. Drain and mash.

3 Transfer the mashed potatoes to a large mixing bowl, stir in the yeast, flour and stock and mix to form a smooth dough.

4 Add the garlic, rosemary and 75 g/2¾ oz of the cheese and knead the dough for 5 minutes. Make a hollow in the dough, pour in the oil and knead the dough.

5 Cover the dough and leave it to rise in a warm place for 1½ hours or until doubled in size.

6 Knead the dough again and divide it into 3 equal portions. Roll each portion into a 35 cm/14 inch sausage shape.

7 Pressing one end of each of the sausage shapes together, plait the dough and fold the remaining ends under.

8 Place the plait on the baking (cookie) sheet, cover and leave to rise for 30 minutes.

9 Sprinkle the remaining cheese over the top of the plait and cook in a preheated oven, 190°C/375°F/Gas Mark 5, for 40 minutes or until the base of the loaf sounds hollow when tapped. Serve warm.

Potato & Nutmeg Scones

Makes 8

INGREDIENTS

225 g/8 oz floury (mealy) potatoes, diced	1½ tsp baking powder	1 egg, beaten
125 g/4½ oz/1 cup plain (all-purpose) flour	½ tsp grated nutmeg	50 ml/2 fl oz/¼ cup double (heavy) cream
	50 g/1¾ oz/⅓ cup sultanas (golden raisins)	2 tsp soft light brown sugar

1 Line and grease a baking (cookie) sheet.

2 Cook the diced potatoes in a saucepan of boiling water for 10 minutes or until soft. Drain well and mash the potatoes.

3 Transfer the mashed potatoes to a large mixing bowl and stir in the flour, baking powder and nutmeg.

4 Stir in the sultanas (golden raisins), egg and cream and beat the mixture with a spoon until smooth.

5 Shape the mixture into 8 rounds 2 cm/¾ inch thick and put on the baking (cookie) sheet.

6 Cook in a preheated oven, 200°C/400°F/Gas Mark 6, for about 15 minutes or until the scones have risen and are golden. Sprinkle the scones with sugar and serve warm and spread with butter.

COOK'S TIP

For extra convenience, make a batch of scones in advance and open-freeze them. Thaw thoroughly and warm in a moderate oven when ready to serve.

VARIATION

This recipe may be used to make one large scone 'cake' instead of the 8 small scones, if you prefer.

Potato Muffins

Serves 12

INGREDIENTS

175 g/6 oz floury (mealy) potatoes, diced
75 g/3 oz/³/₄ cup self raising flour

2 tbsp soft light brown sugar
1 tsp baking powder

125 g/4¹/₂ oz/³/₄ cup raisins
4 eggs, separated

1 Lightly grease and flour 12 muffin tins (pans).

2 Cook the diced potatoes in a saucepan of boiling water for 10 minutes or until cooked. Drain well and mash until smooth.

3 Transfer the mashed potatoes to a mixing bowl and add the flour, sugar, baking powder, raisins and egg yolks. Stir well to mix thoroughly.

4 In a clean bowl, whisk the egg whites until standing in peaks. Using a metal spoon, gently fold them into the potato mixture until fully incorporated.

5 Divide the mixture between the prepared tins (pans).

6 Cook in a preheated oven, 200°C/400°F/ Gas Mark 6, for 10 minutes. Reduce the oven temperature to 160°C/325°F/Gas Mark 3 and cook the muffins for 7–10 minutes or until risen.

7 Remove the muffins from the tins (pans) and serve warm.

COOK'S TIP

Instead of spreading the muffins with plain butter, serve them with cinnamon butter made by blending 60 g/2 oz/¹/₂ cup butter with a large pinch of ground cinnamon.

VARIATION

Other flavourings, such as cinnamon or nutmeg, can be added to the mixture, if you prefer.

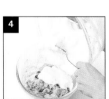

Fruity Potato Cake

Makes one cake

INGREDIENTS

675 g/1½ lb sweet potatoes, diced	3 eggs	125 g/4½ oz dried fruits, such as apple, pear or mango, chopped
1 tbsp butter, melted	3 tbsp milk	2 tsp baking powder
125 g/4½ oz demerara (brown crystal) sugar	1 tbsp lemon juice	
	grated rind of 1 lemon	
	1 tsp caraway seeds	

1 Lightly grease an 18 cm/7 inch square cake tin (pan).

2 Cook the sweet potatoes in boiling water for 10 minutes or until soft. Drain and mash the sweet potatoes until smooth.

3 Transfer the mashed sweet potatoes to a mixing bowl whilst still hot and add the butter and sugar, mixing to dissolve.

4 Beat in the eggs, lemon juice and rind, caraway seeds and chopped dried fruit. Add the baking powder and mix well.

5 Pour the mixture into the prepared cake tin (pan).

6 Cook in a preheated oven, 160°C/325°F/ Gas Mark 3, for 1–1¼ hours or until cooked through. Remove the cake from the tin (pan) and transfer to a wire rack to cool. Cut into thick slices to serve.

COOK'S TIP

This cake is ideal as a special occasion dessert. It can be made in advance and frozen until required. Wrap the cake in cling film (plastic wrap) and freeze. Thaw at room temperature for 24 hours and warm through in a moderate oven before serving.

Pumpkin Loaf

Serves 6-8

INGREDIENTS

450 g/1 lb pumpkin flesh
125 g/ 4¹⁄₂ oz /¹⁄₂ cup butter,
   softened
175 g /6 oz/³⁄₄ cup caster
   (superfine) sugar

2 eggs, beaten
225 g /8 oz/2 cups plain (all-
   purpose) flour, sifted
1¹⁄₂ tsp baking powder
¹⁄₂ tsp salt

1 tsp ground mixed spice
   (allspice)
25 g/1 oz pumpkin seeds

1 Grease a 900 g/2 lb loaf tin (pan) with oil.

2 Chop the pumpkin into large pieces and wrap in buttered foil. Cook in a preheated oven, 200°C/400°F/Gas Mark 6, for 30-40 minutes until they are tender.

3 Leave the pumpkin to cool completely before mashing well to make a thick purée.

4 In a bowl, cream the butter and sugar together until light and fluffy. Add the eggs a little at a time.

5 Stir in the pumpkin purée. Fold in the flour, baking powder, salt and mixed spice (allspice).

6 Fold the pumpkin seeds gently through the mixture, then spoon into the loaf tin (pan).

7 Bake in a preheated oven, 160°C/325°F/ Gas Mark 3, for 1¹⁄₄-1¹⁄₂ hours or until a skewer inserted into the centre of the loaf comes out clean.

8 Leave the loaf to cool and serve buttered, if wished.

COOK'S TIP

To ensure that the pumpkin purée is dry, place it in a saucepan over a medium heat for a few minutes, stirring frequently, until it is thick.

Chilli Corn Bread

Makes 12 bars

INGREDIENTS

25 g/4 1/2 oz/1 cup plain (all-purpose) flour
125 g/4 1/2 oz polenta
1 tbsp baking powder
1/2 tsp salt

1 green chilli, deseeded and chopped finely
5 spring onions (scallions), chopped finely
2 eggs

142 ml/4 1/2 fl oz/generous 1/2 cup soured cream
125 ml/4 fl oz/1/2 cup sunflower oil

1 Grease a 20 cm/8 inch square cake tin (pan) and line the base with baking parchment.

2 In a large bowl, mix together the flour, polenta, baking powder and salt.

3 Add the finely chopped green chilli and the spring onions (scallions) to the dry ingredients and mix well.

4 In a mixing jug (pitcher), beat the eggs with the soured cream and sunflower oil. Pour the mixture into the bowl of dry ingredients. Mix everything together quickly and thoroughly.

5 Pour the mixture into the prepared cake tin (pan).

6 Bake in a preheated oven, 200°C/ 400°F/ Gas Mark 6, for about 20-25 minutes or until the loaf has risen and is lightly browned.

7 Leave the bread to cool slightly before turning out of the tin (pan). Cut into bars or squares to serve.

VARIATION

Add 125 g/4 1/2 oz of sweetcorn kernels to the mixture in step 3, if you prefer.

Cheese & Potato Bread

Serves 4

INGREDIENTS

225 g/8 oz/2 cups plain (all-purpose) flour
1 tsp salt

½ tsp mustard powder
2 tsp baking powder
125 g/4½ oz Red Leicester cheese, grated

175 g/6 oz potatoes, cooked and mashed
200 ml/7 fl oz/¾ cup water
1 tbsp oil

1 Lightly grease a baking tray (cookie sheet).

2 Sieve (strain) the flour, salt, mustard powder and baking powder into a mixing bowl.

3 Reserve 2 tbsp of the grated cheese and stir the rest into the bowl with the cooked and mashed potatoes.

4 Pour in the water and the oil, and stir all the ingredients together (the mixture will be wet at this stage). Mix them all to make a soft dough.

5 Turn out the dough on to a floured surface and shape it into a 20 cm/8 inch round.

6 Place the round on the baking tray (cookie sheet) and mark it into 4 portions with a knife, without cutting through. Sprinkle with the reserved cheese.

7 Bake in a preheated oven, 220°C/425°F/Gas Mark 7, for about 25-30 minutes.

8 Transfer the bread to a wire rack and leave to cool. Serve the bread as fresh as possible.

COOK'S TIP

You can use instant potato mix for this bread, if wished.

VARIATION

Add 50 g /1¾ oz chopped ham to the mixture in step 3, if you prefer.

Mini Focaccia

Makes 4

INGREDIENTS

350 g/12 oz/3 cups strong
    white flour
$\frac{1}{2}$ tsp salt
1 sachet easy blend dried yeast
2 tbsp olive oil
250 ml/9 fl oz tepid water

100 g/3$\frac{1}{2}$ oz green or black
    olives, halved

TOPPING:
2 red onions, sliced
2 tbsp olive oil
1 tsp sea salt
1 tbsp thyme leaves

1 Lightly oil several baking trays (cookie sheets). Sieve (strain) the flour and salt into a large mixing bowl, then stir in the yeast. Pour in the olive oil and tepid water and mix everything together to form a dough.

2 Turn the dough out on to a lightly floured surface and knead it for about 5 minutes (alternatively, use an electric mixer with a dough hook and knead for 7-8 minutes).

3 Place the dough in a greased bowl, cover and leave in a warm place for about 1-1$\frac{1}{2}$ hours until it has doubled in size. Knock back (punch down) the dough by kneading it again for 1-2 minutes.

4 Knead half of the olives into the dough. Divide the dough into quarters and then shape the quarters into rounds. Place them on the baking trays (cookie sheets) and push your fingers into the dough to achieve a dimpled effect.

5 Sprinkle the red onions and remaining olives over the rounds. Drizzle the olive oil over the top and sprinkle each round with the sea salt and thyme leaves. Cover and leave the dough to rise again for 30 minutes.

6 Bake in a preheated oven, 190°C/375°F/Gas Mark 5, for 20-25 minutes or until the focaccia are well cooked and golden. Transfer to a wire rack and leave to cool before serving.

Sun-Dried Tomato Rolls

Makes 8

INGREDIENTS

225 g/8 oz/2 cups strong white
  bread flour
1/2 tsp salt
1 sachet easy blend dried yeast

100 g/3 1/2 oz/1/3 cup butter,
  melted and cooled slightly
3 tbsp milk, warmed
2 eggs, beaten

50 g/1 3/4 oz sun-dried tomatoes,
  well drained and chopped
  finely
milk, for brushing

1 Lightly grease a baking tray (cookie sheet).

2 Sieve (strain) the flour and salt into a large mixing bowl. Stir in the yeast, then pour in the butter, milk and eggs. Mix together to form a dough.

3 Turn the dough on to a lightly floured surface and knead for about 5 minutes (alternatively, use an electric mixer with a dough hook).

4 Place the dough in a greased bowl, cover and leave to rise in a warm place for 1-1 1/2 hours until the dough has doubled in size. Knock back (punch down) the dough by kneading it for a few minutes.

5 Knead the sun-dried tomatoes into the dough, sprinkling the work surface (counter) with extra flour as the tomatoes are quite oily.

6 Divide the dough into 8 balls and place them on to the baking tray (cookie sheet). Cover and leave to rise for about 30 minutes until the rolls have doubled in size.

7 Brush the rolls with milk and bake in a preheated oven, 230°C/ 450°F/Gas Mark 8, for 10-15 minutes until the rolls are golden brown.

8 Transfer the rolls to a wire rack and leave to cool slightly before serving.

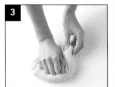

Cheese & Onion Pies

Makes 4

INGREDIENTS

3 tbsp vegetable oil

4 onions, peeled and sliced finely

4 garlic cloves, crushed

4 tbsp finely chopped fresh
  parsley

75 g/2³/₄ oz mature (sharp)
  cheese, grated

salt and pepper

PASTRY (PIE DOUGH):

175 g/6 oz/1¹/₂ cups plain (all-
  purpose) flour

¹/₂ tsp salt

100 g/3¹/₂ oz/¹/₃ cup butter, cut
  into small pieces

3-4 tbsp water

1 Heat the oil in a frying pan (skillet). Add the onions and garlic and fry for 10-15 minutes or until the onions are soft. Remove the pan from the heat and stir in the parsley and cheese and season.

2 To make the pastry (pie dough), sieve (strain) the flour and salt into a mixing bowl and rub in the butter until the mixture resembles breadcrumbs. Stir in the water and mix to a dough.

3 On a lightly floured surface, roll out the dough and divide it into 8 portions.

4 Roll out each portion to a 10 cm/4 inch round and use half of the rounds to line 4 individual tart tins (pans).

5 Fill each round with a quarter of the onion mixture. Cover with the remaining 4 pastry (pie dough) rounds. Make a slit in the top of each tart with

the point of a knife and seal the edges with the back of a teaspoon.

6 Bake in a preheated oven, 220°C/425°F/Gas Mark 7, for 20 minutes. Serve hot or cold.

COOK'S TIP

You can prepare the onion filling in advance and store it in the refrigerator.

Red Onion Tart Tatin

Serves 4

INGREDIENTS

50 g/1¾ oz/10 tsp butter
25 g/1oz/6 tsp sugar
500 g/1 lb 2 oz red onions,
    peeled and quartered

3 tbsp red wine vinegar
2 tbsp fresh thyme leaves
250 g/8 oz fresh ready-made
    puff pastry (pie dough)

salt and pepper

1 Place the butter and sugar in a 23 cm/9 inch ovenproof frying pan (skillet) and cook over a medium heat until melted.

2 Add the red onion quarters and sweat them over a low heat for 10-15 minutes until golden, stirring occasionally.

3 Add the red wine vinegar and thyme leaves to the pan. Season with salt and pepper to taste, then simmer over a medium heat until the liquid has reduced and the red onion pieces are coated in the buttery sauce.

4 On a lightly floured surface, roll out the pastry (pie dough) to a circle slightly larger than the frying pan (skillet).

5 Place the pastry (pie dough) over the onion mixture and press down, tucking in the edges to seal the pastry (pie dough).

6 Bake in a preheated oven, 180°C/350°F/Gas Mark 4, for 20-25 minutes. Leave the tart to stand for 10 minutes.

7 To turn out, place a serving plate over the frying pan (skillet) and carefully invert them both so that the pastry (pie dough) becomes the base of the tart. Serve warm.

VARIATION

Replace the red onions with shallots, leaving them whole, if you prefer.

Fresh Tomato Tarts

Serves 6

INGREDIENTS

250 g/9 oz fresh ready-made
    puff pastry (pie dough)
1 egg, beaten
2 tbsp pesto

6 plum tomatoes, sliced
salt and pepper

fresh thyme leaves, to garnish
    (optional)

1 On a lightly floured surface, roll out the pastry (pie dough) to a rectangle measuring 30 × 25 cm/12 × 10 inches.

2 Cut the rectangle in half and divide each half into 3 pieces to make 6 even-sized rectangles. Leave to chill for 20 minutes.

3 Lightly score the edges of the pastry (pie dough) rectangles and brush with the beaten egg.

4 Spread the pesto over the rectangles, dividing it equally between them, leaving a 2½ cm/1 inch border on each one.

5 Arrange the tomato slices along the centre of each rectangle on top of the pesto.

6 Season well with salt and pepper to taste and lightly sprinkle with fresh thyme leaves, if using.

7 Bake the tarts in a preheated oven, 200°C/400°F/Gas Mark 6, for about 15-20 minutes until well risen and golden brown.

8 Transfer the tomato tarts to warm serving plates straight from the oven and serve while they are still piping hot.

VARIATION

Instead of individual tarts, roll the pastry (pie dough) out to form 1 large rectangle. Spoon over the pesto and arrange the tomatoes over the top.

Provençal Tart

Serves 6-8

INGREDIENTS

250 g/9 oz ready-made fresh
puff pastry (pie dough)
3 tbsp olive oil
2 red (bell) peppers, seeded and
diced

2 green (bell) peppers, seeded
and diced
150 ml/¼ pint/⅔ cup double
(heavy) cream

1 egg
2 courgettes (zucchini), sliced
salt and pepper

1 Roll out the pastry (pie dough) on a lightly floured surface and line a 20 cm/8 inch loose-bottomed quiche/flan tin (pan). Leave to chill in the refrigerator for 20 minutes.

2 Meanwhile, heat 2 tbsp of the olive oil in a pan and fry the (bell) peppers for about 8 minutes until softened, stirring frequently.

3 Whisk the double (heavy) cream and egg together in a bowl and season to taste with salt and pepper. Stir in the cooked (bell) peppers.

4 Heat the remaining oil in a pan and fry the courgette (zucchini) slices for 4-5 minutes until lightly browned.

5 Pour the egg and (bell) pepper mixture into the pastry case (pie shell).

6 Arrange the courgette (zucchini) slices around the edge of the tart.

7 Bake in a preheated oven, 180°C/350°F/ Gas Mark 4, for 35-40 minutes or until just set and golden brown.

COOK'S TIP

This recipe could be used to make 6 individual tarts – use 15 x 10 cm/6 x 4 inch tins (pans) and bake them for 20 minutes.

Celery & Onion Pies

Makes 12

INGREDIENTS

PASTRY (PIE DOUGH):
125 g/4¹/₂ oz/1 cup plain (all-
    purpose) flour
¹/₂ tsp salt
25 g/1 oz/6 tsp butter, cut into
    small pieces

25 g/1 oz mature (sharp) cheese,
    grated
3-4 tbsp water

FILLING:
50 g/1³/₄ oz/10 tsp butter
125 g/4¹/₂ oz celery, chopped
    finely

2 garlic cloves, crushed
1 small onion, chopped finely
1 tbsp plain (all-purpose) flour
50 ml/2 fl oz/¹/₄ cup milk
salt
pinch of cayenne pepper

1 To make the filling, melt the butter, add the celery, garlic and onion and fry for 5 minutes or until softened.

2 Remove from the heat and stir in the flour, then the milk. Heat gently until the mixture is thick, stirring frequently. Season with salt and cayenne pepper. Leave to cool.

3 To make the pastry, sieve (strain) the flour and salt into a mixing bowl and rub in the butter with your fingers. Stir the cheese into the mixture together with the cold water and mix to form a dough.

4 Roll out three quarters of the dough and using a 6 cm/2¹/₂ inch biscuit (cookie) cutter, cut out 12 rounds. Line a patty tin (pan) with the rounds.

5 Divide the filling between the rounds.

Roll out the remaining dough and, using a 5 cm/2 inch cutter, cut out 12 circles. Place the circles on top of the pies and seal. Make a slit in each pie and chill them for 30 minutes.

6 Bake in a preheated oven, 220°C/425°F/ Gas Mark 7, for about 15-20 minutes. Leave to cool in the tin (pan) for about 10 minutes before turning out. Serve warm.

Asparagus & Goat's Cheese Tart

Serves 6

INGREDIENTS

250 g/9 oz fresh ready-made
    shortcrust pastry (pie dough)
250 g/9 oz asparagus
1 tbsp vegetable oil
1 red onion, chopped finely

200 g/7 oz goat's cheese
25 g/1 oz hazelnuts, chopped

2 eggs, beaten
4 tbsp single (light) cream
salt and pepper

1 On a lightly floured surface, roll out the pastry (pie dough) and line a 24 cm/9½ inch loose-bottomed quiche/flan tin (pan). Prick the base of the pastry (pie dough) with a fork and leave to chill for 30 minutes.

2 Line the pastry case (pie shell) with foil and baking beans and bake in a preheated oven, 190°C/375°F/Gas Mark 7, for about 15 minutes.

3 Remove the foil and baking beans and

return the pastry case (pie shell) to the oven for a further 15 minutes.

4 Cook the asparagus in boiling water for 2-3 minutes, drain and cut into bite-size pieces.

5 Heat the oil in a small frying pan (skillet) and fry the onion until soft. Spoon the asparagus, onion and hazelnuts into the prepared pastry case (pie shell).

6 Process the cheese, eggs and cream in a

blender until smooth, or beat by hand. Season well, then pour the mixture over the asparagus, onion and hazelnuts.

7 Bake in the oven for 15-20 minutes or until the cheese filling is just set. Serve warm or cold.

VARIATION

Omit the hazelnuts and sprinkle Parmesan cheese over the top of the tart just before cooking in the oven, if you prefer.

Onion Tart

Serves 6

INGREDIENTS

250 g/9 oz fresh ready-made
   shortcrust pastry (pie dough)
40 g/1½ oz/8 tsp butter
75 g/2¾ oz bacon, chopped
700 g/1lb 9 oz onions, peeled

and sliced thinly
2 eggs, beaten
50 g/1¾ oz Parmesan cheese,
   grated
1 tsp dried sage

salt and pepper

1 Roll out the pastry (pie dough) on a lightly floured work surface (counter) and line a 24 cm/9½ inch loose-bottomed quiche/flan tin (pan).

2 Prick the base of the pastry (pie dough) with a fork and leave to chill for 30 minutes.

3 Heat the butter in a saucepan, add the chopped bacon and sliced onions and sweat them over a low heat for about 25 minutes until tender.

If the onion slices start to brown, add 1 tbsp water to the saucepan.

4 Add the beaten eggs to the onion mixture and stir in the cheese, sage and salt and pepper to taste. Mix well to combine all the ingredients.

5 Spoon the onion mixture into the prepared pastry case (pie shell).

6 Bake in a preheated oven, 180°C/350°F/Gas Mark 4, for about

20-30 minutes or until the tart has just set.

7 Leave to cool slightly in the tin (pan). Serve the tart warm or cold.

VARIATION

For a vegetarian version of this tart, replace the bacon with the same amount of chopped mushrooms.

Pissaladière

Serves 8

INGREDIENTS

4 tbsp olive oil

700 g/1 lb 9 oz red onions, sliced thinly

2 garlic cloves, crushed

2 tsp caster (superfine) sugar

2 tbsp red wine vinegar

350 g/12 oz fresh ready-made puff pastry (pie dough)

salt and pepper

TOPPING:

2 x 50 g/1³/₄ oz cans anchovy fillets

12 green stoned (pitted) olives

1 tsp dried marjoram

1 Lightly grease a swiss roll tin (pan). Heat the olive oil in a large saucepan. Add the onions and garlic and cook over a low heat for about 30 minutes, stirring occasionally.

2 Add the sugar and red wine vinegar to the pan and season with plenty of salt and pepper.

3 On a lightly floured surface, roll out the pastry (pie dough) to a rectangle 33 × 23 cm/ 13 × 9 inches. Place the

pastry (pie dough) rectangle on to the prepared tin (pan), pushing the pastry (pie dough) well into the corners of the tin (pan).

4 Spread the onion mixture over the pastry (pie dough).

5 Arrange the anchovy fillets and green olives on top, then sprinkle with the marjoram.

6 Bake in a preheated oven, 220°C/425°F/ Gas Mark 7, for about 20-25 minutes until the

pissaladière is lightly golden. Serve piping hot, straight from the oven.

VARIATION

Cut the pissaladière into squares or triangles for easy finger food at a party or barbecue (grill).

Mini Cheese & Onion Tarts

Serves 12

INGREDIENTS

PASTRY (PIE DOUGH):
100 g/4^1/$_2$ oz/1 cup plain (all-
 purpose) flour
^{1}/$_4$ tsp salt
75 g/2^3/$_4$ oz/^{1}/$_3$ cup butter, cut
 into small pieces
1-2 tbsp water

FILLING:
1 egg, beaten
100 ml/3^1/$_2$ fl oz/generous
 ^{1}/$_3$ cup single (light) cream
50 g/1^3/$_4$ oz Red Leicester cheese,
 grated

3 spring onions (scallions),
 chopped finely
salt
cayenne pepper

1 To make the pastry
(pie dough), sieve
(strain) the flour and salt
into a mixing bowl. Rub in
the butter with your
fingers until the mixture
resembles breadcrumbs.
Stir in the water and mix to
form a dough.

2 Roll out the pastry (pie
dough) on to a lightly
floured surface. Using a
7.5 cm/3 inch biscuit cutter,
stamp out 12 rounds from
the pastry (pie dough) and
line a patty tin (pan).

3 To make the filling,
whisk together the
beaten egg, single (light)
cream, grated cheese and
chopped spring onions
(scallions) in a mixing
jug (pitcher). Season to
taste with salt and
cayenne pepper.

4 Pour the filling
mixture into the pastry
cases (pie shells) and bake
in a preheated oven,
180°C/350°F/Gas Mark 4,
for about 20-25 minutes or
until the filling is just set.

Serve the mini tarts warm
or cold.

VARIATION

*Top each mini tartlet with
slices of fresh tomato before
baking, if you prefer.*

COOK'S TIP

*If you use 175 g/6 oz of
ready-made shortcrust pastry
(pie dough), these tarts can
be made in minutes.*

Curry Pasties

Serves 4

INGREDIENTS

225 g/8 oz/1¾ cups plain
  wholemeal (whole wheat)
  flour
100 g/3½ oz/⅓ cup vegetarian
  margarine, cut into small
  pieces
4 tbsp water

2 tbsp oil
225 g/8 oz diced root vegetables
  (potatoes, carrots and
  parsnips)
1 small onion, chopped
2 garlic cloves, chopped finely
½ tsp curry powder

½ tsp ground turmeric
½ tsp ground cumin
½ tsp wholegrain mustard
5 tbsp vegetable stock
soya milk, to glaze

1 Place the flour in a mixing bowl and rub in the vegetarian margarine with your fingertips until the mixture resembles breadcrumbs. Stir in the water and bring together to form a soft dough. Wrap and leave to chill in the refrigerator for 30 minutes.

2 To make the filling, heat the oil in a large saucepan. Add the diced root vegetables, chopped onion and garlic. Fry for 2 minutes, then stir in all of the spices and mustard, turning the vegetables to coat them with the spices. Fry the vegetables for a further 1 minute.

3 Add the stock to the pan and bring to the boil. Cover and simmer for about 20 minutes, stirring occasionally, until the vegetables are tender and the liquid has been absorbed. Leave to cool.

4 Divide the pastry (pie dough) into 4 portions.

Roll each portion into a 15 cm/6 inch round. Place the filling on one half of each round.

5 Brush the edges of each round with soya milk, then fold over and press the edges together to seal. Place on a baking tray (cookie sheet). Bake in a preheated oven, 200°C/400°F/Gas Mark 6, for 25-30 minutes until the pastry is golden brown.

Brazil Nut & Mushroom Pie

Serves 4-6

INGREDIENTS

PASTRY:

225 g/8 oz/1³/₄ cups plain wholemeal (whole wheat) flour

100 g/3¹/₂ oz/¹/₃ cup vegan margarine, cut into small pieces

4 tbsp water

soya milk, to glaze

FILLING:

25 g/1oz/6 tsp vegan margarine

1 onion, chopped

1 garlic clove, chopped finely

125 g/4¹/₂ oz button mushrooms, sliced

1 tbsp plain (all-purpose) flour

150 ml/¹/₄ pint/²/₃ cup vegetable stock

1 tbsp tomato purée (paste)

175 g/6 oz brazil nuts, chopped

75 g/2³/₄ oz fresh wholemeal (whole wheat) breadcrumbs

2 tbsp chopped fresh parsley

¹/₂ tsp pepper

1 To make the pastry, rub the margarine into the flour until it resembles fine breadcrumbs. Stir in the water and bring together to form a dough. Wrap and chill for 30 minutes.

2 Melt the margarine for the filling in a pan, add the onion, garlic and mushrooms and fry for 5 minutes until softened. Add the flour and cook for

1 minute, stirring. Slowly add the stock, stirring until the sauce is smooth and beginning to thicken. Stir in the tomato purée (paste), nuts, breadcrumbs, parsley and pepper. Cool slightly.

3 Roll out two thirds of the pastry (pie dough) and use to line a 20 cm/8 inch loose-bottomed quiche/flan tin (pan). Spread the filling in the pastry case

(pie shell). Brush the edges of the pastry (pie dough) with soya milk. Roll out the remaining pastry (pie dough) to fit the top of the pie. Seal the edges, make a slit in the top of the pastry (pie dough) and brush with soya milk.

4 Bake in a preheated oven, 200°C/400°F/Gas Mark 6, for 30-40 minutes until golden brown.

Lentil & Red (Bell) Pepper Flan

Serves 6-8

INGREDIENTS

PASTRY:
225 g/8 oz/1³/₄ cups plain
wholemeal (whole wheat)
flour
100 g/3¹/₂ oz/¹/₂ cup vegan
margarine, cut into small
pieces
4 tbsp water

FILLING:
175 g/6 oz red lentils, rinsed
300 ml/¹/₂ pint/1¹/₄ cups
vegetable stock
15 g/¹/₂ oz/3 tsp vegan margarine
1 onion, chopped

2 red (bell) peppers, cored,
seeded and diced
1 tsp yeast extract
1 tbsp tomato purée (paste)
3 tbsp chopped fresh parsley
pepper

1 To make the pastry (pie dough), place the flour in a mixing bowl and rub in the vegan margarine with your fingertips until the mixture resembles fine breadcrumbs. Stir in the water and bring together to form a dough. Wrap and chill for 30 minutes.

2 To make the filling, put the lentils in a pan with the stock, bring to the boil and simmer for 10 minutes until the lentils are tender and can be mashed to a purée.

3 Melt the margarine in a small pan and fry the onion and red (bell) peppers and fry until soft.

4 Add the lentil purée, yeast extract, tomato purée (paste) and parsley. Season with pepper. Mix until well combined.

5 On a lightly floured surface, roll out the dough and line a 24 cm/ 9½ inch loose-bottomed quiche tin (pan). Prick the base of the pastry (pie dough) with a fork and spoon the lentil mixture into the pastry case (pie shell).

6 Bake in a preheated oven, 200°C/400°F/ Gas Mark 6, for 30 minutes until the filling is firm.

Index